M

The Tragedy of Property

New Russian Thought
The publication of this series was made possible with the support of the Zimin Foundation.

Maxim Trudolyubov, *The Tragedy of Property*

The Tragedy of Property

Private Life, Ownership and the Russian State

Maxim Trudolyubov

Translated by Arch Tait

polity

First published in Russian as *Люди за забором: Частное пространство, власть и собственность в России [People Behind the Fence: Private Space, Power and Property in Russia]*. Copyright © 2015 by Novoye Izdatelstvo. This edition is a translation authorized by the original publisher.

This English edition © Polity Press, 2018

This book was published with the support of the Zimin Foundation.

Polity Press
65 Bridge Street
Cambridge CB2 1UR, UK

Polity Press
101 Station Landing
Suite 300
Medford, MA 02155, USA

ISBN-13: 978-1-5095-2700-7
ISBN-13: 978-1-5095-2701-4 (pb)

A catalogue record for this book is available from the British Library.

Library of Congress Cataloging-in-Publication Data

Names: Trudolyubov, Maxim, author.
Title: The tragedy of property : private life, ownership and the Russian
    state / Maxim Trudolyubov.
Description: Cambridge, UK ; Medford, MA : Polity Press, [2018] | Series: New
    Russian thought | Includes bibliographical references and index.
Identifiers: LCCN 2017059735 (print) | LCCN 2018006032 (ebook) | ISBN
    9781509527045 (Epub) | ISBN 9781509527007 (hardback) | ISBN 9781509527014
    (pbk.)
Subjects: LCSH: Property and socialism--History. | Property--Russia
    (Federation)--History. | Property--Soviet Union--History. | Russia
    (Federation)--Politics and government. | Soviet Union--Politics and
    government.
Classification: LCC HX550.P7 (ebook) | LCC HX550.P7 .T78 2018 (print) | DDC
    306.3/20947--dc23
LC record available at https://lccn.loc.gov/2017059735

Typeset in 10.5 on 12 pt Sabon by
Servis Filmsetting Ltd, Stockport, Cheshire
Printed and bound in Great Britain by Clays Ltd, Elcograf S.p.A.

For further information on Polity, visit our website: politybooks.com

CONTENTS

Acknowledgements   viii
Foreword by Alexander Etkind   ix

Introduction: The Tragedy of Property   1

1 The Entrance   7
   Homeless people   7
   From city dwellers to citizens   11
   Reflected modernity   12
   The capital of succeeding generations   16

2 The Fence: Russian Title   22
   Good fences make good neighbours   22
   The permanence of the fence   25
   Life without property rights   28
   Russian title   32

3 Behind the Fence: The Privatization of Utopia   37
   Private palaces   37
   The privatization of utopia   41
   The birth of private life   46
   The Dutch carpenter's house   47

4 Private Property: My House Is My Castle   50
   The myth of Sparta   50
   The *domus* of our forebears   53
   Mine and yours   58
   Life, liberty and property   61

v

Christianity and utopia   65
Utopia without property   68

5 Territory: Ambitions of Colonialism and Methods of
   Subjugation   73
   Yermak the conquistador   73
   Stewardship and extraction   77
   A natural resource irony of history   81

6 The Lock on the Door: The Priority of Security   87
   The collapse of monarchy in the West   87
   Success in the East   88
   Control as the top priority   91
   Security as a threat   96

7 Labourers: Moral Economics and the Art of Survival   100
   The plough, the scythe and the axe   100
   Moral economics   104
   The commune versus the private farmer   109
   Dictatorship of the collective   113

8 Masters: The Tragedy of Domination   118
   Owners and rulers   118
   'Let not the nobility be dispossessed of their estates
      without due process of law'   120
   The birth of free people   125
   Traduced and sacred law   127
   The attempt to share   131

9 Architecture, Happiness and Order   136
   The project we live in   136
   Stalin's orders   140
   Khrushchev's social revolution   144
   Happiness and order   152
   Russian order   154

10 The Halfway House   157
   Favour from the tsar   157
   Property without the market   162
   A market without property   168

11 Two Options: Finish Building the Home, or Emigrate   173
    Property without property rights   173
    Democracy without the rule of law   176
    Law enforcement without the rule of law   178
    The open door   183

Conclusion   191

Epilogue: In Search of Real Ownership   198
    Moral hazards of the present   198
    The invisible hand of the past   201
    Still a halfway house   203

Notes   206
Index   224

ACKNOWLEDGEMENTS

My wife, Inna Beryozkina, has provided invaluable assistance during the writing of this book, as have Matvey Trudolyubov, who grew up along with it, and Maria and Pyotr Trudolyubov.

The book, and not only the book, has benefited immensely from my good fortune in knowing and conversing with: the philosophers and founders of the Moscow School of Civic Education, Yelena Nemirovskaya and Yury Senokosov; historian Vasiliy Rudich; economists Sergey Guriev, James Robinson, Konstantin Sonin, Oleg Tsyvinsky, Kirill Yankov and Vladimir Yuzhako; political scientist Ivan Krastev; political analyst Ellen Mickiewicz; Russian language and literature specialist Mikhail Gronas; architect Nikita Tokarev; businessmen Alexey Klimashin, Sergey Petrov and Bulat Stolyarov; Matthew Rojansky, director, and William E. Pomeranz, deputy director, of the Kennan Institute at the Woodrow Wilson Center, Washington, DC; and my colleagues at *Vedomosti* – Pavel Aptekar, Boris Grozovsky, Andrey Sinitsyn, Nikolai Epple and Nikolai Kononov. The book would never have seen the light of day without the active participation of editor Andrey Kurilkin, who agreed to read the manuscript in the first place, accepted it and helped to improve it.

The high professionalism and intellectual distinction of my associates cannot guarantee a finished product of equally high quality, and culpability for shortcomings and errors lies squarely with me.

FOREWORD

In 2014, the revolution in Ukraine forced President Viktor Yanukovych to flee to Russia. The rebels entered his private, well-fenced residence near Kiev, which previously had been secured by dozens of heavily armed guards. In post-Soviet history, it was probably the first – but surely not the last – break-through into the intimate life of power. What the public – mostly students and impoverished intellectuals – saw in the residence was ridiculous rather than sublime. Palladian columns, gilded walls and pseudo-rococo furniture produced a strange feeling of bad taste with historical resonances: here the reminiscences of Austro-Hungarian glory, there the replicas of socialist realism, plus some imitations of the slave-holding American South to boot. Well connected and even better protected, Mr Yanukovych now lives in a smaller mansion near Moscow, where his neighbours cannot help but think about his fate.

In this book, Maxim Trudolyubov depicts contemporary Russia from an unusual but uniquely relevant perspective – the history of space. This perspective is relevant because in many ways Russia is equal to its space, and contemporary Russia particularly so. It is the integrity of space that has been the highest political value for Russian rulers, and the disintegration of the Soviet Union added fresh and traumatic undertones to this age-old sentiment. Even the ruling party calls itself 'United Russia' rather than, say, 'Happy Russia'. The largest country in the world by landmass, Russia has developed its historical particularities in the millennial effort to capture, protect and cultivate the enormous territory of northern Eurasia. Sustaining life in this space has, historically, not been a trivial issue, and unusual instruments of indirect, communal organization were developed for the purpose. In the massive literature on Russian history, Trudolyubov's book is unique in presenting the long and tortured story of Russian property arrangements in one coherent narrative. From land communes to communal apartments to late Soviet condominiums to the exorbitant inequality that is characteristic of contemporary Russia, we feel a bizarre, contingent logic to these twisted and often inverse developments. Introduced by the state, property regulations partially resolved and partially exacerbated the enormous difficulties and complexities of space and property in Russia.

Our neoliberal age has translated the problems of Russian space into legal regulations of private property on land, housing, apartments and, inevitably, fences. Trudolyubov demonstrates the ambivalent and tortured, even tragic, nature of the process. Russian history is a history of self-colonization, and Trudolyubov elaborates on this dictum. From the patriarch of Russian historiography, Vasiliy Kliuchevsky, to my recent *Internal Colonization* (2011), this story of Russia's external and internal colonization has been told mostly from the perspectives of political, cultural and economic history. Independently of its declared purposes, colonization leads to tragic results. This book demonstrates that there is no better perspective on the unique character of Russian history than its space management, property regulations, privatization campaigns, enclosures and fences. This book is also about the tragedy of post-socialist capitalism, a massive but peculiar version of political and cultural economy that is still waiting for its Adam Smith.

From Ukraine to Russia to the Central Asian republics, post-Soviet states lead the world indices of unhappiness, a coherent tendency that cannot be explained by purely economic causes but has deep historical underpinnings. One common denominator for post-Soviet grievances is a lack of trust, a corrosive legacy of the socialist past with its huge, and hugely abused, public spaces and institutions. Trudolyubov's book adds a good deal to our understanding of this overwhelming mistrust. Another consistent cause of Russia's tragic underdevelopment goes deeper in history, but it takes new forms with its every turn. This is a malicious split between the ruling elite and the working masses – a total decoupling between labour and capital. The political rulers build the economy in such a way that it provides them with monies that do not depend on the population. In a resource-bound economy, the more space the rulers control, the more resources they exploit, and the less they are dependent on the population: this is the best-kept secret of Russia. In its contemporary form, this political-economic decoupling results from the increasing reliance of the output of the country and the prosperity of its rulers on natural resources such as oil, gas and metals. According to some estimates, the Russian elite now has as much wealth abroad as the state and the people, including the same elite, own domestically. When these oligarchs and bureaucrats invest their petrodollars and gasorubles in a labour-bound economy – a hotel, a private bank, a university endowment – they prefer to do it abroad.

In the mid-nineteenth century, the Russian Empire openly admitted that its aim was to hold back development, and this demodernizing sentiment led the country to defeat in the Crimean War. With the new tsar, the reforms did occur; but although they deferred the disastrous revolution, they could not prevent it. In the early twenty-first century, we see a similar combination of a one-man show, cultural panic and political adventurism, with the eye of the cyclone again focusing on the Crimea. But of course we do not know the future. All we can do is study the past in order to make sense of the present.

Alexander Etkind
European University Institute, Florence
20 December 2017

Dedicated to the memory of my parents, Margarita
and Anatoly Trudolyubov

INTRODUCTION

The Tragedy of Property

The enserfment and emancipation of the peasants, the Russian Revolution and collectivization, a massive residential building programme and, finally, the transfer of newly privatized apartments to their occupants are all landmarks in Russia's history that have an impact on us today. They are all about land and the ownership of property, whether people are tied to the land or released from that tie; they are about the confiscation of property and the reacquiring of it.

These events affected literally every Russian. Tens of millions of people lost all they owned in the early 1930s; tens of millions had privacy returned to them as a result of residential building on a massive scale between the 1960s and the 1980s (see chapters 1, 10 and 11). *Homo sovieticus* was a product not so much of the revolution as of an acute housing shortage in the rapidly expanding cities. Character was formed and careers were made in cramped living conditions, through squabbles and friendships as neighbours battled over square metres of floor space. For millions of people in the USSR, possessing their own home was their ultimate dream.

The aspiration to privacy is an issue future generations will still have to address, but there has been a qualitative change affecting everyone in Russian society: the difficult transition from collective homelessness under the Soviet state to personal, private life has been achieved.

Giving its members a private life is a major step forward for any society. Today, the opportunity of being alone with yourself and your loved ones seems to us only natural. We feel that our four walls, our family affairs, our feelings and words belong to us alone; that is now not only an aspiration but a right enshrined in the constitution. In Russia, however, it is a very recent achievement, something that, in

1

historical terms, happened only yesterday. Actually, it has not been around in the rest of the world for all that long.

Throughout history, human beings have existed primarily as a unit within a tribe, a group, a commune, an army, a guild, a community, a church. There has been no respite from need and want and pressure from their fellow humans. Humans may be social animals, but they value privacy.

For most of history only a privileged few, leaders and saints, have been able to withdraw into their shells. For the common man or woman, the path to a life apart has been long, arduous and slow, and it has come by way of the Industrial Revolution, the expansion of trade and the emergence of the middle class. The end result has been creation of the space essential for private life, the home exclusively for just a few people, immediate family. Before he could live in a separate apartment or house in a town, the working man who was neither a leader, a feudal lord nor a gangster boss had to rise above the threshold of hand-to-mouth living to become more ambitious and bring in more than subsistence wages. That became possible as he gradually escaped from a barrage of restrictions and as monopolies on trade and power were eroded. Geographical exploration, private ownership of land, new technologies and, with them, new ways of making money have all helped to promote the concept of private life (see chapter 3).

The acquisition of a home of your own would have been an impossibility in Russia without a new recognition of the importance, and the introduction on a massive scale, of the right to own private property. The sense of ownership of the place you live in goes back, no doubt, to the very beginnings of human culture, but awareness of one's own personal identity and consolidating the boundaries of private life is even now a work in progress (see chapter 4). At the same time, agreement is developing on what an individual may or may not consider legally his or her own property.

In all cultures, including Western cultures, there have always been alternatives to private property, in the form of public and state-owned property. Many countries are seeing increasing adoption of forms of temporary or shared use of goods. Cars, apartments and second homes are often rented rather than purchased outright. It is a curious fact that in countries with the most venerable tradition of private property, the percentage of home owners among town dwellers is substantially lower than in Russia. In Switzerland it is less than 50%, in Germany it is just over, and in the United Kingdom it is around 68%, as against 85% in Russia.

In Russian culture, the various types of property ownership evolved differently. There is nothing mystical about that; it has nothing to do with the mysteries of the Russian soul, although it is just possible that a lack of freedom and the constraints on life in such a vast country bear some relation to the nature of our society and state.

In centuries past, Russia's rulers extended their domains and exercised control over vast territories by centralizing power rather than negotiating and delegating it. The fact that the Russian state saw its main aims as territorial expansion and security inevitably affected the way society developed, and the predominance of such sources of wealth as furs, peasant labour, timber, grain and oil facilitated the emergence of a particular style of rule.

Its priorities emerged as the Muscovite state was taking shape, and they were the creation of robust defences against external enemies, and extraction of natural resources for the benefit of a small elite. Development of a professional bureaucracy and improvement of arrangements at district level were conspicuously sluggish, which suggests they were of little concern to that elite. There is a marked difference in the welfare and mood of citizens between countries whose leading figures interest themselves in improving social conditions and countries where they do not. The latter tend to be colonies, or otherwise states where the ruling elite are interested only in exporting natural resources and other goods (see chapters 5 and 6).

Russia is an odd country, because it is simultaneously a colony and a colonizer. The paradoxical outcome of its centuries-long expansion has been that, despite having a great deal of territory, it feels overcrowded; and it feels overcrowded because so little of its vast territory has been intelligently developed.

The fact that there exists one single, overriding source of easy money sets the ground rules. If these reward a particular type of behaviour, savvy players will adopt it. If one route for advancement is far more rewarding than any other, everybody will head in that direction: to St Petersburg, to Moscow, to the state treasury, to the decision-making centre. The extraordinary concentration of resources in the two capitals and neglect of the provinces are related: underdevelopent of the latter is the direct consequence of a strong, centralized regime. We have too little space because we have too much regime.

In Russia the universal human desire for personal well-being constantly collides with a political system that puts maintaining order (in terms of class, ideology and the state) above economic development. Unlike in the West, private property has not been a badge of citizenship, conferring rights and involvement in public affairs.

The institution was not well regarded either before the Bolsheviks' revolution or after the revolution of Yeltsin and Gaidar in the 1990s. For some, property was, and is, a legitimate means of retaining their dominant position, for others it was, and is, evidence of a profoundly unjust social system (see chapters 7 and 8).

Many scholars have linked the languishing of the institution of private property in Russia with peculiarities of the country's political development. The best known examples are Richard Pipes' *Russia under the Old Regime* and his *Property and Freedom*,[1] in which he correlates the extent to which private property develops in Russia with the level of political freedoms.

There has, however, been no lack of private property in Russia: it has existed in one form or another throughout our history, and in the last 150 years of the St Petersburg period it was even more radically 'private' than many European analogues. The problem is just that property and freedom in Russia are entirely separate: they occupy parallel universes.

At one time it was customary in Anglo-American discourse to talk about the 'tragedy of the commons', which was held to show the impossibility of sharing resources equitably and to demonstrate the superiority of private property. In Russia, it seems to me, we need to talk rather about the 'tragedy of private property'. The history of attitudes to property here is different from that of the West. In Russian political culture, private property has not provided a foundation for awareness of other civil rights. Those championing property and those championing human and civil rights have often been on opposite sides of the political divide. Private property, particularly large amounts of it, has been perceived in our culture as unearned and hence not deserving to be defended. It was used negligently and foolishly, with the result that society did not see it as having any great moral value and readily repudiated it during the social upheaval of the 1917 Revolution. 'If private property was easily swept away in Russia, almost without resistance, by the whirlwind of socialist passions,' S.L. Frank wrote in 'Property and Socialism', 'that was simply because belief in the rightness of private property was so weak; even the robbed property owners, while they excoriated those who had robbed them on a personal level, did not themselves, deep in their hearts, believe they had legitimate title to their own property.'[2]

One of the basic premises of the Soviet project was that life would be organized on rational, scientific principles, which implied management of the economy from a single centre. The leaders of the communist state promised the world they would put right the deep, inherent unfairness of capitalism and economic relations based on private property, thus doing away with social inequality and a dearth of coordination of human activity. If there was no private property, there would be none of the selfishness of those who owned it, who inevitably tried to pull more than their fair share of the blanket to their side of the bed. The Marxist ideal proved impracticable, however, perhaps because human nature proved more powerful than reason, and the Soviet economic project collapsed under its own weight.

The post-revolutionary pendulum swung back incredibly strongly in 1990s Russia. The right to own the residential property they currently occupied was officially conferred on the sitting tenants, and privatization vouchers were offered to virtually the entire population. That was not enough, however, to make people property owners in spirit, even though the right to their property, no matter how vulnerable because of the imperfections of the new Russian state, was entirely real. Somehow it was not the magic wand capable of transforming the population into citizens, and voters into masters of their country. They gained possession of certain things but not of their country. People were searching desperately for an understanding of their own identity, of how they related to their homeland, and of the sense in which they could be said to own it.

The rehabilitation of private property in the new Russia opened up unprecedented opportunities but raised new problems. There was no way those who now began to control and exploit the country's natural resources and formerly public assets, created by the united efforts of the population in the Soviet era, were going to be viewed by society as having earned it honestly by their own hard work. Neither was that something the state wanted; indeed, it had every intention of ensuring that no property owners, not only those who had been handed the country's natural resources on a plate, but even the owners of small or medium enterprises, should be allowed to feel independent. No trustworthy legal underpinning or stable definitions were created for property owners in Russia. This was partly because it was always possible to have recourse to the legal systems of other countries, but partly also because keeping owners uncertain of the rules suited the regime's upper echelon nicely. Under the new dispensation, the right to own property was placed once more, as in earlier times, in a category separate from other civil rights.

The post-Soviet years have seen Russian society pass through a period characterized more by appropriation than creation. There was a boom, a tsunami, of appropriation; everything was up for grabs.

Vladimir Bibikhin tried twenty-five years ago to discriminate between the sense of 'mine' felt for appropriated property and the sense of genuine ownership of property acquired by intelligence and hard work. He suggested the difference was between 'mine', when it meant only 'not yours', and the sense of ownership of something truly one's own.[3] To this day Russian society has failed to master the distinction.

This book is structured as a progress through an imaginary private home. We will be contemplating the fence, the space of the courtyard, the land the house is built on, and the issues of its security, price and the design to which it was built. There are chapters about the people who live in this house, whether as 'workers' (from the peasants to our contemporaries) or as 'owners' (from before 1917 and in the present day). We shall consider the history of Russia's property institutions and propose a view on how far we remain in thrall to the past, and this will lead on to discussion of the future.

— 1 —

THE ENTRANCE

Homeless people

In 1970, nobody was more delighted with the move than my grandfather. A separate, three-room apartment in a new, nine-storey block was now his, conferred on him as a senior electrician and war veteran. He was fifty-five, his grandson had just been born, and he was happy. This was not a makeshift roof over his head, not a room shared between several families, but an actual, separate address. This was the culmination of a forty-year journey from the countryside to the city, and it came with documentary confirmation and a passport with the best residence permit in the world, for Moscow. It was a journey that had started when he was fifteen and fled Perevitsky Torzhok, a village in Ryazan, 200 km southeast of Moscow.

Perevitsky Torzhok stands on the River Oka, on steep hills above the township of Konstantinovo, where the poet Sergey Yesenin was born in 1895. Even today art students are brought here to sketch: the place is almost unspoiled, and at the time my grandfather was living there must have been breathtakingly beautiful, with a high hilly bank affording a view over plains that stretched endlessly beyond the river. In 1930 there had been no time to admire the view, however: my grandfather got out of Perevitsy Torzhok after the local people were forced to join a collective farm and it became impossible to carry on living as an extended family in the traditional way. He said he left because of the system of communal remuneration. 'We started working for "worked-day credits". You do a day's work, you get a note in your record book, and that's it.'

He loved to recall how picturesque the countryside he left behind had been, and claimed their village was even more beautiful than Konstantinovo. He told us how he and the other boys would leap off a steep bluff into the river, and that a hill called Makovishche that rose up directly opposite their house was actually an ancient burial mound where you could dig up Tartar and Russian skulls. He recounted these stories, though, without emotion, and thought back to the past only rarely, like an émigré long out of touch with the old country.

His first job in the city was riveting boilers at an asphalt factory in Moscow, and to start with he and the other workers actually lived under the boilers. It was terrible work, literally deafening, but he felt no urge to go back to his family home on that beautiful hillside. I never detected any sense of attachment in my grandfather to the sundry places he had lived in. A scrap of land between a platform and the tram turnaround hardly counted as home. So he was proud of the apartment he had been awarded in recognition of his labour and army record, although I always felt he took an even greater pride in the documents confirming the award. He had no interest at all in the new district of Belyaevo where he now lived.

He was one of eight children in a large peasant family and there was no time for schooling, but he became a man with urban ways and urban ambitions. He loved his job as an electrician, loved books, reading newspapers, going for walks in the park and making a career. He enjoyed the moving from one job to another, climbing the ladder step by step, and celebrated every new advancement by unselfconsciously drinking himself silly. He accepted the rules of a city of newcomers, moving ahead and paying little attention to anything else. There were more ladders in the city than in the countryside, always giving something new to aim for.

My grandfather's career was typical, and what he experienced was the experience of the majority. He was born in a country where 85% of the population were, like him, peasants. His fortunes changed, like those of everybody else, in 1929–30 with the mass collectivization of agriculture. He went to the front, like most men of his age, but, unlike many, survived. That was the second big event in his life. The third was when he was awarded a separate apartment, and that, too, occurred at much the same time as for many of his generation. He died in a country where a large majority, 74% of the population, were, like him, town dwellers.[1] In the country my grandfather was born in, the majority of people were under thirty. At the time of the 1917 Revolution, over 60% of the population of the Russian Empire were young. In the country in which he died, there were already more elderly people than young. Nowadays less than 40% of the population are under the age of thirty.[2]

This incredible transformation took place in less than one lifetime. Millions, like my grandfather, fled the countryside, famine and the new ways of doing things, and those who survived settled in cities. It was young people born, like my grandfather, to large families in the year of the revolution – or a little earlier or a little later – who became the first 'new generation'. It was new in the sense that the lives of such a vast number of people were to bear no resemblance to the lives of any previous generation of Russians. The aspiration to earn wages and gain an education had, of course, brought peasants to the cities before this, but never on such a scale. Millions of new proletarians, in cities or on collective farms, had to learn to live in an entirely new way, where the experience of their parents could only be a hindrance. The traditional way of life could no longer feed them, large families were an unsustainable burden, and they were forcibly converted from their old religion to a new one.

The introduction of collectivization, the liquidation of the more successful 'kulaks', and the policy of breakneck industrialization 'convulsed the lives of the Soviet Union's more than 130 million Soviet peasants'.[3] In their scale and consequences, the end of 1929 and the first months of 1930 are more significant than the revolutionary events of October 1917. Nicholas Riasanovsky likened collectivization to the christianization of Rus. '[B]ecause it affected most Russians in a fundamental way, the year 1929 marked the most important turning point in all Russian history, with the probable exception of the year 988,' he writes in his book on Russian identities.[4]

These young, strong, homeless people were forced, before they could become fully attached to the old way of life, to master the new way. They were a blank sheet of paper, willing to listen, understand and work. They provided a demonstration of just how much privation a human being can endure and what sort of conditions he can survive. For them, sleeping in a proper bed rather than under a boiler, the opportunity of earning extra rations, meant more than being part of the great national construction project. Riasanovsky writes that steadfastness and endurance rather than enthusiasm for work were the norm for most of these people. Steadfastness is not one of Aristotle's political categories, but it had a political role to play. It helped to hold the Nazis at bay at Stalingrad, and also helped people to endure all the trials of Soviet history.[5]

These stoical people were, moreover, accommodated in atrocious conditions, in utility rooms, dugouts, barracks, huts, hostels and communal apartments. The homelessness of an enormous number of Russia's citizens was actually a deliberate policy decision on the part of the regime. Firstly, this was because housebuilding was one of the casualties of the 'great turning point' of 1929–30. A conscious decision to concentrate limited resources on defence and heavy industry doomed the rest of the economy, including housebuilding, to be starved of funds. Investment in housebuilding was cut, and by 1940 even the statutory norms of floor space per person had been almost halved. Needless to say, no explicit policy of creating homelessness is to be found in Party documents, but it is entirely reasonable to infer this was a policy decision.

Secondly, the housing famine made it easier for the political leaders to direct labour at will. Most people were allocated accommodation through the enterprises for which they worked, and were only too willing to go wherever housing would be 'given': square metres were more readily available to those working in priority sectors. Thirdly, there was the system of residence permits, which, in a slightly modified form, is still in force today. Mandatory registration of citizens' place of residence made it easier to monitor them, both through official channels and with the aid of volunteers keen to assist the Party: unmasking an enemy of the people among your neighbours enabled you to lay claim to the room thus vacated.

What millions of new proletarians and collective farm peasants were unwittingly caught up in was an unprecedented experiment, an attempt by the political elite to achieve a predetermined result (a communist society, otherwise known as 'the radiant future') by radically accelerating and rigidly directing the historical process. It was a controlled social explosion. The theoreticians and practitioners of Leninist communism were planning to imitate, and indeed improve on, a process that in Europe had taken several centuries.

The hunger and deprivation were invariably presented as the price of the Party's march towards the radiant future, and that ideal really become rooted in citizens' minds. As a result of the homelessness to which the Soviet strategists doomed most of the USSR's citizens, the radiant future they really aspired to, however, was a separate, private apartment. This dream of private accommodation and a private life has, as we shall see, been crucial to how Russia developed, in both the Soviet and post-Soviet eras.

In Russian history, there have been no few rulers who believed the historical process was as malleable as metal and lent itself to technical manipulation. Peter the Great was certain he could, within a generation, turn Russia into a European state governed under the rule of law and complete with competent officials and army officers. The Soviet leaders were sure they could create an urbanized, industrialized country without having to pass through all the stages of organic growth of cities and industry. The post-Soviet leaders supposed they could establish a market economy without the institutions of private property and an independent judiciary. It would not be true to say that nobody has ever been able to leapfrog history – rapid transformations are possible – but success is never guaranteed and, more often than not, the result is far from what was intended.

From city dwellers to citizens

The rise of cities in Europe saw not only a rise in the urban population, but also a strengthening of its role in administering the cities and later the country. Yesterday's peasants, Europe's new citizens, had to defend the fruits of their labours from both feudal lords and monarchs, and this was the context of their efforts to organize themselves into guilds, parliaments and various popular movements.

The rulers needed the townspeople. Without their cities, the monarchs would never have been able to create nation states: the city was an ally in the struggle against the centrifugal forces of the provincially based hereditary aristocracy. During the fourteenth and fifteenth centuries, when modern states were being formed, European monarchs relied increasingly on the growing urban population, seeking agreements with representative institutions and taking into their service citizens with the benefit of a university education. Thus was the bureaucracy born, the upper level of the 'third estate'. 'With the development of industry, however, the third estate became too powerful for its former ally, the monarchy, to control, especially if the central government was weak or corrupt,' historian Vasiliy Rudich tells us. 'This led to bloody revolutions in Europe, and then to the birth of the modern age.'[6]

The city dwellers helped modern society to take shape. Industrialization and urbanization involved more than a mere growth in output and crowding of increasing numbers of people within cities' walls. Over long years, the city dwellers won what philosophers call designated rights. The rights to private life, freedom and the inalienability of property were formed over many centuries of deal-making between monarchs, the Church, the aristocracy and the city dwellers. In the course of all this bargaining, the city dwellers became citizens.

A crucial part in demonstrating the very possibility of private

11

property ownership on this earth was played, perhaps surprisingly, by the Church. It was the Fathers of the Church who brought back into intellectual currency classical authors whose works provide the starting point for any discussion of property to this day. Mediaeval scholars were preoccupied with proving it was legitimate for the Church to own property, and with defending that property against encroachment by monarchs. The monarchs for their part sought to prove that, within their territories, they alone were the fountainhead of legitimate ownership. Aristocrats and city dwellers alike needed a means of protecting their property from both Church and monarch. None of the parties succeeded in clinching victory, but then neither could anybody claim to be the sole authority for granting legitimate ownership. Neither the emperor nor the Church nor any association of citizens could gain the role of supreme arbiter. That role was constantly contested, which led to conflicts and wars, but precisely because there was no single victor, private property became what it is in Western culture today.

Perhaps that is why it is so difficult to replicate the institution in other cultures without a similarly long period of urbanization and industrial growth. It has proved especially difficult in cultures such as that of Russia, where no balance was ever achieved between the public and the aristocracy, and state power and property ownership fused into a single entity with a single arbiter. (For more detail, see chapter 4, which is devoted to the concept and institution of property.)

Reflected modernity

What happened in the USSR between the 1930s and the 1950s is also conventionally described as industrialization and urbanization. Certainly, in the decade before the Second World War and in the 1950s, an unprecedented number of factories, mines and power stations were built; schools, higher education institutions and research institutes, theatres, concert halls and pioneers' palaces were opened. None of that would have been imaginable without a new labour force, the city dwellers. By the early 1960s, the urban population in the USSR was level pegging with the rural population. That was a hundred years after England reached the same point, but only ten years later than the average in Europe, which is not all that much.

If we look more closely at the reality, however, the Soviet Union's performance, despite that statistic, was less than dazzling. The economic surge of the 1920s and 1930s, interrupted at the time of collectivization, continued until it returned to the long-term trend that had existed before the First World War. It slowed in 1940, before the start, for Russia, of the Second World War. So the rapid economic growth during the Stalin period before the war (variously estimated at 4% to 6% per year) may have been no more than a return to the long-term pre-revolutionary trend. Not even the stated objectives of Stalin's Great Leap Forward were actually achieved: not one of the five-year plans was fulfilled, and the decline in draught animals on the collectivized farms was not compensated for by tractors and other mechanization until the mid-1950s.

On average, over the course of the whole experiment, beginning with the 'anti-Christianization' of 1929–30 and until the last full year of the existence of the Soviet Union in 1990, per capita GDP grew by only 2.6% per year, and that despite a terrible cost in human and material terms.

Recent studies have shown that, in economic terms, the USSR was at its most successful towards the end of the 1970s, when per capita GDP rose to 38% of the US level. In 2012, Russia's per capita GDP stood at approximately 30% of that of the United States, which is close to where it was in 1908 and 1990.[7] Thus, taking a long-term view, Stalin's Great Leap Forward did not change Russia's economic weight relative to other key players in the global economic system. 'If the communist social system did have any economic objective, it was not achieved. Many countries, not only in Europe but in Asia and Latin America, showed higher growth rates with far less restriction of rights and freedoms.'[8]

The gap with Europe was not that startling, and Chinese per capita GDP was one-sixth that of the USSR (by 2012 it had already risen to half the Russian level). Literacy had become almost universal and education and medical care were more accessible than at any time previously in Russian history. We now had an educated urban population, but as a result of the dramatic reduction in family size we had an 'elderly' country. We are close to European modernity; we have almost caught up.

The result of the controlled social explosion our grandfathers experienced is, however, different from the outcome of several centuries of hard bargaining in Europe. Russia's modernity gives every impression of being perfectly standard. Who can doubt it? The same products, the same technology, the same clothing – but the similarity is external. Experimentally gestated in its Soviet test tube, our modernity has something missing. And what is missing is what was cast aside in the course of the experiment: the free will, the naturalness, the organic development it had in Europe. A draining of population from the countryside and into the cities is a natural process that almost all societies have experienced, but in Russia it was contrived and pushed through at high speed. Those in charge of the great project called the USSR deliberately set out to improve the course of history.

Developing the right to own property or the right of citizens to play an active role in the political growth of their country, so fundamental to the evolution of Western culture, had no place in Russia's scheme of things, because from the outset there was no intention of bargaining with anyone. Something Western society arrived at by an untidy process of trial and error, Soviet ideologists planned to transcend by the more hygienic procedure of building utopia to a blueprint.

By definition, however, utopias cannot be realized. Most are paper architecture, projects never intended to be implemented literally The American historian Martin Malia believes that the Bolsheviks made a 'mistake of Columbus': they went looking for socialism and found something quite different. 'The Party set sail for socialism but instead stumbled on Sovietism, thereby landing Russia in an inverted modernity.'[9]

The Soviet Union developed as a reaction to the West. The experimentally grown Soviet modernity can be seen as a reflection – as Western society on the other side of Alice's looking-glass.[10] In the final two and a half decades of its existence, the Soviet version of modernity looked increasingly authentic. This was when the USSR gained a reputation as a major power in science and space exploration. Grigoriy Khanin calculates that between 1951 and 1960, the USSR's GDP rose by 244%. Extraction of oil and gas was put on a more professional footing, and technology was imported to mass produce consumer goods. The lifestyle of my parents' generation in big Soviet cities began to bear at least some comparison with that of their peers in Europe and the United States. As a result of a massive programme of housebuilding, growing numbers of people were able to afford their own apartments. Life became more comfortable, owning a car became more affordable, as did seaside holidays and travelling around the country. It became possible to think seriously about the education and free time of your children.

A Soviet childhood was the same for everyone and had a limited set of components familiar to everyone. Identical buns were sold in identical breadshops. After school, you could visit any of your friends in an apartment just like your own. There you could be told off for the same misdemeanours and given the same meal as you would have had at home. The lucky ones had the same colourful tomes of The

14

Library of World Literature. The schoolmistresses, trained to teach us the same syllabus in identical schools, all seemed remarkably similar and had identically daunting hairdos.

Who could grow in this incubator other than identical little homunculi? In fact, however, those who emerged were remarkably varied, curious and lively people, and what saved them was the art of combination. For me, the elements available were school, books, the pioneers' palace and the summer. In the mornings, I had to go to school and attend the same classes as everybody else. In the summer, I had to go to the obligatory summer camp like everybody else, which was the same as last year only with a new cohort of tormentors.

The pioneers' palace was what I liked best because it was not obligatory. Here you could choose an activity, find your secret interest, something nobody else had. Your hobby could be the only thing that distinguished you from your friends, and ultimately the result was different just because of that distinctive ingredient. My good friend in the art studio at the pioneers' palace also went to Italian classes, and learned the language so well he got a job as a translator and went on to set up his own business in Italy. I know people who, thanks to the pioneers' palace, later became painters and actors. For most of the children, however, their hobby of learning Japanese and painting, or photography, or acting and geology, remained no more than a hobby. It was never intended that they should be more, but it was those extra-curricular activities that broadened your horizons, gave you a choice and prepared you for an unknowable future better than the rigid school curriculum. They helped us to become convertible currency in a world that overnight, in early 1992, became completely unpredictable.[11]

The pioneers' palaces were a splendid feature of Soviet civilization, but there were few others. Soviet industry could not supply citizens with ideal analogues of all the products manufactured on the other side of the iron curtain. An economy that knew nothing of competing for customers just could not match the quality of Western consumer goods. Soviet cars and products often looked like copies of Western originals that someone had glued together from whatever was available. Soviet vocal and instrumental ensembles did not sound like British rock groups. Materials and fabrics were not right. Clothing did not look the way it did on foreigners.

However, we did have books, including some by foreign authors in brilliant translations. There were wonderful societies with talented people prepared to donate their time and energy to children. Unfree people had a deep respect for 'free art', that is, what spiritually free

15

people produced. Possibly this was because people who, in a free market-based civilization, would have been busy making money and becoming famous were exposed to no such blandishments in Soviet civilization. They could conduct proper conversations, devote themselves to translation, write books and teach children. That was a real luxury, unplanned by the Soviet regime.

Many believed it would be enough to eliminate the shortages of goods to achieve a draw in the competition between Western originals and Soviet imitations. The problem of shortages did, however, prove less straightforward than Soviet planners had expected, and the only thing that helped to overcome it was the forcible introduction of free prices. It is the existence of a workable price mechanism that distinguishes the reality of today's Russia from that of the 1970s. Our imitation today looks considerably more like the original because the materials and fabrics are finally up to scratch. We buy the best, latest models of cars, and we can always invite genuine musicians from anywhere in the world. Our modernity, though, still lacks something crucial, something an external observer might not notice, because it is intangible. It is still those same ingredients the Communist Party left out of Soviet modernization: the genuine right to own property, and the right to participate in the country's affairs. Our modernity is still a reflection, and we are still stuck in Alice's Wonderland.

The capital of succeeding generations

The rungs of the ladder my grandfather climbed were: survive, get enough food, find a roof over your head, find a room, get a residence permit, get a separate apartment and, if you were lucky, the acme of success, get a dacha and a car. By the end of his life, a dacha and a car were within reach. The dacha he turned down, feeling no urge to go back to anything reminiscent of living in the countryside. He did, however, get a car. As a veteran wounded in the war, he was entitled to have a Moskvich conferred on him by the city. Unfortunately he was no longer in any state to drive, and could only look down from the window to see his car parked outside. From above, the Moskvich looked like a real car, his car, and grandfather could consider his life a success.

There was nothing wrong or laughable about climbing that apartment–dacha–car ladder, but my grandfather, like millions of his peers, paid too high a price for these urban tokens of success. He did not know how much he had been overcharged because, thank

God, he knew nothing of the recent research on the Soviet economy quoted above. He did not know that for every chair, table, carpet, shelf of books, cupboard of crockery, for every metre of roadway constructed, every house built and car manufactured, he had paid many times more than people of his age in countries beyond the iron curtain. He had nothing with which to compare his life, which was much like the lives of the people he saw around him. He had no managerial view 'from above' or from the sidelines. When I asked him why people in his time put up with all that was being done to them by those in charge, he gave no answer, and I do not think he really understood the question.

It is only now I have begun to think that even asking the question was cruel. It was only for my parents and me that there were dissident writers like Alexander Solzhenitsyn and Varlam Shalamov, while for him and most of his peers, those who were imprisoned and those who were not, their own experiences were quite enough. The generation that lived through collectivization, the labour camps and the war had a moral right not to know the full truth about Soviet history. That, however, is the only generation for whom it is excusable. Later generations have no such right.

The heroism of my grandfather's generation did not lie in denouncing an inhumane regime and rebelling against it. Their heroism was in the fact that, uprooted from their natural environment, all these millions of homeless people who began life in inhuman conditions stuck it out to see a day when life was at least tolerable; to see a radiant future which, unlike communism, was achievable; to obtain a private apartment. They had passed through a bloodbath, but managed at the end of their lives to look as if there had been no such thing. A table, a carpet, china, crystal, an apartment, a dacha, a car – these were, of course, only possessions, but for our grandmothers and grandfathers they were as blessed as the Promised Land was for the generation of Moses, and Moses only got to glimpse it, not to live in it.

Millions of families had grandparents who had lived through the Soviet bloodbath for the sake of something approximating to a proper life. They were able to sample this almost proper life of consumerism only when they were very old, which is why they so valued it. Their message to the next generation, whether they articulated it or not, was, 'We paid the price, now you live the life.'

In a country that had nullified everything that went before, they began life with a clean slate, either never having had anything or having lost everything. As they passed through life, everything was again repeatedly nullified. In a country where life evolves, every

17

generation builds on what, in cultural and material terms, it has inherited from its predecessors. In Russia, though, it has been as if these props were deliberately knocked from under people's feet. Vladimir Yuzhakov calls this the 'decapitalization of the generations'.

> For the bulk of the population, it was not only consumption that was restricted, but even the possibility of accumulation. Expropriation, nationalization, collectivization, the proscribing of entrepreneurship and punishment visited on any attempt at it, a mobilization economy of depressed wage levels, forced and practically unpaid labour in the countryside and in camps specially created for the purpose, compulsory 'voluntary' loans to the state, state terrorism that exterminated huge swathes of the population, including its most active members, to say nothing of the vast loss of life in the Civil War and the Second World War and from famines that catastrophically diminished the potential of the generations: even that is not a complete list of the factors and methods by which generations of Russia's citizens were 'decapitalized'.[12]

We often say that most people in Russia cannot kick the habit of waiting for handouts from the state. It sometimes seems almost a cultural characteristic, but neither my grandfather nor millions like him had any delusions about the paternalism of the state. He preferred not to perish in exile, not to live on the verge of starvation in the countryside, and instead went to build a new life with his own hands. The state's collectivization of agriculture deprived him of the cultural and financial legacy of his father, but for my grandfather and his son, my father, that same state was their mentor and employer and they knew no other. The dependency culture of most people in Russia is an inevitable feature not of our culture but of our history. It is a rut we live in, created by the path we have travelled. The majority are, of course, unaware of this peculiarity and could not put it into words, but it is a fact of our lives.

'With each successive generation, Russians became increasingly dependent on the state,' Yuzhakov says. 'The opportunities for people of each succeeding generation to solve their problems for themselves did not increase: they decreased.'[13] And even when they did not decrease, everything had to be started from scratch, when it was lost at the time of the revolution, when it was confiscated during collectivization, again after the war, and again after the collapse of the USSR. Let us not forget that at the end of 1991, the previous generation's capital was again nullified, and that the loss of value and fall in consumption at that time are entirely comparable with what occurred at the time of the Bolshevik Revolution. A way of life in which every generation suffers the loss of its financial and cultural capital is bound to be peculiar.

Our explosive, and constantly nullified, history has many consequences. The most important are: firstly, a perpetual expectation of help from the state and, if that is disappointed, a readiness to go into opposition; secondly, the repetitiousness of the main topics discussed by generation after generation. We have the books on our bookshelves, but many insights from the past have been erased from living memory, so that for the umpteenth time we find ourselves arguing about how Russia should develop, its place in the world, and about values. Every generation seems to set about accumulating cultural capital as if nothing had ever gone before.

The same has been true of material capital. A third consequence is that those who do have an opportunity to accumulate set about it with limitless ambition and total disregard for other people or the country's interests. They take what is up for grabs while they have the chance. When I see the city outskirts built up with villas, the country estates large and small, the mansions Russians buy abroad, I see this reflex of accumulation at work. I can see that the children and grandchildren of grandparents like my own are still living by their precepts and cannot restrain themselves: one more property make-over, one more car, one more second home, everything bigger, everything higher.

This makes it easier to understand the vast, ornate palaces. They result from that same set of values, only they have gone haywire and veered off into a 'bad infinity': if grandfather fought for his 5 m², his son wants 500, but preferably 5,000 along with 30 hectares of land and a modest palace with fountains – although actually, better still, would be 10,000 m² of floor space and a full 60 hectares. In purely human terms, it is possible to understand the psychology behind 'Miller's Palace',[14] and 'Putin's Palace',[15] because those people, too, belong to the generation to which that happy, consumerist future was bequeathed. They have taken the message too literally, and seem fixated on making sure the homelessness can never come back by endlessly increasing the number of square metres they own.

We do not have to follow their example. I would like very much to know what the post-Putin generations are thinking, the third generation, and the fourth hot on its heels. I would like to believe that those born, like myself, in the 1970s or younger have more on their minds than just accumulating possessions and real estate. The inertia is no doubt great, but it seems unthinkable that this scratched gramophone record should go on repeating endlessly.[16]

We have said that Russia has been modernized in a very odd manner, with something missing. What remains unmodernized is basically the intangibles: rights are not protected, most segments of the population have no representation at state level and the state itself is archaic and corrupt. The obvious recommendation is for the new generation to see its mission as being to complete the task of modernization. That may be over-optimistic, but one goal really should be the protection of property rights, more precisely of life and liberty, and of property as the guarantor of all other rights.

If the goal of the first twenty post-Soviet years was a continuation of the Soviet hankering after a 'radiant future', by which the last Soviet generation meant a private life at all costs, then logically the next, long-overdue goal should be the protection and development of what has already been built and accumulated. People have made money as best they could, without the benefit of laws or regulation, but now, if property is to be protected, laws and regulation are essential. Rights of ownership can be defended in jurisdictions abroad, which is what many people already do. If, however, expatriating assets and despatching children abroad remain the only way to guarantee reliable accumulation, Russia will in effect be permanently saddled with the status of a colony. It will remain a resource base for people who do not live in the country but only make money out of it. (More on this in chapter 6.)

There are different ways of reading the message from the older Soviet generation. How should you live? Should you grab yourself more apartments, dachas and cars? Build an even bigger mansion? A better mansion? Here size is not what matters. The younger Soviet generation, and all future generations, have no right not to know Soviet history. That means we need to take an interest not only in the number of square metres, but also in their quality and beauty. We need also to be mindful of all the things Russian society was artificially deprived of because of the peculiarities of the history of the Soviet period: protected property rights and the public representation of private interests. Without civic society, private interests are too vulnerable. Here you find the state intruding in the city, preventing you from having a normal car journey because, unlike you, its officials have a flashing beacon on their car; here you find it intruding in the courtyard of your apartment block, building a flashy garage where there used to be a public space to enjoy; here it is invading your house or apartment to check your residential registration; and it is even sneaking into your bed to check you are not 'promoting homosexuality'. That is the lesson recent years have taught us, and it is our agenda of what to fix in the years to come.

'Decolonization' and establishing the stable rule of law in Russia will be no easy matter and will, most probably, lead to conflict, but if we despair and declare the problems cannot be put right, it makes no sense to plan to continue to live, and build your home, in Russia.

However, first things first. Let us begin our discussion of home at the beginning, that is, at the boundary fence.

— 2 —

THE FENCE
Russian Title

Good fences make good neighbours

In 1914, Robert Frost wrote a poem, 'Mending Wall'. It is about how he and his neighbour walk along a stone wall separating their farms. They do so every spring to fix stones that have become dislodged over the winter. In the episode described, the poem's protagonist is trying to get his neighbour to discuss how sensible this is. Do they even need the wall?

> My apple trees will never get across
> And eat the cones under his pines, I tell him.
> He only says, 'Good fences make good neighbors.'
> Spring is the mischief in me, and I wonder
> If I could put a notion in his head:
> 'Why do they make good neighbors? Isn't it
> Where there are cows? But here there are no cows.
> Before I built a wall I'd ask to know
> What I was walling in or walling out,
> And to whom I was like to give offense.
> Something there is that doesn't love a wall,
> That wants it down.'[1]

The poet fails to sow doubt in his neighbour's mind. The poem begins with an enigmatic sentence: 'Something there is that doesn't love a wall,' and ends as the neighbour walks away, repeating the old saying, 'Good fences make good neighbours.' This ironic meditation leaves open the question of why people should need fences.

'Mending Wall' is open to many interpretations, but we can safely

22

say that the poem was never intended to be applied to practical, let alone political, purposes. By the early 1960s, it had become an American classic. The saying it featured was constantly quoted, and indeed the entire poem was cannibalized for quotations. When President John F. Kennedy was in West Berlin and inspecting the wall newly erected by the East German side, he recalled Frost's 'Something there is that doesn't love a wall.'[2]

The poem became almost a symbol of American–Soviet rivalry, focused at that moment on the problem of partitioned Berlin. The meaning was not, of course, limited only to the physical wall and Cold War foreign policy. The soft-spoken poem, delicately posing the question of good-neighbourliness and good walls, much to the poet's surprise, resonated very far from his farm in New Hampshire and suddenly found itself at a flashpoint where Russian and Western attitudes to walls, fences, private property and politics collided.

In late August 1962, as the Khrushchev thaw was in decline and one year before Robert Frost's death, the poet visited the USSR. 'Mending Wall' was one of the poems published in the Soviet press to mark his visit. A curiosity is that Frost later said the Russians had, for political reasons, removed the first line about there being something that didn't love a wall, while leaving in the words about 'good fences', which they evidently found to their satisfaction. 'I could've done better for them, probably,' he joked, suggesting,

Something there is that doesn't love a wall,
Something there is that does.[3]

There was some misunderstanding over the first line of Mikhail Zenkevich's translation, which was shown to Frost. The line is there, but the word 'wall' is replaced by 'barrier'.

Frost met Soviet writers and literary bureaucrats, the young Yevgeny Yevtushenko and Andrey Voznesensky, Korney Chukovsky, Konstantin Paustovsky, and even Anna Akhmatova. The visit culminated in a conversation with Nikita Khrushchev, during which the almost ninety-year-old Frost seems to have been more belligerently inclined than his host. '"God wants us to contend,"' [Frost] said; "you have progress only in conflict."'[4]

Khrushchev said in response that the fundamental conflict between the two countries needed to be in 'peaceful economic competition', and assured Frost that the USSR and its satellites had greater potency than the Americans. The socialist states were young, healthy and full of energy, while the United States and Western Europe were weighed down by a millennium of history and a decaying economic system.

At this point, Khrushchev mentioned an episode described in Maxim Gorky's memoir of Leo Tolstoy where Tolstoy complained that 'there was such a thing possibly as a nation's getting like the bald-headed row at a leg show so it enjoyed wanting to do what it could no longer do.' Frost laughed and said he had the same feeling, but that the United States was still too young to have any worries in that department. 'Noble rivalry' was the right theme for 'two nations laid out for rivalry in sports, science, art and democracy', Frost added.[5]

The episode that really showed the height of the 'wall' (or the depth of the gulf) between the two cultures was Frost's meeting with Anna Akhmatova. In order to prevent their American visitor seeing the conditions Akhmatova lived in, the meeting was arranged at the dacha of Professor Mikhail Alexeyev. ('What would Frost have said if he saw "The Shack", the doghouse Akhmatova lived in?' Joseph Brodsky wondered.) Akhmatova always found the episode comical when she reminisced.

> On one side sat Frost, decorated with all the honours and medals and prizes ever possible or imaginable. And on the other side there I sit, I, festooned with all the dogs in existence. The conversation proceeds as if everything were perfectly normal. Until he asks me, 'And what, madame, do you do with the trees on your land? I, for example, make pencils out of my trees.'[6]

Frost evidently asked the question to lighten the conversation and be friendly. What could be more straightforward and helpful for bridging cultures than their everyday, human concerns about their own plot of land? Anatoly Naiman adds that Frost asked Akhmatova what profit could be made from making pencils out of the pine trees in Komarovo (the creative artists' settlement where she lived). Akhmatova decided to respond in an equally businesslike register and told him, 'We get fined 500 rubles for cutting down a tree in the communal grounds.'[7]

Whether Frost detected the irony, there is no telling, and in any case the conversation was being conducted through a translator. It had been decided it should be in Russian so the secret police minders sitting in on it would understand what was being said. What Akhmatova perceived as an alien streak of the farmer in Frost was just the mistake of someone not very well informed about the USSR who took owning a house and land for granted. Pastoral rural delights were as exotic for her as the May Day Parade was for her American colleague. She lived in a country where property was seen as something that used to belong to aristocrats, or as a sign of special services rendered to the state, like the Soviet dacha in which the conversation was taking place.

Frost lived in a country where property ownership had shaped a nation and defined its national character. In his 1941 poem 'The Gift Outright', he wrote, 'The land was ours before we were the land's.' The newcomers seized the lands of America, but then the land seized them and made them American. The West was yet to come, 'still unstoried, artless, unenhanced'. Frost says here that through the histories told, through art and its inherent power, the land takes possession of its inhabitants. In the process, he denies ownership of the land to Native Americans, and overlooks the fact that the territory captured by the colonizers had already been storied in the myths and legends of the American 'Indians'. Now Frost had arrived in a land attempting to uproot the very concept of private property. He had proposed that 'something there is' within us that 'doesn't love a wall' and that shies away from strict demarcation of 'mine' and 'yours', but can have had no idea of the extent of the privation to which people had been subjected in a world where the attempt was being made to subjugate the private to the communal.

In debate with Khrushchev, Frost said that competition between the two systems was indispensable, and that 'conflict is the driving force of progress'. 'We and Russia,' he said on returning to America in September 1962. 'Two hundred years may pass before this conflict is resolved.'[8] The poet had no inkling that just one month after his departure there would be the Cuban Missile Crisis, which very nearly became the last crisis in world history. Neither was he to know that the economic and political rivalry between the two superpowers would abate in the 1990s and 2000s, and then resume as a farce.

The permanence of the fence

When Peter I ('the Great') founded St Petersburg, one of the eighteenth century's 'most deliberate cities', there was to be no place for fences. From the outset, buildings were constructed with their façades right on the building line, which in Russian cities was more usually where the front railings were placed.

Comparing the American and Russian capitals, Blair Ruble notes that both cities were created to look their best in good weather, despite the fact that both were in areas with highly inhospitable climates. These two self-conscious capitals were intended to demonstrate the ability of politicians to design cities, but real life sported with their dreams of imperial splendour. The long straight lines and ornate façades concealed hundreds of souls whose visibility would have ruined any dinner party.[9]

Europe's coldest capital required 'serious amounts of firewood', so 'the real economy of storage, stables, workshops, outhouses' and huge piles of firewood was hidden behind the classical façades in the extensive St Petersburg courtyards.[10]

Tsar Fyodor III (1676–82), brother of the future Peter the Great, started his reign by decreeing that all the storage porches and fences on Moscow's Red Square were to be dismantled. Catherine the Great, intending to build a new palace in Moscow, in 1773 ordered demolition of the Kremlin wall itself, part of which, along the riverfront, actually was demolished (but later restored). The city authorities hoped that after the fire of Moscow in 1812, the city's streets would at last be graced by elegant architecture rather than dominated by fences, but, as usual, the fences won.

The Soviet authorities proclaimed their new architectural policy by demolishing the Kitai-Gorod wall and the shops that clung to it in the 1930s, but the apogee of their building plans for Moscow was the wall surrounding communism's greatest white elephant, the never-completed Palace of Soviets. During the Soviet period, many such walled-in empty sites were created, and sometimes even built to completion. Behind enclosures, public buildings were erected; behind high fences, the Party leaders lived and prisoners laboured. Industrial enterprises in the Soviet Union would have been unthinkable without security fences: factories, plants, warehouses and ports had security befitting strategic military facilities, to protect them from the people who worked there no less than from outsiders.

For Vladimir Papernyi, emphasis on the importance of borders and secrets is an integral component of what he calls 'Culture Two', of which the culture of the Stalin period is an example. This kind of culture glorifies the state border and insists on secretiveness, immobility and strict hierarchy. Its opposite, 'Culture One', exemplified by the culture of the avant-garde constructivism of the 1920s, aspires to be international. The architecture of 'Culture One', he suggests, considers itself already the equal of foreign culture and accordingly has no need of frontiers.[11]

In fact, however, fences have been needed at every stage of Russian history. In our times, they have begun protecting not public but private territory. A fenced camp with watchtowers has again become a common sight, because that is now the look of gated communities of mansions which people freely choose to live in, and pay a great deal of money for the privilege of doing so. Fortress-like walls and armed guards at a security checkpoint are a significant factor enhancing the price of residential property on the outskirts of cities.

Fences, together with Russian society, have survived through all the changing political systems and social upheavals. They are our constant, and clearly the outward manifestation of some internal need that none of the forms of government has been able to satisfy. Indeed, the opposite is true: the changing regimes have rather fuelled the human propensity to hide behind fences. I believe there are at least three reasons for this persistence. Firstly, they were and are a monument to a still not fully satisfied longing for privacy. Secondly, they serve as a false solution to the lack of legitimacy and compromised security of private property. Thirdly, they are a physical manifestation of people's distrust of each other.

Enclosure serves these purposes everywhere, but in Russia the sense of needing it is stronger and more enduring than in other societies. There have been just too many political and social changes, those 'nullifications' discussed in chapter 1, signalling yet another redistribution of everything we feel belongs to us. A fence is a subconscious attempt to barricade oneself in, away from unwelcome changes of that kind.

For an American farmer, a wall is primarily a demarcation to prevent disputes over property boundaries and thereby maintain good neighbourly relations ('Good fences make good neighbors'). For us Russians it is more a defence. There has, after all, been a constant need to protect ourselves, whether against the imposition of collectivism or simply from our neighbours. In a society where everyone lived in fear of invasion by the state and individuals, a fence symbolized the longing for peace and privacy. Extreme inequality in the way private space is distributed in a vast country is a direct consequence of forced industrialization and its accompanying urbanization, which was at its most acute in Russia between the 1920s and the 1960s. Over those fifty years, the population distribution pyramid between town and country was almost upended. From 15% of the population living in towns, the figure rose to over 70%. Tens of millions of people moved to cities that were not ready for them: there were not enough apartments or roads, and transport was inadequate. The people themselves were not ready. We are living with the social and town-planning consequences of that revolution to this day.

The amazing privilege of having your own territory was allocated individually and in strict accordance with a hierarchy. For those who possessed that privilege, their fence was an immensely significant and desirable status symbol. Those who had no right to their own territory just helped themselves to it, appropriated it, built houses and erected makeshift fencing around them. For them, their fence was the badge of the pioneer. Soviet and post-Soviet suburban building is still a largely unexplored phenomenon, and has much the same legal basis as the favelas of Brazil or the shanty towns surrounding the megacities of Latin America and Asia. Over 30% of buildings in Russia are not officially sanctioned. The Russian Horticultural League calculates that only 20% of owners of plots of land have legal title to them.[12]

Life without property rights

This is a common state of affairs. Globally, and particularly in poor and developing countries, there is more unregistered property than registered. The only difference from Russia is that usually what is unregistered is people's actual, permanent place of residence, not their summertime second homes. US lawyer Winter King estimates that 85% of town dwellers in developing countries are occupying 'their' property illegally.[13] For the most part, these dwellings are slums.

The Peruvian economist Hernando de Soto says that 70% of the world's population have no legally recognized property rights. Informally held property he calls 'dead capital', and he claims the world could be transformed by giving people a standard, universally recognized title deed certifying that they own their home. Their capital would become 'live': it could be used as collateral for loans and provide a foundation for developing entrepreneurial activity, thereby raising the living standards of vast numbers of people. Credit and capital arise on the basis of property rights, never the other way round, according to de Soto. As soon as property is registered on a title deed, universal and convertible, accepted by any organization and bank in the country, you have capital and, consequently, money.[14]

In de Soto's homeland of Peru, the intention was that registration of property rights should play another important role. The foundation of the success of local radical movements was the help they gave the poor to defend their homes and land from encroachment by others, including the state. 'By creating a civilized alternative, a legally effective property system,' de Soto says, 'we took away the extremists' political legitimacy.'[15] Inadequate property rights he sees as a political, rather than an economic, failure: it is possible to create a system to solve the problem, but you need to be careful how you go about it. Liberals' advice to introduce the basics of a market economy is ineffective, he explains, because the present generation of people in the West take for granted the legal framework needed to support private property. It was the great-great-grandfathers of today's liberals who created the present legal system, and it is no good asking such liberals for help. De Soto decided he needed a better grasp of history, so he studied the evolution of the law in various countries before trying to create a modern programme to overcome the failures of earlier politicians. Over the past twenty years, he has initiated a worldwide set of 'titling programmes' to disseminate property rights.

These programmes really have contributed to the creation of a lot of new value, and that is something their organizers can be proud of, but the macroeconomic effect de Soto envisaged has not been forthcoming. There is no reliable evidence to suggest that those in possession of the title deeds to their homes stand a better chance of obtaining credit. In fact, there is even some evidence that banks are less willing to provide credit, because they recognize it will be more difficult to seize property if a borrower defaults.[16] The probability is that the positive results the Peruvian government achieved in the fight against terrorism in the 1990s had less to do with the issuance of title deeds than with a strengthening of the state and the implementation of anti-terrorist campaigns based on force. De Soto has done a lot to draw the world's attention to the problem of property, but the cure he proposed is evidently less effective than he hoped.

The Russian situation is, of course, different; we are not talking about slums but often about entirely respectable buildings that really do have potential as capital. If they were legitimized, they might well play a more substantial role in the economy than the humble dwellings of the Latin Americans. On its own, however, a title deed is not enough. Those organizing programmes to 'bring capital to life' aim to provide citizens with legally enforceable titles of ownership, but institutionalizing property rights is, as we shall see below, a complex and difficult business. It is so intimately tied up with history and political development that attempting to introduce it by purely bureaucratic means in a few short years is likely to fail.

If we are to embark on such a programme, we need not just to issue title deeds but also to undertake a complete overhaul of the mechanisms of the state. For property to be secure, an honest police force is essential, as is integrity all along the line of law enforcement, from the police officer on the beat to the judiciary themselves. The acquisition of private property by a large number of people will generate disputes, and these will need to be resolved by a workable court system that none of the parties can simply bribe. Without that, property rights are a nonsense. If your dishonest business partner can just go to the court investigator and commission a criminal case against you, there is no real right to own property in your country. If a representative of the state, a governor or a president, can treat the finances of major corporations as a supplementary source of budgetary funding, the shareholders have no genuine property rights but only a circumscribed right of tenure.

No matter how ornate a title deed may be, it does not determine the practical reality of the law. Where the state does not honestly respect the right to property, fails to give it proper protection, regards all property as its own patrimony – that is, where it does not provide a service of genuine law enforcement and law courts with integrity, does not share power and property – we see the emergence of quasi-state or anti-state forces. They sell themselves to citizens as supposed guarantors of their rights, arbitrators and trouble-shooters, usurping the functions exercised in a developed state by the police force and law courts. In Latin America, these 'services' are provided by armed gangs of various kinds;: in today's Russia, they are provided by personnel working in law enforcement but acting in a 'private' capacity.

Failure to assert property rights in the developing world thus leads to displacement of the state from everyday life and the creation of a market of private services that substitute for those of the state. Citizens who resort to the services of this black market do so at their own risk. A 'privately employed' police officer or investigator who solves a client's problem by instigating a fabricated criminal investigation in return for payment may perfectly well be destroying someone who had been his own paying client in the past.

The state should in, theory, have a major interest in ensuring the rule of law, because this enshrines its role as protector and arbiter, which increases its power. The only modern states interested in strengthening the law, however, are those in which autonomous institutions have priority over 'hands-on control' from above.[17] Where a hands-on control regime generates generous benefits for particular officials, they will actively work against consolidating the institution of private property.

The development of robust institutions to protect rights, wider distribution of property rights and the market growth that would accompany it mean, at the very least, increased tax revenues for the state budget. At best, they would also provide a basis for citizens to take an informed interest in the policies of the state. If people are paying direct taxes and are fully aware of parting with their money, they have a quite different attitude to the way the state spends it.

The introduction of property taxation has been under discussion in Russia for many years now. Its advantages in terms of redistribution of resources within the community are obvious: it would penalize the owners of investment apartments, meaning that the system would provide less subsidy for the lifestyle of those living on unearned income than it does at present. Land and real estate, dividends and capital gains are taxed very leniently in Russia, and there is no direct inheritance or luxury goods tax.[18]

The regime is, however, in no hurry to act. When he was at the height of his fame, Hernando de Soto was invited to come to Moscow and talk about his theory and programme to the presidential administration, but nothing followed from that. As in Soviet times, most taxes are not paid by Russians personally but deducted by our employer from wages or salaries, so we have no direct awareness of paying for the services provided.

The problem is deeper than that, however. Introduction of the institution of legally safeguarded private property in a country leads to the emergence of autonomous players and a limiting of the state's influence. From there it is no distance to introducing the full rule of law, which interposes between the state and the individual an arbiter beholden to neither of them. Historians and political scientists tell us that this kind of major change does not come about without conflict, because why would a ruling elite voluntarily relinquish power? The transition from authoritarian rule to a democratic system takes too much from those running the state, bringing in numerous new constraints and challenging the inertia of their ways.

For all that, Russia is a country where tectonic shifts in rights, if admittedly they did not extend to the whole population, are by no means unknown. Property rights were granted to the nobility under Catherine the Great (r. 1762–96); serfdom was abolished under Alexander II (r. 1855–81); and Pyotr Stolypin's land reform was introduced in the reign of Nicholas II (r. 1894–1917). These are all instances of a voluntary reduction by the ruler of some of his or her powers. In each case there were radical changes to the system of ownership, and these had profound long-term consequences which can justifiably be described as revolutionary.

It is not beyond the bounds of possibility that at some future time the modern Russian state, too, will find that it cannot develop further without some degree of self-limitation and that there will be another tectonic reallocation of rights, another revolution from above. At present it is difficult to see that happening, because the elite would have voluntarily to share out both their power and their property with the rest of society. Moreover, a separation of power and property would result. In place of the under-capitalized generation discussed in chapter 1, we would see a capitalized generation of new property owners. They would inevitably pay more taxes, but they would also be more demanding of those who spend their taxes, and would have fit-for-purpose institutions to protect their rights.

Those who currently represent the Russian state are probably aware of the magnitude of this task and the consequences of undertaking it. One consequence would be that they would cease to be 'the regime' in the present Russian sense of the word. The new society would also want answers from them over a number of issues. Sooner or later, that is inevitable. Governments and elites may come and go, but the issue of the absence of a genuine right to own private property will continue to dog the country until it is resolved.[19]

Russian title

A fence in Russia, then, is a symbolic replacement for several missing institutions. In Soviet times, everyone had to wait and apply if they wanted to show they enjoyed the status of a person who owned at least something of their own. The yearning for the minimum of privacy essential for self-esteem burst out immediately after the change of political regime in 1991–2, and has not been satisfied to this day. Concrete, brick, metal fences and railings the height of a three-storey house have the distinct look of overcompensation for vulnerability and an attempt to tell the world, 'All this is mine.'

It is a characteristic of Russian fences, traditionally expected to be stationary, that they are constantly on the move. Fences may burn down in fires or be demolished by the authorities, but they very soon spring up again. Both citizens and the authorities have always been adept at exploiting the movability of fences enclosing land, but land can also just be enclosed and thereby become someone's property. In Russian cities, fences were often on the move immediately before roads were built or railway tracks laid. Even today, every dacha owner knows there will be no untoward consequences if a fence is discreetly moved a bit closer to the road.

For many centuries, fences, field boundaries and markers were movable even in Western Europe. From the fifteenth and sixteenth centuries right up until the early nineteenth century, European landowners made fortunes by 'enclosing' communal land. Peasants were driven off their land so that sheep could be grazed and their wool sold. Enclosure was a neat way of seizing land that nobody else owned, and even if they did.

One of the signs of a developed society is the ability to reach consensus on certain rights, which come to be more important than physical barriers. In the absence of property rights, a fence is no more than a gesture. No matter how much concrete you pour, no matter what armour cladding you give it, without the rule of law your fence will afford poor protection. No number of security guards will help, even though Russia is a world leader in the number of security guards it has. Of the 70 million economically active members of our population, more than 600,000 are security guards, private or institutional, and that is before we count the police. That, believe it or not, is a reduction: in 2003 the number of guards peaked at 1 million.[20] China, by way of comparison, has some 2 million people employed as guards but its population is ten times larger.

And then we have Russia's ongoing problem with doors, most of which are kept locked. When Soviet architects were designing public buildings – ministries, theatres, shops and stadiums – they never stinted on doors. In the ideal world for which they were designing huge buildings, people were going to be entering and exiting in droves. Great torrents of them would sweep up gigantic flights of steps and flood through perhaps five, even ten, doors. These tended to be enormous and carved if they were made of wood, or with grilles if they were metal.

In the real world, though, for some reason it was only ever thought necessary to open one half of the door, morning and night, winter and summer, and some doors were never opened at all. People had to pass through in single file, perhaps so the gatekeeper could check who was coming in or going out. Or perhaps he was supposed to be counting the numbers going in each direction.

There would be guards sitting at every entrance of every building, watching television all day, with only one half of the door open. If it was a club or a disco where you had to pay to get in, then no doubt the closed doors were needed to ensure that people paid. The other entrances, even though there were guards for them, were usually closed. It was obviously more congenial for all the guards to sit together, clustered around just one door.

The doors remain closed, despite the fact that there has long been no need for people to come in one by one. There are computer programs that cope admirably with the checking of security passes, the police can be summoned by pressing a button, but companies are willing to pay for security guards and fire officers because the job they are doing is just so important. It is a firm tradition: entrances must not be left without human supervision. Someone must be there to keep an eye on us squeezing through that half of the only available door. Someone must be there to eye us suspiciously as we come in and to scowl at our retreating form as we leave. Without that distrustful scrutiny, an entrance would not be a proper entrance. It is a little frontier, a state border in miniature.

Mistrust is another reason for the tenacity with which we retain our fences and cling to irrational security traditions. The global average for respondents who, if asked if they trust other people, reply 'no' is 56%. In Russia, however, 77% of those surveyed did not trust their compatriots. In the Scandinavian countries, the proportion of the mistrustful rarely exceeds 30%, and on average throughout Europe the figure fluctuates around 40%.[21]

Fear that your neighbour may be a crook has not only psychological, but also more tangible, consequences. This has been demonstrated by Robert Putnam, an American scholar who was among the first to engage in close study of the elusive quality of trust. Comparing standards of behaviour and levels of civic engagement, willingness to give mutual assistance and cooperate in different regions of Italy, he found there were variations. Moreover, the present-day level of trust in a community might have deep historical roots, and depend on whether in the past the province had been under papal jurisdiction or belonged to one of the independent principalities. 'Trust itself is an emergent property of the social system as much as a personal attribute.'[22]

At the national level, a low degree of mutual trust hampers economic development. Studies show that in countries with a high degree of trust, the government intervenes less in the work of enterprises and the daily life of citizens, and this reflects positively on economic growth. When horizontal links are strong in a society and there is a high propensity for cooperation, people are able to resolve conflicts themselves, without outside intervention. When people are afraid of each other, they tend to demand the intervention of their superiors, the police, security or the 'iron fist' of a leader.

The growth of trust is part of the transition of a society from 'survival values' to 'self-expression values'. When people have provided for themselves, when they feel security in their everyday life, they no longer aim simply to earn money (survival values), but to earn it by doing something interesting (self-expression values predominate). Moving on from the survival model leads to a change in social and political values. For example, more people speak out in favour of private rather than public ownership of enterprises, and people more often say that education and work are equally important for men and women. There is also a link between values and political systems: among the countries where self-expression values are more common, there is not a single dictatorship.[23]

Until that transition occurs, a society composed of many frightened people carries more and more costs for protection against theft, and threats from competitors and the state. That inhibits growth of the economy and reduces its efficiency. Resources allocated to protection and security are withdrawn from development, but fail to contribute meaningfully to peace of mind. Mistrust between citizens leads to the demand for a 'firm hand', while authoritarian rule further fuels fears and mistrust of each other.[24] The citizens have no illusions about what kind of people officials and law enforcement officers are. Opinion polls reveal that officials are seen as pursuing only their own selfish interests, but mistrust of one's neighbour evidently outweighs mistrust of the state. Ultimately everyone is on their own in looking out for themselves and their property.

Perhaps this also explains the strength of the tradition of putting railings and fences round the graves in Russian cemeteries. Is it an attempt to stake out territory for oneself and one's loved ones, if not in this life then at least in the next? Here too a physical fence is performing the important existential function of telling the living that the deceased now finally has undisputed ownership of something. The railings in cemeteries are often more conspicuous than the memorials themselves, and come to be seen as being the memorial.

Of course, a fence is no real guarantor of property: it can neither protect owners from attack nor hide them from a hostile world; power and money are stronger than any fence. Nevertheless, flying in the face of logic, fences are greatly prized in Russia. They are at least the token of a right, a recognized symbol, a talisman of planks, bricks or concrete.

The architect Alexander Brodsky has an artwork: a plot of land on which there is a bed with a fence round it. It is a very elegant and precise statement of the issue, a metaphor of an unsatisfied longing for privacy and a statement about private property. Perhaps it is also an allusion to Leo Tolstoy's parable 'How Much Land Does a Person Need?'

This enables us to summarize the significance of a fence in Russia, which, as we can now see, has not only a utilitarian but also a symbolic function, defending the orderliness of society. Apart from that primary function, the fence serves perhaps ten other purposes, being also the border separating a person from the state, private from public life; it serves as a proxy for a title deed to the property, a means of grabbing land, a means of protecting it, a status symbol, a talisman against evil spirits, a minor architectural form, a work of art and a monument.

— 3 —

BEHIND THE FENCE

The Privatization of Utopia

Private palaces

As a child, I knew that behind a fence – if it was splendid enough, of wrought iron and with pillars topped with plaster spheres – you would usually find a palace. This might be a museum devoted to people with no longer existent names like Sheremetiev or Yusupov. Behind less ornate fences were different palaces – of pioneers, culture or sport. I knew those palaces were public and so did not belong to anyone, unless, at a pinch, to Lenin. They had fascinating turrets, oriel windows, attics and other bits that stuck out. I wanted to live in them because details like those help you to be different. They are not standard.

> Like any child growing up in the Soviet Union and not knowing any-thing different from a standard apartment, I dreamed of a palace. In fact I was really very lucky: our apartment was quite sizeable, and my father had a dacha that went with his job. I always longed, though, for something out of a fairy tale, the sort of fantasy that has a prince on a white horse, only I also wanted to have a castle where I could tether the horse and proceed into the inner chambers. Secondly, I wanted a house in the country but, thirdly, it would be really boring just to build an ordinary house. I liked mediaeval Gothic. I imagined building it for more than five years. I did, of course, want to amaze everybody else, but that was not what mattered most. What I really wanted was to give myself a big treat.[1]

Telling us all about his residence in Moscow province, TV presenter Maxim Galkin reminds us that the precept of our fathers and grand-fathers remains in force. Their message, 'We paid: you live!', has been heard and, thanks to this popular actor's large and appreciative audience, it has even been writ large. Not everyone talks openly about the things they privately cherish, but for Galkin publicity is his profession, and for some years now he has been telling us in the newspapers and on television about his home. The images are very striking, with the result that there are probably even more people dreaming of living in a great, fairy-tale mansion nowadays than there were before.

So here is the tale of another palace. In December 2010, entrepreneur Sergey Kolesnikov published an open letter on the Internet to the then Russian president, Dmitry Medvedev, informing him that, on the Black Sea coast near Gelendzhik, a huge palace was being constructed 'in the style of an Italian palazzo, with a casino, a winter theatre and summer amphitheatre, a chapel, swimming pools, a sports centre, helipads, landscaped parks, and teahouses'. Kolesnikov went on to say he was sounding the alarm because the palace was intended for the then prime minister, Vladimir Putin, was being built with the involvement of state institutions, on money donated for other purposes, and was costing a billion dollars.[2]

That this 'leisure centre' belonged to Putin was officially denied, but later, in February 2011, *Novaya gazeta* published documents indicating a link between the palace and the presidential administration, so there certainly was something a bit governmental about it.[3] In early March, it was bought by a businessman, previously completely unconnected, for an amount substantially lower than Kolesnikov had mentioned.[4] A lot gets written about palaces nowadays. It is a topic people find interesting.

There are numerous photographs on the Internet, so anyone can look at them, read what is written and compare these palaces. 'Putin's Palace', built to an Italian design, is, of course, bigger and more grandiose than Galkin's, but Galkin's is a palace without quotation marks around it. Who owns it is a matter of public record, and its owner can talk openly about his pet project because he is a highly paid actor who prides himself on his good taste. His 'mediaeval Gothic' architectural gem may not be to everybody else's liking, but at least there is no conflict here between what is public and what is private.

Such is not the case with 'Putin's Palace'. The then prime minister may also as a boy have dreamed of palaces, and he, like Galkin, probably thought it would be boring to build an ordinary house, but he is in no position to flaunt his caprice. Who really owns the Italian palazzo in Praskoveyevka has to be kept secret.[5]

Publicity is always a nuisance, but cannot always be avoided when the line between public and private gets blurred. A passion for building on a royal scale gives away who the owner is. Public curiosity about unusual private homes has increased in recent years, and is more easily satisfied than people who secretly own property might like to imagine. It is possible to look over the fence with the aid of Google Earth, people in the vicinity can take photographs, because nowadays nearly every phone has a camera, and social networks make it possible to disseminate video stories. Indeed, Alexey Navalny, Russia's anti-corruption crusader, has made it his trademark to scout, with the assistance of aerial drones, for unaccounted properties that might be illegally owned by state officials.

So in due course we will know all there is to know about secret palaces. Perhaps civic curiosity and social media will together help us to do something that is always difficult: to grow out of attitudes and institutions left over from the past. In this case, we are talking about a Soviet institution whose time is up: the nomenklatura, or class of privileged officialdom, and its carefully guarded opportunities for consumption. The nomenklatura was a secret category of the most important and lucrative positions in the ruling party, the state bureaucracy and the economy. It has proved exceptionally persistent and survives to the present day.

During the Soviet era, a nomenklatura position gave its occupant access to benefits unavailable to the majority of people. These included houses, dachas, sanatoriums and official residences. Today's cashless consumer economy for the nomenklatura, who nowadays are called 'the elite', is in direct succession to the Soviet version. It is largely financed through compulsory levies on big business which used to be in the public sector. It does, of course, also help itself to state funds, but is essentially an alternative 'elite' budget whose resources are unavailable to the majority of the population. Something to bear in mind is that, just as in Soviet times, 'residences and analogous facilities ... are considered part of the infrastructure of government and, as such, information about them is a state secret.'[6] This makes it difficult for journalists to unearth how much all this is costing, and easy for businessmen with links to officialdom to enrich themselves from the gravy train.

Just over a score of residences for the president and head of the government are the meagre pickings left over from the true luxury of Soviet times. The other castles and palaces are attempts by private individuals to imitate, at their own expense, the quality of life enjoyed by the nomenklatura. A famous example is 'Miller's Palace', built by Alexey Miller, executive director and a major contractor of Gazprom for the top managers of the Russian gas monopoly. As soon as this story became public through social media and the press, Gazprom disowned the project, and the baroque palace, covering a territory the size of several football pitches, was transformed into a large dacha owned by an individual completely unconnected with Gazprom.[7]

It is difficult to find a rational explanation for the expenditure, running to tens of millions of dollars, on such projects, especially when we take account of the scale of the embezzlement while they are being built. It is irrational behaviour, which the economist and sociologist Thorstein Veblen a hundred years ago suggested calling conspicuous, or status, consumption. The American moneybags written about by Veblen openly sought to shock the public with their displays of opulence. In the case of Russia, status consumption is provocatively gross, but the owners try to conceal it or play it down. Ridiculously oversized properties often originate as lavish gifts given to top officials by grateful contractors who grew rich on state concessions. The donors often avoid transferring property rights to the official in question. Distant relatives, friends, even fake charities are used as nominal owners, which makes proving the connection to an official difficult. In numerous cases, activists have shown either family connections or the facts of use of the facilities by officials. The officials in turn have always denied ownership.[8]

I see this as an indication that, in the first two decades since the break-up of the USSR, the social utopia of the Soviet Union has moved to the private sector. More precisely, it has fragmented into a multitude of private utopias in a process that began not with the collapse of the Soviet Union, but far earlier. We were born in a country where palaces could be either public, like the metro, or the domain of the nomenklatura and hidden from sight. Such public goods as the army, the navy, armaments, the space programme, heavy industry, healthcare, education, science, children's sports schools, pioneers' palaces, public transport, public spaces and central squares were an economic speciality of the Land of the Soviets and were maintained by the state on a middling or inferior level, but they were maintained.

In the 2000s, when the official rhetoric was all about restoring the grandeur of the state, what actually happened was that the production of public goods was transferred, officially and unofficially, into private hands. Uniformed individuals to whom the constitution granted the right to use force in the interests of society began trading in that right for their personal profit. Construction of roads, railways and other infrastructure projects – that is, works for the public good – became an area where people close to the regime made gigantic private fortunes. The same was true of healthcare, especially in the provision of medical equipment and medicines. After the Soviet period, where they became public, palaces are now once again becoming private, as they were in tsarist times.

The word 'palace' was deliberately applied in the Soviet period only to premises open to the public. They might be museums, former palaces seized by the power of the people from their owners and thrown open to everyone. They might be pioneers' palaces, palaces of sport or palaces of culture, all of them public institutions. It is a cause for celebration that the pioneers' palaces, and in particular the modernist Moscow Pioneers' Palace on the Vorobiov ('Sparrow') Hills, were successfully saved from privatization. Many other public facilities, however, passed into private hands. There is a symbolism in the fact that sometimes a building confiscated by the Bolsheviks from its owners and nationalized has now in the post-Soviet period reverted to private ownership. Such has been the fate of the Yusupov Palace in Moscow.

It may be that the wheel has come full circle and that the palaces will eventually be open to the public again. The private utopia is showing signs that its time is up. The 2014 political crisis in Ukraine led to President Viktor Yanukovych fleeing the country and his private residence being opened to the gaze of the public. Russia's leaders and oligarchs have yet to start donating their palaces to the people, but we are already hearing some declare their intention to return the wealth they have accumulated to society and the state.[9]

The privatization of utopia

The Bolshevik state, from the first years of its existence until Stalin's forcible 'turning point' at the end of the 1920s and early 1930s, appealed to the masses to create collectives and encouraged a communal way of life. The ideal lifestyle was to be collective, work was to be collaborative, emotions were to be shared. The family was regarded as an outdated institution. New People were not to cook and eat, do their laundry or bring up their children individually, and accordingly, in the 1920s, the regime supported the building of hostels, communal dining rooms, industrial kitchens and laundries. There were to be no family kitchens in the communal housing, and there were none even in many of the apartments in the House on the Embankment, a residential building for the Soviet Party and state elite built in 1928–31 by Boris Iofan.

The constructivist architect Konstantin Melnikov proposed a

'Sonata of Sleep' project that was to provide accommodation with a collective musical dormitory for 600 people. The sleeping area was also communal in a house Melnikov built for himself and his family, which had six compartments with beds. It was, nevertheless, a private urban house: quite a rarity in the USSR.

Of course, for most people life was collective not by design but simply because there was a catastrophic housing shortage. The new enterprises and factories being built throughout the land needed workers, and life in the ever more impoverished, collectivized countryside was becoming more desperate. The urban population was increasing at an unprecedented rate and the city soviets began moving people from place to place, redistributing and equalizing the living space occupied by citizens of different classes. Apartments abandoned by more affluent city dwellers were filled with new tenants; apartments where, in the view of the authorities, there were too few occupants had additional people moved into them. In order to destroy the old hierarchy of classes, the new state resettled workers from the suburbs in the houses and apartments of the rich in the city centre. As a result of this kind of migration, the percentage of workers living within the Garden Ring Road in Moscow rose between 1917 and the end of 1920 from 5% to between 40 and 50%. By 1924, a total of over 500,000 workers and family members had been resettled in requisitioned houses in the capital.[10]

The new regime demanded that the old city dwellers move over and make room. At first it even proposed fixed quotas. The aristocrat Lenin thought in terms of rooms, so proposed billeting the new residents in requisitioned apartments in accordance with the formula: $N = K - 1$, where N is the number of occupants and K is the number of rooms. There should, accordingly, be one more person in each apartment than there were rooms. This, in his opinion, would prevent them from feeling they were rich.[11]

Even today, not every family in Russia can boast of having reached the level of privacy prescribed by Lenin's formula, but until a start was made on mass construction of residential accommodation under Nikita Khrushchev, housing was allocated in terms not of rooms but of square metres, which, for some reason, were constantly being reduced.

People were renting not a room but a 'corner', that is, part of a room. They lived in corridors and in kitchens. Home for a family might be a boiler room, a doorkeeper's cubbyhole, a cellar or a space under the stairs. The most urgent and frequent issue in citizens' appeals to the authorities was accommodation. Sheila Fitzpatrick quotes a letter in which the children of a Moscow family of six begged for rescue from their accommodation in a windowless cubbyhole under a staircase totalling 6 square metres.[12] Benedict Sarnov recalls trying to exchange a room in a communal apartment for one better suited to his family, and had almost reached agreement with the owners when he discovered the new apartment had the family of a prosecutor living in the bathroom,[13] much as in Mikhail Zoshchenko's famous story, 'The Crisis' (1925).

Private life began making a comeback in the early 1930s, but always as a privilege, for special people, in return for services rendered. New apartment blocks in cities were designed and built as one-off projects and clearly could never solve the problem of the massive housing shortage.

Stalin was determined to assert his personal authority and dissociate himself from the previous era. He wanted to demonstrate that the state had now entered a period of stability. The emergent totalitarian system of power sought to replace mobility with stasis, egalitarianism with hierarchy, the horizontal with the vertical, the collective with the individual. In cinema, the state now began to favour individual characters rather than the heroic masses. Standardization and uniformity were no longer of interest to the system, which now favoured individuality both in styles of clothing and in accommodation.[14]

It even became possible to get a separate apartment and a dacha, but only if you were a special kind of person. Distribution of the good things in life became more personalized and, inevitably, was unequal and strictly hierarchical, because in a poor country there was not enough food or clothing, let alone accommodation, to go round.

Titles and honours, abolished by the proponents of proletarian culture, returned; ranks and insignia reappeared in the army; uniforms came back in schools and certain state organizations. In the field of culture, honorary titles were introduced: Distinguished Actor, People's Actor. Your place in the hierarchy determined your access to the good things and to a more or less decent way of life.

A genuine private life was thus attained by a select few. A separate apartment, a home, privacy, personal transport did appear, but they were luxury goods.

It is hardly surprising that for most people the longing to have their own home, and the privacy essential to a sense of their own human dignity, built up for years and burst out immediately the USSR collapsed in 1991. Even now that yearning for privacy has not been fully satisfied. Perhaps it is to this process of creating a personal world for individuals rather than a socio-political change that we should be referring as 'getting off our knees', a phrase President Vladimir Putin has used on many occasions to describe Russia's newly assertive stance.

The Soviet experience profoundly discredited collectivist enthusiasms, and not only in Russia. These survived until, perhaps, the middle of the twentieth century. Collectivist management of the economy, planning from a single centre of every aspect of production and consumption, communal living, public palaces, parks and museums, support for the sick, and communal bringing up of children in special camps – they were all part of a myth of utopia created over centuries. A classic feature of many of these ideal states was acceptance that a special caste of leaders should be separated out: the best people, talented and dedicated to the motherland. It hardly needs to be said that the Communist Party, envisaged as just such a caste of leaders, failed to live up to expectations and undermined faith in the very possibility of selfless service of that kind.

Then, of course, there was the matter of private property. For Thomas More, who coined the word 'utopia' and wrote the best-known book on the subject, this was a concept that did not exist in his imaginary ideal state. Money is not used on the island of Utopia and its citizens treat precious stones and gold with contempt: diamonds are mere toys for children, and gold is used to make chains for slaves, and chamber pots.[15]

A striking image can prove to possess astonishing power. Some 400 years later, Lenin, the leader of the world's first socialist state, who was, of course, well familiar with More's book, wrote that when the communists conquered the world they would install public conveniences made of gold in the streets of several of the world's greatest cities.[16] His words evidently made a big impression on, among others, Lam Sai-Wing. A gold trader in Hong Kong who grew up in communist China, he has repeatedly told reporters that Lenin's words inspired him to install a gold toilet in his showroom.[17]

The gold-plated toilet has acquired mythical status in post-Soviet society. There are firms that manufacture and sell them, and articles about them appear in the popular press. After their president fled the country, the Ukrainians, we are told, looked for a gold toilet in his former residence.

For centuries, people, horrified by social injustice, sought intellectual refuge in the collectivist utopia, but the general disillusionment with the socialist ideal caused the pendulum to swing far in the opposite direction. Post-Soviet Russia was indeed a realm of the privatized utopia, a kind of escape, characterized by a desire to bury our heads in the sand and not see what was going on around us.

I grew up in a socialist country myself, and no one is less inclined to idealize the myth of an ideal society. I heard plenty of talk about it, but never saw it. I read about that kind of world in Plato, in Nikolai Chernyshevsky and in Ivan Yefremov, but books about ideal lands should not be dismissed as children's fiction. As Lewis Mumford wrote in *The Story of Utopias*:

> [Utopias] exist in the same way that north and south exist; if we are not familiar with their classical statements we at least know them as they spring to life each day in our own minds. We can never reach the points of the compass; and so no doubt we shall never live in utopia; but without the magnetic needle we should not be able to travel intelligently at all.[18]

Utopias, of course, discredited themselves in the twentieth century. Most, on closer examination, proved to be closed societies whose main goal was the prevention of human development. Mumford complains that, like Procrustes, the authors of utopias either stretched man to fit the size of bed they had arbitrarily chosen, or amputated whatever was too big for it. Apart from the cruelty, though, utopians did have something to offer in their thinking. They did, if only in imagination, pay due attention to human interaction with the environment in which we live, the relationship between social institutions and human aspirations. Those who think in utopian terms see life as an integral whole: not as a random mix but as an organic unity of component parts that can be rationally organized and which need to be kept in balance, as in any living thing if it is to grow and survive.

There is no reason why utopian thinking should have to die along with the USSR. Thinking about a society as an integrated whole has a very long and worthy history. A fulfilling private life cannot be lived in a vacuum, in disregard of economics and architecture, of rights and laws for which people sometimes have to demonstrate in city squares. It is fair to say that we spent the greater part of the twentieth century struggling for ourselves, our right to a private life, our own house, apartment or dacha. There was nothing petty about that struggle, nothing 'bourgeois'; it is entirely deserving of respect. Perhaps later and at a higher price than others paid, Russian society did make its way from collectivism to individualism, from the general to the specific, and is now on the verge of a new phase of seeking common values.

Everybody travels this path, each in his or her own way, and, by the measure of history, it is a fairly recent development for us Russians. The examples of aristocratic and bourgeois private life we customarily take as our guidelines are far from ancient. The privately owned town house has not existed all that long, perhaps just over 300 years, perhaps less.

The birth of private life

For Russia, private life has grown out of utopia, out of the notion of the best way to live, and perhaps that is why we surrender ourselves to it so wholeheartedly. It is just as much a new religion as the ideal of socialism was in earlier times. In European culture, privacy evolved quite differently. There the path to an individual, private life was a long, difficult process of evolution. It was associated with the Industrial Revolution, the growth of trade, the emergence of the middle class and, as a consequence, the emergence of the space needed for privacy: a private house to accommodate one family.

In mediaeval Europe, home was a public place. There was no division into rooms. In shared accommodation, usually located above a shop or studio, food was cooked and eaten, visitors were received, business was discussed, people worked and slept. Benches, coffers, tables consisting of planks on trestles, collapsible beds (also consisting of planks on trestles) were essential attributes even in well-off families. Furniture was moved around, put up and taken down depending on the time of day and what was needed. If necessary, the whole lot could be loaded on to a cart and moved to another house, of which wealthy families might have several. Furniture was highly prized and, accordingly, moved together with its owners, hence its alternative name of 'movables'.

The interiors of mediaeval houses reconstructed by historians look as if they were designed by modern minimalists. A typical European house, if it had not been touched by the hand of a Renaissance architect, consisted of one or two large empty spaces with a few benches and tables. In reality, the house would not have been empty but full of people. In addition to family members, there would constantly have been students, apprentices, servants, customers, friends and partners; a house could have twenty-five or thirty people living in it. Its occupants knew nothing remotely resembling privacy.

People sat, stood, lay on the floor, on benches, coffers and beds which could be enormous, big enough for several people. Children might sleep in the same bed as their parents, in a pull-out bed underneath it or in an adjacent bed. Sleeping places for servants were sometimes provided on the floor at the feet of their employers. 'Designer' beds were a luxury that people were as proud of as today we might be proud of a stylish car; they were often situated on the ground floor so that visitors or passers-by looking in the window could be impressed by the prosperity of their possessors. In Shakespeare's time, a decent canopied bed cost half the annual salary of a typical schoolmaster.[19]

Guests at an inn, entirely unacquainted with each other, might be offered a place not just in the same room but in the same bed. There were even famous 'communal' beds. Shakespeare mentions one in *Twelfth Night*, 'the bed of Ware in England', which, it was said, could accommodate four couples.[20]

European town dwellers endured the discomfort of overcrowding and insanitary conditions. Comfort and convenience as we understand them today, with small, separate rooms, soft sofas, heating, convenient kitchens, toilets and bathrooms, simply did not exist. Home comforts had yet to be invented. 'What our mediaeval ancestors did lack was the awareness of comfort as an objective *idea*.'[21]

What really typifies people living before modern times was not gripes about inconveniences, which were not perceived as such, but awareness of their place in a strictly organized world: the estate they belonged to, their title, their place at court, their position within the estate, guild or workshop, and even their place at the dinner table. Most people, with the exception of kings and hermits, never experienced a space of their own. Rooms did not have a designated purpose, spaces were not separated out from one another; your whole life was lived in full view of those around you. Our grandfathers and great-grandfathers would find that reminiscent of the residential huts or communal apartments in the Soviet period; we today are reminded of life in the barracks or at a Young Pioneers' camp. We can talk this way because we know what privacy and home comforts are. Witold Rybczinski is sure the idea of home as we know it today evolved over a lengthy period. The mediaeval way of life long outlasted the Middle Ages. For the private house to become possible, several random and non-random factors had to come together, and this they did in early seventeenth-century Holland.[22]

The Dutch carpenter's house

The success of the Dutch at this time evoked the same sense of alarm among their neighbours as Japan did in the 1980s or as China does today: people were puzzled and tried to work out why they were being so successful. Holland had been fighting the monarchy of Spain

47

and the Catholic Church for several decades and, when it finally liberated itself, discovered it was now an independent, urbanized and successful trading nation.

Unlike England, there were no landless peasants here. Unlike France, there was no all-powerful aristocracy. The 'landscape' of Dutch society was almost as level as the landscape of the country itself. Dutch historian and philosopher Johan Huizinga wrote that this landscape, devoid of beauty and undulation and familiar from childhood to every Dutch person, fostered a corresponding national character.[23] If there were no natural wonders, the whole country was full of man-made miracles. Indeed, it was to some extent itself man-made, because it consisted in part of land reclaimed from the sea. The economic progress of the Dutch was attributable to the success of the country's middle class: the land-owning farmers, merchants and craftsmen. In the main Dutch provinces the population was, already in the seventeenth century, predominantly urban. At a time when the prosperity of other European countries depended heavily on the fruits of the toil of the rural population, Holland was rapidly becoming a state where growth and development resulted from its own manufactures and trade.

The Dutch did not, as a rule, take in lodgers. They could afford to own their own house, even if it was modest in size. Families had few servants or none at all: not a dozen like in wealthy houses in France and England. This was partly due to aspects of Protestant culture and partly due to the policy of the Dutch state, which levied a tax on the hiring of servants. As a result, most households consisted of a single couple and their children. The fact that the children were living at home was also something new. It was a centuries-old tradition that craftsmen and traders sent their children to learn from other craftsmen,with the result that they became members of a different family. These changes were unspectacular, but viewed from a historical perspective they were revolutionary. The mediaeval 'great house', full of servants, workers and visitors, gave way to the small house.

The actual physical conditions necessitated a smaller scale because the unavoidable expense of constructing canals meant frontages had to be limited. Houses were narrow and built in close proximity to each other. Builders erecting them on pile foundations on land reclaimed from the sea had to devise ways of making the buildings lighter. The main weight was borne by the side walls, so, in order to save on the foundations, façades were made as light as possible, with large windows, which were also an advantage before the introduction of gas and electric lighting. The interiors of Dutch houses were flooded with light during the day, which was something new.

The need to make the buildings less heavy was due also to their being built of wood and brick rather than of stone. A brick façade did not lend itself to carved or moulded ornamentation, hence the severe, standard-looking exteriors. Even public buildings were constructed of brick, and little effort was put into making them spectacular. The rhythm of repetitive façades lined up along canals and decorated only with large windows was a major Dutch contribution to architecture. The Danish architect Steen Eiler Rasmussen wrote that, if the French and Italians created amazing palaces, the Dutch designed amazing cities.[24]

We are still able today to peep into the private family house in the era when it was born thanks to the work of artists of the time. The economic boom of the Netherlands in the seventeenth century also saw a boom in Dutch painting. Artists there were among the first to experience a revolution in the market for paintings. For a thousand years, their main customer had been the Church, but after the Reformation, there was no longer any demand in the Protestant regions of Europe for altarpieces and paintings of the saints. The only customer now was the prosperous town dweller. For the first time, art became a tradable commodity, and this led to specialization: customers and dealers would come to a particular artist for seascapes, to another for ribald scenes, to a third for interiors.

The novelty of the interior scenes of Pieter de Hooch and Johannes Vermeer was precisely the prominence they gave to private life. There might be a moral or proverb encoded in them, as had been the practice in earlier Dutch painting, but everyday life in someone's home was no longer mere illustrative material: it had become a fit subject for art.

In this chapter, we have recalled how our sense of personal identity has evolved through our repudiation of the imperial past, through the dream of a social utopia, followed by disillusionment and a turn to extreme individualism, which has itself in turn brought no small measure of disillusionment.

There are many indications that Russian society does not consider even the most fundamental concepts of the communal and the private, or the very institution of private property, as settled once and for all: they remain open to discussion.

— 4 —

PRIVATE PROPERTY

My House Is My Castle

The myth of Sparta

An important piece of history for understanding the issue of private property is the stand-off between the ancient city states of Athens and Sparta (Lacedaemon). The Athenians and Spartans belonged to similar cultures, had the same problems to solve, but came up with different solutions. Sparta is seen as symbolic of a stable, monolithic society subordinated to a single goal, shielded from the deleterious influence of the rest of the world, and as having renounced wealth, luxury and art. Athens symbolizes freedom, disorder, art, political extremes and instability. Both are literary stereotypes related only tenuously to historical reality.

These myths are, however, important to us, particularly the myth of Sparta. It is the way ancient writers discussed the ideal state of Lacedaemon that has so strongly influenced theorists and practitioners of the art of politics in every age since. The understanding those writers had of Sparta was only partly based on historical fact, but their narrative was very coherent and, as a result, Sparta has had a good press from conservative thinkers for thousands of years, from Plato and Xenophon to the ideologists of the Nazi regime in Germany. Sparta's bad press has come from those who were freedom-loving and democratically inclined, in a time when people had learned to distinguish fact from opinion.

The crucial reform that the ancient Greeks themselves believed had helped both *poleis* to a resurgence was a redistribution of land. The mythical lawgiver Lycurgus in Sparta, and the entirely historical lawgiver Solon in Athens, were faced with the problem of rescuing their city states from a profound crisis, and they did it in wholly different ways.

Lycurgus divided the land into equal portions, which were to be passed by primogeniture from father to son but could be neither sold nor divided. The land that remained in communal ownership was worked by state slaves, the helots. Crafts and other manufacturing were carried out by villagers, the perioeci, who, although they lacked the rights of citizens, were not enslaved. The income from their holdings was to suffice to maintain the citizens' health and strength, so that the head of each family could devote himself entirely to sport, war and politics. No citizen was to enjoy a standard of living superior to that of any other. According to Plutarch, Lycurgus' own assessment of the results of the reform was, 'All Laconia looks like a family estate newly divided among many brothers!'[1]

In Athens, Solon resolved the city state's debt crisis by declaring an amnesty. People who had become enslaved through debt were released, and it was forbidden henceforth to make loans against the pledge of a citizen's freedom. Solon did, however, encounter a problem with insider dealing. History relates that three friends with whom he discussed his reform borrowed large amounts on the eve of the amnesty. When this became known, the whole future of the reform was called into question, since the integrity of the legislator was seen as having been undermined. Confidence was restored only after it became known that Solon had himself lent large sums of money, which he lost as a result of his reform.[2]

Solon also devalued the currency, standardized weights and measures and encouraged cultivation of more profitable crops. There was no redistribution of property. Indeed, a property qualification was introduced for occupying political office. A citizen's right was reaffirmed to sell, give and bequeath land however he pleased. In other words, Solon made no attempt to do away with inequality and, indeed, strengthened the right to own private property, which Sparta denied. He also urged citizens to respect the practical crafts despised in Sparta. Plutarch summarizes the difference in their approaches as follows: Sparta was

> flooded with a multitude of Helots, whom it was better not to leave in idleness but to keep down by continual hardships and toil, – it was well enough for him to set his citizens free from laborious and mechanical occupations and confine their thoughts to arms, giving them this one trade to learn and practice. But Solon, adapting his laws to the situation, rather than the situation to his laws, and observing that the land could give but a mere subsistence to those who tilled it and was incapable of

supporting an unoccupied and leisured multitude, gave dignity to all the trades, and ordered the council of the Areiopagus to examine into every man's means of livelihood, and chastise those who had no occupation.[3]

Sparta adopted a more radical approach to solving the problems of inequality and internal dissension than most of the ancient Greek *poleis*. The ancients saw inequality as the principal cause of unrest, and many wanted to even it out, but no one attempted to impose complete equality of ownership. Sparta was a 'commune of equals', but its equalizing of property has mistakenly been perceived as an equalizing of wealth. More on that below.

What Sparta's admirers particularly liked was the all-embracing system for educating its citizens, which called for health in body and mind: military discipline, repudiation of usury, a lifestyle of severe simplicity, and unchallengeable subordination to the law. To this list was added a high opinion of the Spartan system in general, which seemed to combine the advantages of monarchy, aristocracy and democracy.[4]

But now from the myth to the reality: the theoretically benign rule of law in Sparta, the supposed general respect for it, rested on some harsh political facts. This commune of equals applied to only a very modest proportion of the overall Spartan population: just 5% of the inhabitants of Lacedaemon had full citizenship, and that minority was literally at war with the majority. At the start of every year, the country's regime declared war on the helots. This was done so that citizens could, where necessary, kill slaves without incurring the stigma of murder. In effect, in Sparta, murder was legal. Moreover, young citizens had to go through a kind of initiation rite that included night-time raids to murder helots.

'Indeed fear of their numbers and obstinacy even persuaded the Lacedaemonians to the action which I shall now relate, their policy at all times having been governed by the necessity of taking precautions against them,' Thucydides writes.[5] Subordination of every aspect of the country's life to the struggle against internal and external enemies was integral to Spartan ideology.

The Spartans (unlike the Athenians) regarded themselves as conquerors of their own country, and the perioeci and helots as the spoils of victory. If the citizens of other city states periodically went off to create colonies in different lands, the citizens of Sparta were committed colonizers of their own country. Accordingly, they all had to be professional soldiers and their *polis* had to be an army camp with life spent in barrack-like conditions, with communal meals. Children had to be taken from their parents at birth and brought up away from their families, in want and undergoing constant training. Only in this way, the Lacedaemonians believed, could their country be maintained as a perfect war machine.

Who won in this historical contest? The Spartans were an invincible military power. They ended the domination of Athens in the Greek *oecumene*, but after winning the Peloponnesian War their military successes became fewer. As a result of casualties in battle, the number of citizens decreased and the army lost its combat capability. Later notions that there was strict compliance with the law in Sparta were an exaggeration, and even the admirers of its system had to admit that the reality of life in Sparta did not correspond to the ideal of a commune of equals.

Sparta gave the world the myth of an ideal state built on the breeding of a new, ideal human being, on unity, on rejection of property in both a material and an intellectual sense, on rejection of art.[6] The Spartan approach to organizing life was holistic, total and utopian (in adapting circumstances to fit the law). Plato was already comparing the Spartan preoccupation with producing strong, healthy people with the breeding of thoroughbred animals. In the nineteenth and twentieth centuries, these ideas reappeared in theories of eugenics, the 'science' of improving human hereditary characteristics, and in the crimes of the Nazis.

What did Athens give the world? Science, poetry, drama, architecture, the decorative arts, democratic culture (which has upset many people) and, of course, philosophy (including anti-democratic philosophy). The Athenian approach to life varied at different times, but overall was more inclined to remain realistic and not aim at totally transforming society by abolishing property and revising all traditions. The Athenians fitted the law to the circumstances.

The *domus* of our forebears

For a family to be living in a house of its own is a fairly recent achievement, as we saw in the previous chapter. However, the separateness of their residence, its economic autonomy and security, are also recent, and they are social rather than personal achievements.

Our attitude to the house is based not only on the instincts of self-preservation and greed; to a large extent, through culture, books and laws, we owe it to people who have thought about these things before us. If we take the ancient Greeks and Romans as our guides and starting point, we will see they have given us various constituents of our notion of home. For the Greeks, the home was primarily an economic unit (the word 'economy' derives from the Greek *oikos*). They associated it with notions of good housekeeping and order. The concept of the home as a stronghold, a refuge, a sanctuary and a piece of property protected by law comes more from the Romans.

Unlike the Greeks, who had to go to the public square to worship their gods, the Romans had the option of worshipping them at home. The Roman *domus* was a sanctified private world where there were domestic shrines and representations of their ancestors. The ancestors were not only venerated but also obeyed: the basis of Roman law was 'the way of our elders' (*mos maiorum*). Temples were the dwelling place of the gods, but Roman homes, too, were temples, the dwelling place of numerous household deities.

Here is what Cicero had to say on the subject:

> What is there more holy, what is there more carefully fenced round with every description of religious respect, than the house of every individual citizen? Here are his altars, here are his hearths, here are his household gods: here all his sacred rites, all his religious ceremonies are performed; here he prays. This is the asylum of every one, so holy a spot that it is impious to drag any one from it.[7]

St Augustine, looking down on the pagan world from the heights of his Christianity and expending much sarcasm on the unconverted, wrote that the gods of the Romans kept an eye on every detail, right down to the door hinges.

> Every one sets a porter at the door of his house, and because he is a man, he is quite sufficient; but these people have set three gods, Forculus to the doors, Cardea to the hinge, Limentinus to the threshold. Thus Forculus could not at the same time take care also of the hinge and the threshold.[8]

The Penates were the divine guardians of the hearth and patrons of humans and their labour. It was believed that there were Penates for every state, town, village and family. Their wooden images standing by the hearth were a symbol of this family living in this place, conjoining the place and the people. Virgil's *Aeneid* is the epic not only of its hero's travels but also of the safe removal of the Penates to a new location from Troy when it was captured by the enemy. The Penates theme runs through the entire poem and ultimately Latium becomes the home and motherland of Aeneas, with its centre where the city of Rome will stand in the future.

The Romans regarded the Lares as spirits that guarded property. Ovid likens them to dogs:

> But a dog, carved out of the same stone, used to stand before their feet. What was the reason for its standing with the Lar? Both guard the house: both are faithful to their master: cross-roads are dear to the god, cross-roads are dear to dogs: the Lar and Diana's pack give chase to thieves.[9]

It is worth remembering that initially the principal deity of the Roman pantheon, Janus, was the god of entrances and exits. All gates, passages and doors enjoyed his protection.

Historians and anthropologists believe that the ancient Romans' belief in household gods and their special attitude to entrances as the boundaries of sanctified domestic territory contributed to the formation of Roman property law. In all cultures, access to the hearth and the dwelling is governed by ancestral tradition, but it was the Romans who codified these customs into written law.

A Roman had the right to take an offender to court for bursting into his home or breaking a door. Less drastic action – throwing stones onto a neighbouring plot or polluting it with smoke – was also considered actionable. Roman law, the Laws of the Twelve Tables, viewed an intrusion during the night more severely than one during daytime. A houseowner who killed a burglar at night in self-defence would be acquitted in court. During the day it was permissible to use a weapon only if the wrongdoer was also armed. Intruding in someone's home during the day and in the absence of the owner was punished less harshly. All these rules were interpreted differently in different countries and later times, but in one way or another they became incorporated in modern legal systems, which usually recognize a right to self-defence.

Even the procedure for summoning the accused or a witness to court was subject to certain restrictions. Notice of the requirement to appear in court was to be delivered courteously. It was forbidden to forcibly remove a person from his house and drag him there. In the second century BC, the Roman lawyer Gaius noted that nobody was to be taken by force from his home to be brought to court, because the home is a safe refuge and shelter for everyone.[10]

We should note that the Romans were well aware of a dividing line between the authorities and private property, between *imperium* and *dominium*. The precise meaning of the word 'property', and the fact that it must be obtained by lawful means and be absolute and perpetual, were refinements added in later periods, but at its core there is a distinction between power and property. Property is something to which the authorities may not lay claim, or, if they may, then only in certain circumstances.

For a Roman, a house's entrance doors were a sacred boundary: it was deemed improper to enter a house uninvited, improper for the authorities, for friends and for enemies. On the days when a Roman patrician was receiving his clients, the doors to the atrium (the first courtyard of the house) were left open, a tacit invitation to enter. Those not allowed in by the gatekeeper had to stand at the entrance. Those who considered they had been aggrieved could dress as if in mourning, go to the house of whoever had offended them, no matter how powerful that person might be, and stand there, literally in mute reproach. If the owner left his house, the aggrieved party could follow him silently, but might also shout out his or her claims and grievances. A houseowner who tried to chase his pursuer away might only further damage his reputation by offending against ancient tradition.

The representatives of the 'plaintiff' could make a lot of noise and shout insults at the 'defendant' right under the walls of his house. This was often done at night, which was considered particularly effective.

> Then [Verres] himself, being roused, comes forth. . . . He is received by all with such a shout that it seemed to bring before his eyes a resemblance to the dangers of Lampsacus. . . . People began to talk to one another of his tent on the shore, of his flagitious banquets; the names of his women were called out by the crowd . . . .[11]

Events could take a more serious turn, with a crowd throwing stones at the house or setting fire to its door. In that extremity, the design of a Roman *domus* was very helpful, because it had solid walls, with no windows facing the street: all the living was done in the inner courtyards. As the door was the most vulnerable part of the building, the wrath of those who felt they had been wronged was vented on it.

The house was a kind of passport, and could even in some instances stand in for its owner. If a politician was exiled, his house might be destroyed, as happened to Cicero himself. His speech 'Concerning My House', from which the words quoted above about the sanctity of the hearth are taken, is in fact devoted to an episode in his life when he was banished from Rome and his house was pillaged and destroyed by plebeians – at the instigation, Cicero claims, of his principal enemy, Clodius.

Historians doubt that Cicero was quite as innocent as he tries to portray himself in this speech, but what is of relevance for us is the insight we gain into a special attitude towards homes from the vengefulness of the representatives of one party towards the house of an opponent. This kind of destruction was an extreme measure, intended to indicate termination of the exile's membership of the community, the rooting out of even the memory of a person who had committed an offence. Similarly, a return from exile signalled the restoration of rights and of his home. Cicero tells us as much:

> For this return of mine, O priests, and this restoration consists in recovering my house, my possessions, my altars, my hearths, and my household gods. And if that fellow [Publius Clodius] with his most wicked hands tears up their dwellings and abodes, and, with the consuls for his leaders, as if the city were taken, has thought it becoming to destroy this house alone, as if it were the house of its most active defender, still those household gods, those deities of my family, will be by you replaced in my house at the same time as myself.[12]

The house served a Roman as his castle in a very direct sense. There were many instances in history where defendants in court cases and debtors hid from their pursuers at home, in the homes of their patrons, the house of the emperor or just generally any other dwelling. The notion of home as the principal place of refuge was germane not least because, despite a whole system of laws and customs, Rome was not a state under the rule of law in the modern sense. One's position in society was determined by one's place in the hierarchy of estates, and links were formalized as relationships between patrons and clients (citizens dependent on them). A Roman who lost favour after a dispute with a man of influence had recourse only to the traditional refuge of his home.

It was the provision in Roman law that saw the home as a place of refuge that is the origin of the modern comparison of a home to a castle. Russians tend to associate that with England, perhaps because in modern times the first to articulate the idea was the seventeenth-century English lawyer Sir Edward Coke, who was, of course, familiar with the Roman sources: '[T]he house of every one is to him as his castle and fortress, as well for his defence against injury and violence as for his repose. . . . And the reason of all the same is, because *domus sua cuique est tutissimum refugium*.' This last phrase, 'his house is the safest refuge for each man', Coke quotes from Gaius, mentioned above.[13] This could take the English lawyer only so far. European countries were still far behind the Romans in respect of the inviolability of a person's home. Coke was ruling little more than that, if the king's sheriffs were making an arrest or serving a warrant, they should knock and ask permission to enter before bursting into the house.

During the English Civil War, freedom from arbitrary searches and arrests was one of the key demands of supporters of the parliament, and Sir Edward Coke had been a parliamentarian and opponent of absolute monarchy. His words about an Englishman's house being his castle struck a note with his contemporaries and were repeated in speech after speech. One of the most famous assertions of the castle-like status of the domestic stronghold came from William Pitt the Elder, who lived in the latter half of the eighteenth century: 'The poorest man may in his cottage bid defiance to all the forces of the Crown. It may be frail, its roof may shake, the wind may blow through it, the storm may enter, the rain may enter – but the King of England cannot enter!'[14]

Fine words, but again, at the time they were spoken, probably wishful thinking. Of course the forces of the king could break into a house, but the aspiration to limit their powers as far as possible during searches and summonses to court was enduring, and eventually led to the emergence of modern legal standards.[15]

Despite the fact that reality lagged far behind the desires of lawyers and politicians, the saying about an Englishman's house being his castle became proverbial. Those who took it up knew nothing of the lawsuit in the course of which the words had been uttered, or that they alluded to Roman custom. The words 'My house is my castle' just sounded right, and were taken to be restating (but in fact creating) a proper attitude towards the home as a family sanctuary. The English state was not yet ready to extend full protection to private property, but English common law, through the efforts of judges and a parliament independent of the king, had already embraced the crucial principle of protecting a home from arbitrary invasion.

Mine and yours

It is fundamentally important to distinguish property from wealth. Wealth is an accumulation of value not tied to a place or a country of origin. It is a creation of value that is liquid, especially in the present day. It can take the form of plots of land, ships, planes, houses, banks, money, metal, stones or paintings. Property, on the other hand, is not so much value denominated in units of currency as the fact of having a connection with a place. No matter how large or small my home, it signals that I am part of the nation and provides the evidence of my right to participate in the life of my city and my state.

Philosopher Hannah Arendt wrote,

Originally, property meant no more or less than to have one's location in a particular part of the world and therefore to belong to the body politic, that is, to be the head of one of the families which together constituted the public realm. This piece of privately owned world was so completely identical with the family who owned it that the expulsion of a citizen could mean not merely the confiscation of his estate but the actual destruction of the building itself. Not to have any property means not to have a generic place in the world that could be called your own; that is to be someone invisible to the world and to the body politic organized within it.[16]

Property, understood in this way, was the basis of the rights of a free citizen and was wholly unconnected with the notion of wealth. Poverty did not deprive a citizen of his rights, and wealth did not give the rights of citizens to those who did not already have them, which in the city states of the classical world meant foreigners and slaves. It will be very helpful in what follows if we remember that property and wealth are not the same thing.

Even Plato, one of the first opponents of private property, did not dispute the notion of property-based citizenship. For him it was simply a reality. He was thinking about what the state *should be* like. Aristotle, the student and opponent of Plato, sought to understand what the state actually *was* like. Plato the utopian and Aristotle the analyst from the outset established two trends in thinking about property. The first considered it an unavoidable evil; the second saw it as a way of relating to things that was more in harmony with human nature than other approaches. For Plato what mattered was the integrity, the unity of an ideal society, and for him ownership of property was an obstacle to that. Aristotle, on the other hand, firmly believed it was in the interests of the unity of society that property was not pooled but clearly demarcated.

In Plato's ideal state, worries about property should not be allowed to distract the highest caste from devoting themselves to philosophy and governing a country consisting of ideal people. What preoccupies Aristotle is that there should be a clear distinction between 'yours' and 'mine', because that is in accordance with human nature. He was thinking about a country consisting of people as they actually are.

Plato finally 'allowed' property in his last dialogue, 'The Laws', but even here, describing a second-best state, he insists that the best state would be one without property:

The first and highest form is that in which friends have all things in common, including wives and property, – in which they have common fears, hopes, desires, and do not even call their eyes or their hands their own. This is the ideal state; than which there never can be a truer or better – a state, whether inhabited by Gods or sons of Gods, which will make the dwellers therein blessed.[17]

Actually, no, it would not be sensible to make fears, eyes, hands, wives or property communal, Aristotle retorts. That is no way to achieve unity! Quite the contrary. The state is a multiplicity of individuals. If the individual has nothing that is his own, he will be dissolved in the whole and lose his individuality, and without individuals there will be no whole.[18] This is bad news for the economy too. Aristotle understands incentive:

[T]hat which is common to the greatest number has the least care bestowed upon it. Every one thinks chiefly of his own, hardly at all of the common interest. . . . For besides other considerations, everybody is more inclined to neglect the duty which he expects another to fulfil; as in families many attendants are often less useful than a few.[19]

Aristotle also takes account of the fact that people have different abilities and capacities. 'If they do not share equally enjoyments and toils, those who labour much and get little will necessarily complain of those who labour little and receive or consume much.'[20]

Does that sound sensible? Those arguments, which two thousand years later we can label 'utilitarian', have been heard again and again, but for some reason every culture and every age has needed to debate the matter afresh and come up with new answers to old questions. Something has made people reluctant to accept the fact that dividing things up as 'mine' and 'yours' is the best way to reach agreement on the rules of living together – as if such division is somehow coercive and evil. The idea that has given us no peace is the belief that at the origins of the human race there was some primal, original, better world.

The adherents of philosophical stoicism believed human beings are by nature equal, and from them the belief was inherited by the Romans. The notion that there had been a primal egalitarianism automatically led to the view that the world in its current state was distorted, because inequality – with slavery and the difference in incomes among free people – was only too obvious. Educated Romans generally believed that in an original, blissful world there had been no private property: 'To mark the plain or mete with boundary-line – Even this was impious.'[21]

As Seneca writes: 'What race of men was ever more blest than that race? They enjoyed all nature in partnership. Nature sufficed for them, now the guardian, as before she was the parent, of all; and this her gift consisted of the assured possession by each man of the common resources.'[22] The Romans were not themselves inclined to dream up ideal countries, but they accepted the notion of a natural, better state of mankind, compared to which all the subsequent stages of its development had seen changes for the worse. The appearance of private property had been a reaction to one of those changes: '[A] varice broke in upon a condition so happily ordained, and, by its eagerness to lay something away and to turn it to its own private use, made all things the property of others, and reduced itself from boundless wealth to straitened need.'[23]

Everything that takes humans away from nature may, by definition, be bad, but, the Romans conceded, one needs to be realistic. Perhaps ideally all property should be communal, but in the here and now, relations between people need to be regulated in order to bring a modicum of order to this depraved world. A legally precise wording of the idea that ownership was about having the right to do whatever you want with something, to 'use and dispose' of it at will, came much later; but a legal approach to the discussion, which the Romans adopted more readily than the Greeks, became and remains one of the foundations of Western thought.

Life, liberty and property

One of the approaches to thinking about the structure of society and the rights of the people who comprise it is to posit the existence of a kind of 'social contract', to imagine that at some point in the past people agreed the fundamental principles by which they would live together. During the seventeenth century, a time of profound institutional transformation, there was much debate in England about what the nature of such an agreement might have been.

The first point of disagreement concerned the prehistoric, 'natural', state of mankind: had it been angelic or diabolical? For Thomas Hobbes, man's state of nature had been a state of 'warre, as is of every man, against every man'. 'So that in the nature of man, we find three principal causes of quarrell. First, Competition; Secondly, Diffidence; Thirdly, Glory. The first, maketh men invade for Gain; the second, for Safety; and the Third, for Reputation.' In this daily state of war man lives in 'continuall feare, and danger of violent death'. His life is 'solitary, poore, nasty, brutish and short'. Hobbes was certain there was only one way out: everybody must simultaneously renounce the right to govern themselves and transfer the right to rule over them to a single elected person.

> This is the Generation of that great *Leviathan*, or rather (to speake more reverently) of that Mortall God, to which wee owe under the Immortall God, our peace and defence. For by this Authoritie, given him by every particular man in the Common-Wealth, he hath the use of so much Power and Strength conferred on him, that by terror thereof, he is inabled to forme the wills of them all, to Peace at home, and mutuall ayd against their enemies abroad.[24]

Hobbes was writing in the mid-seventeenth century, when the everyday reality was civil conflict between the monarchy and parliament. By the end of the century, parliament had gained control of the tax regime and the exchequer. This was the beginning of a radical changing of the rules. Prior to the Glorious Revolution of 1688, foreign trade had been in the hands of a small group of players, and entrepreneurship had not developed in England because innovations had no prospect of being implemented. The king would not grant them a patent, and a monopolist could destroy a too successful competitor as easily as snapping his fingers. Economic activity was just more of the same, rather than growth or development. The courts were corrupt.

Abolition of the king's right to grant monopolies, initially within the country but then also in respect of overseas trade, immediately gave new players access to areas of manufacturing and commerce previously closed to them. By the middle of the eighteenth century, the explosive growth of trade with the New World, as well as the introduction of new technologies – machinery, steam engines and factory production – in the context of rapid expansion of the road network and worldwide expansion of entrepreneurial activity, enabled Britain to become an economic superpower. Growth was also helped by the fact that, in these conditions, the English law courts became independent, because now that was needed both by the Crown and by the new property owners and traders represented in parliament. We should note that independent institutions generally develop better where no one force in society is dominant.

The right to private property was at the very heart of all these conflicts. It was being formed and given meaning not by principles taken from writers of the classical world but on the basis of people's own experience. From the end of the fifteenth and throughout the sixteenth and seventeenth centuries, a land revolution was taking place in England, with the gradual destruction of feudal relations and a transfer of land from the Crown, the monasteries and a narrow circle of the upper level of the aristocracy into the hands of numerous property owners. The desire of landowners to make money on the 'wool fever'; their readiness to forcibly evict peasant families from land to which the families had no legal property rights; the inability of the Crown to oppose the House of Commons, which promoted the interests of landowners; Henry VIII's break with the Roman Catholic Church followed by confiscation and sale of monastic property – all this resulted in a much changed situation. Land became a commodity and many new landowners appeared.

In 1450, around 60% of all agricultural land in England was owned by the Crown, the Church and some thirty dukes, earls and barons. By 1700, the nobility, Church and Crown between them owned less than 30% of cultivated land. By the end of the seventeenth century, the population of England had risen to 5 million, of whom 2 million owned land.[25]

The crux of the revolution was that now, without having to defer to Almighty God, the king or the lords, a private individual could obtain profit from the land. He could work on it or not, he could keep it or sell it. All the old foundations of the countryside, the mutual obligations of lord and tenant farmer, the old customs and notions of justice were a thing of the past. The decay of communal values greatly alarmed contemporaries. Thomas Becon, one of the founders of puritanism, wrote in the mid-sixteenth century that even the monasteries, once considered nests of ecclesiastical hypocrisy, seemed very respectable when compared with the new speculators in land: 'They abhorre the names of Monkes, Friars, Chanons, Nounes, etc., but their goods they gredely gripe. And yet where the cloysters kept hospitality, let out their fermes at a reasonable pryce, noryshed scholes, brought up youths in good letters, they doe none of all these thinges.'[26]

This was the context in which Hobbes wrote his treatise, with land beginning to be viewed as a commodity, property being redistributed on a large scale, and a conflict between landowners and the Crown. His vision was of the people transferring the right to govern themselves to the Leviathan without conditions or restrictions. Soon, however, it became clear that these were essential.

The new version of the social contract was suggested by John Locke. Locke believed that once, in the original state of nature, people had been equal, lived in harmony and had not distinguished between property that was theirs or not theirs. With time, however, he supposed it would have become clear that equal rights were less than ideal. If anybody could use anything, there was a risk that two people might want the same thing, and one might be the stronger. Accordingly, it would have been found better to hedge universal equality with restrictions and regulations.

> This makes him willing to quit this Condition, which however free, is full of fears and continual dangers: And 'tis not without reason, that he seeks out, and is willing to joyn in Society with others who are already united, or have a mind to unite for the mutual Preservation of their Lives, Liberties and Estates, which I call by the general Name, Property.
> The great and chief end therefore, of Mens uniting into Commonwealths, and putting themselves under Government, is the Preservation of their Property.[27]

So, for Locke the institution of property is not only material possessions but 'Lives, Liberties and Estates'. This refers us to the idea of a sovereign individual, a man who is already lord of himself and the fruits of his labour, without any need for the state to give him anything. That is the understanding of the institution that came to be accepted in the twentieth century (and to which I adhere in the present work). 'Institutions are the rules of the game in a society or, more formally, are the humanly devised constraints that shape human interaction.'[28]

The institution of property, understood in this way as the sovereignty of the individual, as property in a broader sense, existed before the prerogative of the state and has precedence over it. The state is needed to defend that right and, if it fails to do so, citizens have the right to change their state. That was how the French, rising up against their *ancien régime,* explained their actions in the Declaration of the Rights of Man and of the Citizen in 1789: 'The aim of all political association is the preservation of the natural and inalienable rights of man. These rights are liberty, property, security, and resistance to oppression.' Locke's threefold understanding of property as 'Lives, Liberties and Estates' was incorporated in the US Constitution, whose Fifth Amendment states: 'No person shall ... be deprived of life, liberty, or property, without due process of law.'

These ideas were far from self-evident, and it took considerable time to get them formulated. Since being recognized and articulated, they have commanded widespread respect, and numerous countries, including Russia, have embedded them in their constitutions. By no means all cultures, however, have passed through the stages of development that enabled a legally based attitude towards 'Lives, Liberties and Estates' to evolve in a natural, hard-won way. This may explain why there are so few instances of successful implementation of the

European Enlightenment ideals that are written into the constitutions of so many highly diverse countries. In Russia, we find ourselves still arguing over these issues, in the full knowledge that they have already been debated for thousands of years.

Considerable time had to pass before the old traditions and the new requirements of society led to the formulation of rules binding on all. By the end of the eighteenth century, the philosophers of the Enlightenment and the creators of new states had reached consensus that a truly secure dwelling needed to be protected not only by walls but also by the law. Acceptance of the right to have one's person, dwelling, documents and property safeguarded against unjustified searches and seizures became standard in most of the world's legal systems.

A recognition that the threshold of a dwelling had the status of a boundary has existed for a long time: probably, indeed, since human beings adopted a settled way of life and learned to put a roof over their heads. Nowadays, however, we expect more of our home than the protection of robust walls. We want to be protected from enemies and malevolent people not just by walls and bolts, but also by laws and those called upon to enforce them.

Otherwise we would be obliged, as in the Middle Ages, to have our dwellings clustered around fortresses and castles so as always to have somewhere to take refuge. We would need to be armed in order, if necessary, to defend ourselves. We would be unwise to trust anyone we did not know, and to eat produce other than from our own garden; to travel along the road even to the next village would be a dangerous undertaking. It is in order to live more freely than in the past that we pay taxes, and expect those taxes to be spent on employing people who will provide us with a secure environment for trade and travel, who will enforce the rules and resolve conflicts fairly. That will enable us not to waste precious time and energy on protecting our home and not to confine ourselves to our own back garden. We will be able to live a freer and more prosperous life than in the days when our house was not yet our castle.

Christianity and utopia

For the subsequent history of property, not only has the law been important, but so have faith and beliefs. There has been a view that if, at some time in the past, a life lived in harmony with nature or the divine will required communal ownership of property, then that is an arrangement we should strive to return to. What the learned Stoic Seneca could only speculate about, the proponents of the new faith of Christianity went right ahead and implemented. The first Jerusalem community of Christians was communistic: 'And all that believed were together, and had all things common; And sold their possessions and goods, and parted them to all men, as every man had need.'[29]

For a long time, this description from Acts of the Apostles was regarded as guidance for Christians. Wealth and possessions were a hindrance on the path to salvation. Jesus can easily be seen as preaching poverty. In St Matthew's gospel he directly advises a young man, 'Go and sell that thou hast, and give to the poor, and thou shalt have treasure in heaven.'[30]

We need, however, to bear in mind that the authors of the New Testament were addressing themselves to 'Old Testament people'. Those listening to Jesus would have known the tales of Abraham, David and Solomon, and for them, land, flocks, numerous offspring and treasures were signs of God's favour. Jesus said he was not doing away with The Law (primarily the Ten Commandments, which include a prohibition not only of seizing but even of coveting your neighbour's property). In the parables Jesus used for instructing his listeners, there are plenty of stories about a master and his servants, which indicates that those hearing him accepted this state of affairs as normal. From the perspective of Christianity, proceeding from the Old Testament, property is an ancient institution.[31]

The novelty of the Christian view is that wealth can possess a person. Jesus called on only his closest disciples to renounce their property, and more generally it remained something for each person to decide individually. The New Testament rejects serving the material world as an absolute value. There is in any case no absolute value in land, flocks, gold, diamonds, rubles or dollars: their value is relative and determined by the market. Christianity does not deem the accumulation of relative values a worthy pursuit, advocating instead an absolute value. Some of the saints were rich, others poor, but what they all have in common is that, for themselves, they acknowledged the primacy of spiritual values.[32] The probability is that Jesus did not have any social doctrine, any more than he had a utopian vision of the ideal structure of society. His message was to individuals, not collectives.

The early Fathers of the Church believed property was an inevitable feature of the postlapsarian world. In the West, St Augustine taught that property was established by the secular powers in view of the sinful state of mankind. In the East, St John Chrysostom tried to persuade his congregation with statistics that, if they followed the example of the Jerusalem commune and pooled their property, they would be better off not only spiritually but also materially.[33] Neither saint ever said that having wealth and property was intrinsically sinful. Gold can serve both good and evil: the choice is made not by the gold but by its owner.

The fervour of the ancient Church was cooled by the subtle mind of St Thomas Aquinas. He and his students persuaded Christians that private property is natural and good. In the first place, there was no reason why Christians, if they were pious and generous, should have to be poor. And in the second place, the Church needed property if it was to be independent of the rulers of the world and in order to help the poor. A person does come into the world naked, and that is his natural state, but, St Thomas went on, that is no reason to condemn the wearing of clothes. The concept of what is 'natural' can be seen in different ways. As Richard Schlatter puts it, if a plot of land is viewed in absolute terms, there is no reason why it should belong to one person rather than another; but if we proceed from consideration of the worthy use of the land, there is a need for an owner, as Aristotle demonstrated.[34]

We have already met Aristotle's arguments: people take better care of what they own than of what nobody owns. And if the land and a house need an owner, why should that owner not be the Church, because it will be an exemplary owner. Here we have a piece of virtuoso scholasticism: before our very eyes the unthinkable (the Church as landowner and landlord) becomes not only thinkable but indeed essential.

Renaissance philosophers argued with St Thomas and other scholastics of the Middle Ages over practically everything else, but left the question of property unchallenged. More precisely, of all the many trends of Protestantism, the ones that survived were almost invariably those not too radically opposed to property and wealth. Those that were, came to nothing. The Anabaptists, for example, who believed in baptism only after candidates had reached years of discretion, tried to combat wealth and social inequality, refused to bear arms and called for the socialization of property. Although such views did survive in a number of Christian denominations, they have remained fairly marginal in organized Christianity. Martin Luther, the leading figure in the Reformation and a staunch opponent of Church property, nevertheless insisted on the need to respect the right to own property as a legal principle. Yes, he conceded, some of the first Christians voluntarily made their property communal, but they did not attempt to wrest property from Herod or Pontius Pilate.[35]

Like other leaders of the Reformation, Luther insisted that property was not an end in itself, but justified in order to produce more goods. The reason for doing that was not to have even more to eat or to live in greater luxury, but simply for the sake of producing more. What for? Because it is a sin to waste time (the reasoning behind Benjamin Franklin's 'Time is money'). If you stop working, you cease to glorify God. Working and earning money is good for the soul. More than that, thought another Protestant religious teacher, John Calvin: it was perhaps a sign of being chosen by God.

The German philosopher and sociologist Max Weber inferred from this his theory of the Protestant work ethic, which many find questionable but which remains influential. If the leavening of Protestantism did play a role, it was certainly not the only reason for the rapid economic growth of Protestant countries: widespread private ownership of land preceded the spread of Protestantism. Historians have also pointed out that the Puritans, Methodists and Quakers were religious dissidents who often had to live their lives as a persecuted minority and without any expectation of support from the state. Their inclination to independence, the formation of self-sufficient communities, the high degree of trust between the members of these islands of 'true faith' did more to promote the development of private enterprise than their actual religious doctrines.

Quite apart from Protestant values, economic development was supported by the growth of the mediaeval towns and the emergence of guilds, the private property tradition in England, the ideas of Locke and the fact that the founding fathers of America enacted these ideas into law. Alexander Gerschenkron, an American economist of Russian origin, even believed that Weber had his tongue in his cheek when he proposed the theory, and that it was no more than an elegant intellectual game.[36]

Utopia without property

At all events, Weber was a researcher seeking to describe reality. As soon as the theorists and fantasists piled in, the concept of private property was often presented as being the root of all sorts of mischief. The architects of fantastic utopian states, the French philosophers of the eighteenth century and socialists of the nineteenth century regarded private property as the wellspring of poverty and accordingly proposed that public goods really should be in the most literal sense communal.

Thomas More, the English civil servant already mentioned who authored a book that lent its name to a whole genre, came up with a quite improbably wretched utopia. Identical towns, identical houses and the same sort of clothes, everybody going off to work together and all, at the sound of a trumpet, heading for dinner and supper. Every resident of More's island of Utopia can enter the dining hall, there is no right to own property, and there are not even locks on any doors. The Utopians are obliged to change the place where they live every ten years by drawing lots. Moving around the island of Utopia requires a passport, and the penalty for flouting Soviet-style rules for registering where you live is slavery. The Utopians eat and drink together in public palaces to the sound of music or the reciting of edifying books. Everything they produce is stored in vast warehouses, from where they have issued to them precisely what goods they need and no more. The rulers keep a close eye on everything and redistribute goods and foodstuffs to wherever they are in short supply. People's needs are always constant and are well known, because a total number of residents are being maintained at a constant standard, and their numbers are known not just at the level of the towns but right down to the numbers in individual families. Where families have too many children, these are redistributed to other families that do not have enough. The islanders look down on money, and gold and precious stones are always kept in full view of everyone, in order not to create temptations. As already mentioned, gold is used on the island to make chains for slaves, and chamber pots.

More should have been a bit more careful with what he imagined, but his readers, too, should have had a better understanding of the subtleties of the English sense of humour. The name 'Utopia' is itself a play on words that means both 'a good place' ('*eu-topos*') and 'no place' ('*ou-topos*'). The capital of the republic is on a river called Anydrus (no-water), and the name of the hero-narrator, Raphael Hythlodaeus, is also a witticism and can be translated as 'an archangel learned in nonsense'.[37]

There is no telling now what More was inventing for satirical purposes and what was meant seriously. At least he knew he was dreaming things up, but among the things he foresaw were the Soviet system of central planning, collective farming and communal living, compulsory residential registration, the socialist state, summer camps for Young Pioneers, and even a subversive foreign policy. (The state authorities in Utopia suborn foreigners and provoke wars between other countries.) Although he surely never meant to, as things turned out, he invented all the above for the remote and unknown inhabitants of chilly Russia. Lacking any sense of irony or, very often, much of an education, socialist reformers read More as the literal blueprint of a cheerless socialist state, and to this day we are hostages to their blunder.

More himself and other utopians had a different way of thinking. The ideal of a perfectly functioning society was conceived as a response to the harsh reality of the times, where the oppressive power of money and brute force were becoming intolerable. *Utopia* was written in the early sixteenth century, when enclosure was just beginning, and the power of the property owner was starting to grow. More was witnessing the first shoots of a modern economy based on increasing productivity. In the England of the time, that led to a drastic stratification of society, the emergence of the first large private fortunes and of mass poverty.[38] More was inspired by tales of the first great sea voyages and took as his starting point Plato's *Republic*, which would have been well known to his readers. He wrote an intelligent book for kindred spirits, depicted a contrary, carnivalesque world and studded it with serious ideas. *Utopia* really should not be taken literally, and almost certainly its author was assuming his readers would understand that.

The inhabitants of More's island do not suffer privation, but this is achieved by limiting their aspirations rather than trying to expand and satisfy them, by ensuring they work hard rather than live in idleness. He wanted to convey to his reader the ideal of a fulfilled life, which demands work on oneself and moral discipline. The desire for pleasure is, however, also a worthy aspiration providing it is pleasure in creating rather than destroying things. In this respect, *Utopia* has not dated at all.

The closer the countries of Europe come to modern times, the greater is the number of those doubting the beneficence of the concept of property. The faster the economy develops, the louder are the accusations levelled at it.

One other very influential version of the social contract was proposed by Jean-Jacques Rousseau. In his view, the natural life was not a Hobbesian war of all against all, or Locke's fragile moments of equality. For Rousseau, 'man in his natural state' is a lost paradise: 'The example of savages . . . seems to prove that men were meant to remain in it, . . . and that all subsequent advances have been apparently so many steps towards the perfection of the individual, but in reality towards the decrepitude of the species.' The solution is a new treaty that will rate everything communal above everything private: 'Each of us puts his person and all his power in common under the supreme direction of the general will, and, in our corporate capacity, we receive each member as an indivisible part of the whole.'[39]

Rousseau sees the development of civilization, the transition from the state of nature to the social, as a regression. Laws, including laws concerning the inviolability of private property, are snares imposed by the rich on the poor. They have 'eternally fixed the law of property and inequality, converted clever usurpation into unalterable right'.

> The first man who, having enclosed a piece of ground, bethought himself of saying *This is mine,* and found people simple enough to believe him, was the real founder of civil society. From how many crimes, wars and murders, from how many horrors and misfortunes might not any one have saved mankind, by pulling up the stakes, or filling up the ditch, and crying to his fellows, 'Beware of listening to this impostor; you are undone if you once forget that the fruits of the earth belong to us all, and the earth itself to nobody.'[40]

This famous passage from Rousseau's *Discourse on the Origin of Inequality* proved very influential. Let us note that the utopian (Platonic) ideals here are, before our eyes, turning into what will become 'left-wing' ideas. Unlike the future anarchists and socialists, Rousseau was not categorically opposed to property as an institution, but it was his readers who, in the following centuries, created a firm association in the minds of many between private ownership and injustice.

And this injustice, the socialists were certain, could and should be rectified. Enlightenment philosophy changed the intellectual climate and sanctioned the very possibility of social change. This concept, which was initially only an idea, was subsequently reinforced by economic and political realities and determined the history of the twentieth century. It was now possible to restructure societies in accordance with a 'scientific plan'. By the beginning of the twentieth century, an extraordinary situation had developed: the economy was bringing unprecedented benefits, yet the conviction that a new, more just society was needed had never been stronger.

John Locke considered private property the foundation of prosperity and security, while Jean-Jacques Rousseau saw it as the root cause of the degeneration of society: this divergence of views became one of the foundations of the long and bloody confrontation between left-wing and right-wing ideas. To oversimplify grossly, we can characterize Locke's social contract as bourgeois-republican and Rousseau's as socialist. If we oversimplify even more, we can say that out of Locke there developed the form of government that united the states of North America, while Rousseau spawned the Soviet Union.[41]

Socialism was a theoretical doctrine that claimed the mantle of science and, moreover, of applied science, but the mere existence of an *a priori* blueprint for an ideal society disqualified the 'science' of Karl Marx as science in the traditional sense. Science seeks to study nature, to discover its laws, but not to lead to the attainment of an already chosen goal. Perhaps that is precisely why socialist convictions so appealed to the educated classes in Russia. From the perspective of Marxism, our country was the least promising candidate for the socialist experiment, but that evidently only added to its attractiveness for Russia's dreamers. For Russians, the issue of private property was far more theoretical than for their neighbours to the west. The latter had long ceased to ponder the 'eternal questions' and were doing their best to make sense of their contemporary reality. Russian thinkers, on the contrary, were painting pictures of a possible future.

Their thinking, like the thinking in the past of Plato, Aristotle, St Augustine and Thomas More, went back to basics. Was private property moral? Could human relationships be governed by the written law alone? Bringing this digression to an end, let us at once admit that it oversimplifies the reality. It would be quite wrong to say that Christianity gives blanket approval to property while utopias oppose it. In all ages, there were many Christians who ardently opposed property. The Anabaptists, radical Protestants, reached the conclusion that all property should be communal. In Russian history, there were the famous Non-possessors in the early sixteenth century who, under the leadership of Nil Sorsky, preached asceticism and were against the Church owning any land or other property. Conversely, among the authors of classical utopias there were some who favoured private property, like James Harrington, the author of *The Commonwealth of Oceana* (1656).

Nevertheless, the fact is that Christian churches of different denominations have been a force in history that has tended to favour property, while utopians, from Plato to Fourier, have tended to condemn it.

— 5 —

TERRITORY

Ambitions of Colonialism and Methods of Subjugation

Yermak the conquistador

Cossacks under the command of Yermak left the Urals territories of the Stroganov merchant dynasty behind them and for several months travelled up waterways, dragging their boats from river to river, overwintering, then again proceeding upriver, only in the summer clashing with the Siberian Tatars. After a series of victories over Khan Kuchum, in the autumn of 1582 Yermak entered the town of Sibir (Kashlyk) and began receiving local tribal chiefs who came bearing him gifts of fish and furs. The leaders took an oath to pay an agreed annual tribute or *asak*, and in return the new 'khan' promised to protect the populace from the old khan. Thus did the inhabitants of Siberia become subjects of the Russian tsar.

The long voyage, the battles and the establishment of a relationship of master and client with the local populace looks very much like a page out of the history books of colonization. Hernán Cortés, voyaging to Mexico and subordinating the Aztecs to the Spanish Crown sixty years before Yermak, acted in much the same way, albeit with greater cruelty. The histories are comparable: there is nothing far-fetched about viewing Russia as a colonial power. The topic was as extensively discussed in debates between historians a hundred years ago as it is little discussed today, Alexander Etkind suggests. He has devoted a book titled *Internal Colonization* to propounding a colonial approach to Russian history.[1]

Etkind is talking not just about Russia opening up remote eastern territories, but about the country's history in general. Sergey Soloviov, too, characterized the early period of Russian history as a time of colonization:

> Here was a vast, virgin country waiting to be populated, just waiting for history. Accordingly, early Russian history is the history of a land that was being colonized. The country we are considering was not, however, some colony separated by oceans from a distant metropolis: the focal point of the life of the state was located within it. The needs of the state grew, the functions of the state became increasingly complex, and yet the land did not shake off the character of a country that was being colonized.[2]

We associate colonization with sea voyages to the ends of the earth, with conflict with rivals and trade with natives. For some reason we find it difficult to visualize a terrestrial empire, even though before the advent of the railways it was more difficult to travel long distances by land than by sea. The journey from Moscow to eastern Siberia was certainly no easier, and perhaps more difficult, than from Spain to Cuba.

It was faster and cheaper to transport cargo from Arkhangelsk to London by sea than from Arkhangelsk to Moscow by land. During the Crimean War, Russia's rulers discovered to their horror that troops and supplies could be deployed to Sevastopol more rapidly from Gibraltar than from Moscow. In the early nineteenth century, the cost of supplying Russia's bases in Alaska by sailing round the globe was a quarter of the cost of doing so by land. 'Technically and psychologically, India was closer to London than many areas of the Russian Empire were to St Petersburg.'[3]

A sense of dislocation of the colonies from the centre was as typical of Russian colonization as of any other. What was different was that the subject and object of colonization were not so obviously distinct from each other as in many other cases. In Russia there were no armed foreigners from across the seas, although there certainly was a subjugated local population. There was no white man in a pith helmet and no enslaved dark-skinned native, although vast territories were added to the empire.

The expansion and opening up of Russia continued until the collapse of the empire. Colonists invited from Europe filled empty spaces on the map. Hundreds and thousands of Russian peasants were transported thousands of kilometres to new territories. Russia's colonization was quite unique, but there are many parallels in its history with the incorporation of North and South America, Western Australia and parts of Africa.

What gold was in South America, what spices were in Asia or slaves in Africa, furs were in Russia. Russians moved to the north and east of Eurasia in search of better hunting. Fur was the first commodity to contribute to the development and expansion of the country that was to become Russia. It was both a tradeable good and a currency: furs were collected and paid in tribute; before the discovery of their own reserves of precious metals, Russian princes paid in furs for the silver with which to mint coins.

In the course of two years of campaigns along the rivers of Siberia, Yermak sent back to Moscow 2,400 sable skins, 800 black fox skins and 2,000 beaver skins. That does not, of course, compare with Aztec gold, but it is significant wealth when we consider that in a slightly later period the total number of furs received annually by the treasury was estimated at 50,000 skins. Different estimates put the revenue from the sale of furs at anything from 10 to 25% of the gross income of the Muscovite state in the sixteenth to seventeenth centuries.[4]

Towards the end of the fourteenth century, some 95% of all furs imported by London were of Hanseatic origin, and the greater part of those were deliveries from Novgorod. It was at this time that one of the few Russian borrowings to enter the English language arrived: 'sable' (*sobol'*). Because of the huge demand in the West for this fur, sable was all but hunted to extinction in the European part of Russia by the late sixteenth century.[5] That is why Russia's conquistadors then headed further east.

If the peasantry's opening up of lands depended on the plough, the scythe and the axe, in Siberia the pioneering involved the bow, the snare and the gun. Yermak and the many other colonizers who followed him were not looking for a place to put down roots for the rest of their days and raise new generations of Siberians. Their goal was to get the local community leaders under their control and supplying them with furs. Displacing the old 'elite', they aimed to become a new elite, collecting tribute from the native population. This type of colonization makes Siberia comparable to most of the countries of Latin America.

The colonization of Russia's eastern regions has been compared to the development of North America. America's Wild West probably did have similarities to Russia's Wild East. For many years there were completely lawless areas both in the west of North America and in Siberia where everything was under the control of armed adventurers and unscrupulous go-getters. Attempts by local populations to resist predatory 'trade' were brutally suppressed. The colonizers' superior force, thanks to firearms, enabled them to compel the natives to pay tribute in furs. The colonizers did not shrink from taking women and children hostage, or from murder. In the late nineteenth century, the Siberian historian Nikolai Yadrintsev listed a dozen or so ethnic groups that had been wiped out in the preceding 300 years. According to some estimates, the depletion of the native population in the Russian North as a result of colonization is comparable with the depletion of the North American Indians.[6]

There are unexpected chronological coincidences, too. The Siberian and Californian gold rushes took place at much the same time, during the 1840s to 1860s. The abolition of serfdom in Russia and the passing of the Homestead Act, two events that led to massive settlement of the 'Far East' and the Far West, took place almost simultaneously, in the years 1861 and 1862, respectively. Vladivostok and Los Angeles were also both awarded city status in the second half of the nineteenth century.

There is, however, a crucial difference that determined the further destiny of these regions. Siberia's climate, its remoteness from the capital cities of Europe, together with other factors, led to its being settled primarily in order to extract natural resources and send them back to the centre. The colonizers of the American West, on the other hand, saw themselves as founders of a great independent territory. In this respect, Siberia resembles a traditional colony much more than does California. The colonial nature of Siberia's development was added to by the fact that Siberian settlers were mostly soldiers, and the region was used as a place of exile and forced labour. In the course of Siberia's colonization, from the beginning until 1917, at least two million people were exiled or forcibly resettled there. Towns were created for the purpose of military administration. The transport system was designed more as a link with the centre than between local settlements. By 1909, when Russia completed construction of the Trans-Siberian Railway, the Pacific coast of the United States had four railway mainlines connecting it with the rest of the United States.[7]

This pattern of development and focus on the export of resources has, as we shall see, long-term consequences in holding back the progress of any colony, African, South American or Russian. The outlook for Siberia changed in the Soviet period, particularly after the Second World War. As a result of massive public investment, the mining, metallurgical and energy industries grew apace and Siberia got its own research centres. Its cities became more habitable, and between 1959 and 1989 its population increased by a third. This upsurge came to an abrupt end with the collapse of the Soviet planned economy: Siberian industry was integrated in nationwide networks and proved highly vulnerable to free-market conditions. For a time almost everything came to a standstill and, with few exceptions, there has been no resumption since then of road construction and engineering works.[8]

The seizure of remote territories, subjugation of the local population, forced labour and payment of tribute are all stages in establishing the rules and institutions of domination. If power structures of this kind become established, they tend to last, because they are just too convenient. They enable a small elite to exploit all the fruits of a country's development, and which particular 'national idea' or ideology is currently being propounded is not all that important. The structure of domination is and can remain expedient for regimes, tsarist, Soviet or other, for just as long as that regime can avoid becoming accountable to society as a whole. Revolutions can be fruitless when it is so much easier to change the individuals comprising an elite than to change the rules that underpin their domination of a disenfranchised majority.

Stewardship and extraction

The Spanish nobleman Hernán Cortés set off in the early sixteenth century for the New World in search of glory and money. At that time, the colonizers were interested primarily in islands, Cuba and Hispaniola (the future Haiti and Dominican Republic). Cortés was one of the first to muster sufficient forces to penetrate deeper into the mainland, to the future Mexico, and to reach the Aztec Empire.

He acted in America as the Spaniards had acted during the centuries of the Reconquista, the retaking of the Iberian Peninsula from the Moors and Berbers. The right of ownership of the reconquered lands lay with the Crown, but the individual leading the reconquest of territory was granted an *encomienda*, a 'stewardship', over it. The local inhabitants were now obliged to work for their new governor. The Spaniards said, '*Sin indios non hay Indias*,' 'Without Indians there is no Indies.'[9]

Cortés took over the most valuable resource of the New World, the population. The colonizer was supposed to bring the light of Christianity to those newly converted under his stewardship, and in return the Indians got to work for their new master. In effect, the institution gave him the right to exploit a certain number of serfs assigned to him.

Others did the same. Francisco Pizarro landed on the west coast of modern Peru, discovered the whereabouts of the Inca ruler and took him prisoner. In exchange for his freedom, the Spaniards demanded a ransom of a room filled with gold, and two rooms filled with silver. Upon receiving the gold, Pizarro killed the ruler and moved on. Ultimately, all the Incas' tribal rulers were murdered and their treasures shipped back to Spain. As in Mexico, each of the commanders was granted an *encomienda*, a certain number of captives obliged to work for a white man just as they had worked for their old leader.

The colonizers devised another way of forcing the local population to work for them. When they discovered a huge silver deposit on the territory of what today is Bolivia, they needed workers for the mines. Francisco de Toledo solved the problem by reviving the Incan tradition of compelling a proportion of their subjects to do agricultural work for the aristocracy, priests and army. Like the former rulers, Toledo forcibly recruited one man in seven of the male population of villages adjacent to the mines. The system, known as '*mita*', was abolished only in 1812. Recent studies show that, to the present day, territories where *mita* was practised by the Spaniards remain less developed than those where the colonizers did not recruit workers.

Indeed, whole countries where a colonial regime was particularly harsh remain less developed. There was a time when all the Americas were colonies, but there is a considerable difference between the prosperous United States and less prosperous Mexico. Their development has differed largely because of the direction they were given by their European occupiers.[10]

The English were belated colonizers, too late to seize the gold- and silver-rich lands of the Aztecs and Incas, too late to exploit the 'easy' Indians the Spaniards could force to work for them. The English had to settle for northern lands, where there was less in the way of valuable minerals and stronger resistance to uninvited guests. Another important difference between the English and Spanish colonizers was that the former had the right to take legal ownership of the land. Many of them already had experience of enclosing land and acquiring a guaranteed right of possession.

For the Spaniards in South America, everything was more straightforward. They regarded the New World as a place to get rich and had no interest in negotiating agreements or creating institutions to extend legal rights to everyone: they were interested only in subjugation and control. All their instruments of government, including their 'stewardship', were subordinate to that end. Recent studies have come to the extraordinary conclusion that civilizations which, on the eve of conquest by the Europeans (i.e. around 1500), had been wealthy and civilizations which at that time were poor changed places in the historical pecking order. The empire of the Incas and Aztecs were far more developed and wealthy than the civilizations in the lands that subsequently became the United States, Canada and Australia. Today, however, the US and Canada are a lot more prosperous than Mexico and Peru, which have replaced the domains of the Aztecs and Incas.[11]

The rulers there changed frequently, with the colonizers replaced by local romantic, nationalist leaders, followed by new, military leaders, followed by ideologists of liberty and fraternity, fighters for justice and happiness. The ideologies were dramatically different, swinging from one extreme to another; the only thing that never seemed to change was that all the national wealth ended up in the hands of an elite. There are, alas, far more examples of such adverse continuity than of its opposite.

We have only to look at the experience of impoverished, war-torn Sierra Leone on the west coast of Africa. After the proclamation of independence from Britain in the early 1960s, supposedly 'popular' parties fought among themselves for a while. Following a succession of coups, President Siaka Stevens introduced one-party government, which he headed for many years, adopting and perfecting the art of colonial rule.

The British had established the practice of appointing regional leaders, the more conveniently to maintain control of the country as a whole. Stevens retained that institution and made it more rigorous. He wanted local power in only the most loyal hands. The British colonizers had established a system of marketing offices, which made it easier to collect tax from farmers producing coffee and cocoa. Stevens did not change the system, but imposed even higher taxes. The new government retained the diamond monopoly created by the British, and the single change the revolution brought was that now those on the company's board of directors were relatives of the president. The only institution the postcolonial government weakened was the army, because Stevens saw it as a threat. He relied instead on mercenary detachments directly subordinate to him.

To Russians there is something familiar about all this: the appointment of governors, the monopolies, the jobs for relatives. The levers of power and wealth generation created by the colonizers pass from hand to hand, governments change, but what never seems to change is the inequality, the lack of rights and the poverty of the majority. Tsarist governors are replaced by chairmen of provincial Party committees; those in turn are replaced by governors and heads of federal districts. The titles are not what matters. In the end, the liberators, the supporters of democracy who are supposedly going to replace the oppressors, simply take over the old levers of power, and after a few years the population can see no difference between their new rulers and the old.

Economists trying to work out why some countries are historically better off believe that success depends largely on the nature of institutions, of rules and regulations, and, more specifically, on how widely rights are distributed and protected in a society – those same rights to life, liberty and property described in chapter 4. Daron Acemoğlu and James Robinson distinguish two kinds of institutions in the world today: inclusive and extractive.[12]

If the existing laws and regulations are framed in such a way as to protect private property, support the implementation of laws and contracts, encourage economic activity and the creation of new enterprises and companies, Acemoğlu and Robinson call those institutions 'inclusive'. Such regulations stimulate a person to action and enable people to realize their talents. Their effect is to ensure that an increasing number of people are included in productive and creative endeavour.

Property rights are absolutely central to these inclusive institutions, because only someone whose rights are patently safeguarded will invest money and effort in an enterprise. 'A businessman who expects his output to be stolen, expropriated, or entirely taxed away will have little incentive to work, let alone undertake investments and innovations.'[13]

If the existing laws and regulations protect the property rights of only a minority, if they provide legal safeguards and an orderly environment for only a small group of people, if most are forced to take uncongenial work and face numerous obstacles to starting their own business, the institutions of such a society are categorized as 'extractive'. Extractive institutions exploit the coercive resources of the state to redistribute property, using 'hands-on control' from above, and to create entry barriers for outsiders.

Let us think back to the *encomienda mita*, and Russian landowners' rights over their serfs, and note that there is in today's Russia a small group of politically and economically advantaged individuals. These are all ways of extracting benefits for an elite by subjugating the majority. Those who create such institutions are interested in providing a maximum of benefits for themselves by abusing the freedoms and rights of everyone else.

Under these circumstances, the state ceases to act in the interests of society and becomes a tool defending the privileges of the elite. Studies have shown that this kind of mechanism is well able to keep itself in power for a long time. It is capable of resuscitating itself after revolutions, surviving regime change and blithely staying in place after the transfer of power from colonizers to popularly elected rulers. The problem turns out to lie not with particular conquistadors, aristocrats or oligarchs, but with the opportunities an elite have created to rule and enrich themselves.

A colonial politics creates a colonial economy. Extractive political institutions give rise to economic institutions that enable a small group of people to maximize their revenues at the expense of everybody else. Those reaping all the benefits also get their hands on the resources needed to keep themselves in power.

There is clearly a link between the fact that extractive regimes are often based on extractive industries and mineral wealth. The gold of the Incas, African diamonds, Siberian furs, ores, oil and gas all create a huge appetite to seize them and hold on at all costs to power and property. Unsurprisingly, extractive economic institutions in turn support a political system that protects the interests of the extractive elite, forming a vicious circle.

Immense power and immense inequality make the stakes in the political game very high. There are, however, invariably people prepared, under any political banner, to take that gamble in the hope of winning. The fact is that whoever controls the state gets their hands on almost limitless power and almost limitless wealth.

A natural resource irony of history

Vasiliy Klyuchevsky, a disciple of Sergey Soloviov, extended the notion of colonization to the whole of Russian history. Yes, he wrote, Russia is a country that was colonized at the very beginning of its history, but the process never came to a conclusion. 'Sometimes more, sometimes less obviously, this centuries-long movement continues to the present day.'[14]

The way in which members of Russia's ruling class have been buying up real estate all over the world can be seen as confirmation of their colonizing status as foreign players. For the first time in the post-Soviet period, the territory of Russia itself has been expanded by annexing Crimea.

Crimea marked the end of a long-term trend. Prior to 2014, the Russian elite had been inclined to take over territory by buying rather than annexing it. In the post-Soviet era, which should probably now be considered a thing of the past, the traditional tendency of the Russian population to respond to difficulties by moving away from them found expression in economic migration. Soloviov gave the following memorable description of the Russian national character:

> This feckless, passive habit of moving on at first sight of a problem has given rise to an almost nomadic mentality, a lack of attachment to a particular place, which has dissipated personal morality and habituated people to avoiding hard work, to a lack of thrift, to living mulishly from one day to the next.[15]

We recall another observation by Klyuchevsky. This distinguished historian notes that the dramatic expansion of Russia, which included the sixteenth- and early seventeenth-century enlargement of the borders of the Muscovite state to the north, east and south, coincided with the final enserfment of the peasants. He remarks, 'As the country's territory expanded, as the influence of the Russian people grew abroad, so, in inverse proportion, was its domestic freedom increasingly restricted.' The greater the power of the regime, Klyuchevsky observes, the fewer signs there were of a corresponding upsurge of the spirit of the nation. He considered it one of the central paradoxes of Russia's expansion that, until the mid-nineteenth century, territorial expansion was 'in inverse proportion to the development of the freedom of its citizens'.[16]

In the post-Soviet period, this paradox was much in evidence. The relatively rapid extension of civil rights and freedoms after the collapse of the USSR coincided with significant losses of territory. A kind of 'decolonization' took place. The fact that 2014 was marked by territorial expansion may indicate an attempt by the regime and society to halt this trend. If Klyuchevsky's rule is correct, that territorial expansion and the development of freedom are mutually opposed, it would be entirely natural to anticipate attempts to curb freedoms further.

As in Soviet times, financial and economic flows facilitate the optimal removal of resources from the provinces and their redistribution as the capital sees fit. The structure of transport links and geographical location of cities and enterprises still reflect the imperial and Soviet priorities. Even pension and tax systems operate largely in accord with colonial laws.

Vladimir Mau, one of Russia's leading modern economists who works on strategic development programmes, says only partly in jest that it is impossible to fine-tune the Russian tax system.

The attitude in our country to the tax system has roots going back to the Tatar-Mongol period when the tax-gathering *baskaks* would appear once a year in Russia's towns and villages to collect the tribute owed to the khan of the Golden Horde.

> They yelled, 'Pay up your tax if
> It's the last thing that you do.'
> A lot of grief they gave poor Rus,
> That grasping, motley crew,

as Count Alexey Tolstoy exclaimed. He was absolutely right, not only in that immediate context but in a much longer perspective.[17]

Such a state shows no interest in protecting its citizens' freedom and property. It provides only one service (and there is no guarantee even of that): it does not interfere in your affairs as long as you pay your tribute. How is that different from the relationship between the colonizer and the colonized? In fact, however, even this colonial contract is more humane than the relationship between the individual and the state during the Soviet period. At that time, the state intervened in your life whether you paid the tribute or not. Meddling of that kind is limited today to a number of politically taboo subjects, apart from which the relationship between society and the national government does not postulate any very serious obligations on either side. The state and the citizenry have no wish to enter into a close relationship and prefer to keep a wary eye on each other from a safe distance. This is a step forward relative to the Soviet past, but no better than a step back to pre-Soviet relations between the governors and the governed.

The continuities between the old and new institutions of domination in Russia are striking. Historians will debate endlessly how to apportion the blame for this between the Golden Horde's colonizers, the violent *oprichniks* of Ivan the Terrible and Vladimir Lenin's Bolsheviks, but all Russians know from their own experience, and from their family history, how 'eternal' the relationship seems to be between the elite and society. That is precisely the reason why each successive generation reading Gogol's *The Government Inspector* (1836) and Saltykov-Shchedrin's *History of a Town* (1870) finds in them fresh and entirely relevant social satire.

After the revolution, the place in society that had been occupied by the aristocracy did not remain vacant for long. It was gradually filled by the Soviet nomenklatura – a group of people produced by rules concealed from society. They occupied the top positions in the ruling party, the administrative system of the state and the economy of the Soviet Union. The good news was that the nomenklatura did result from a process of selection, even if it was bureaucratic and corrupt, based on education and proven performance. That is a way in which the Party hierarchy was formally different from the aristocracy. Today, however, the distinction is no longer observable. The nomenklatura's monopoly on power has degenerated into a monopoly on extracting the largest obtainable revenues from acting as the patron (*krysha*) of businesses, an activity no different from long-familiar criminal protection rackets. Admission to the elite now depends only on being one of the 'best people'. The aristocracy is with us again.[18]

The evolution of Party bosses into post-Soviet 'stewards' of business enterprise was entirely predictable, although it dragged on for almost two decades. The foundation was laid in the late 1980s. David Remnick, working at that time in the USSR as correspondent of the *Washington Post*, wrote in his book *Lenin's Tomb*, 'In the West, criminal gangs always move into those areas where there is no legal market economy, such as drug trafficking, gambling and prostitution. The Soviet Union had no market economy. Virtually all economic relations were mafia-based.'[19]

This meant that the whole of the economy was contested. The collapse of the empire and its social system turned into a victory for the elite. The naïve leaders of the Perestroika project believed that sluggish officials were trying to undermine Gorbachev's progressive reforms, which would transform the USSR into a just and economically sound state. The nomenklatura, however, was far from sluggish; it was, on the contrary, very shrewd and thinking one step ahead. While clever commentators in newspapers selling millions of copies were arguing about socialism and capitalism, the elite were creating a profitable economy for themselves, quite separate from the crisis-ridden and loss-making economy of the rest of society.

They were those who were allowed access to the new, enterprising 'Young Communist League economy', to the Centres of Scientific and Technological Creativity of the Young, which were established in the latter half of the 1980s and converted state-owned enterprises' financial reserves into ready cash; to the setting up of joint ventures with foreign firms; to dealing in real estate. They were able to convert the assets of the old administrative systems into new capital, including financial capital. If we look at the Yeltsin elite as a whole, sociologist Olga Kryshtanovskaya estimates 70% of it consisted of various levels of the old nomenklatura.[20]

Today's techniques of 'hands-on control', employed by high-ranking officials exploiting the full panoply of the state's resources, are the Russian version of those extractive colonial institutions whose longevity is making it so difficult for countries in Latin America and Africa to develop.

Such political institutions of domination as a single ruling party, the absence of separation of powers, and manipulation of the judicial system, give rise to and maintain the extractive character of the economy. A substantial proportion of manufacturing and mining is the private property of a small circle of individuals, their property rights secured outside Russia in jurisdictions where private property is more reliably safeguarded.

Throughout the post-Soviet years and until quite recently, the government openly supported this situation by keeping taxation of dividends low. The larger a company, the more probable it still is that its assets will be owned by offshore companies. This is convenient in many ways: it makes possible the concealment of property owned by officials. As a bonus, major businessmen with legal protection in the West are less apt to demand a predictable and transparent judicial system.[21]

Toleration of this pattern of ownership has, however, decreased dramatically in recent years. Business that has technically emigrated can be repatriated, either by creating more attractive conditions for investment, including, obviously, protection of property rights, or by coercion, by administrative pressure and legislative restrictions on owning property abroad. The first option is more difficult, but effective; the second is the easy option, but dysfunctional. At the present time, the regime is choosing the second option.

The persistence of the institutions of domination means that old institutional ways survive. We are reminded of the way the Spanish conquistadors succeeded the leaders of the Incas, of how they were in turn replaced by national governments, but how the institutions for extracting revenues remained unchanged.

In Russia, there never has been, and there still is not, any social contract with the government whereby citizens would pay their taxes and the state would, in return, protect their lives, liberty and property. Relations with the state are straightforward: in effect, those who have resources pay off the government. Those who do not have resources are dependent on the state and are on the receiving end of its tutelage and 'support'. Today's relationship of domination is less flat-footed and brutal than in the past, but this is essentially the same old colonial relationship between a dominating force and a dominated population.

It is an irony of history, Alexander Etkind notes, that the oil- and gasfields that currently provide Moscow with such a comfortable existence are in the same territories the Novgorodians once colonized in order to trade furs with the Yugrans (the Khanty and Mansi peoples). Among the main customers for Russian oil today are many who were once major buyers of Russian furs. Where the pipelines of Gazprom now run was once the trade route for exporting pelts from Moscow, through Poland to Leipzig and further west. The North Stream natural gas pipeline follows almost exactly the route of the trade caravans of the Hanseatic League.[22] There are discussions about extending the pipeline to Britain, once the largest customer for Russian furs. If that happens, history will have come full circle.

If we take the long view, we can see that taxing the trade in natural resources has been and remains a key source of revenue for the Russian state; arranging their extraction has been its main concern; and finding ways to deliver those commodities the length and breadth of Eurasia has been its responsibility. Extraction requires specialized skills lacked by the population at large. Relatively few people are actually engaged in business. The result is that the state has little time for the rest of the population, while the people itself has little time for the state. These are circumstances that give rise to a caste-based society, with the security services becoming indistinguishable from the state.

Our pre-revolutionary history should have taught us that privileged circumstances for a narrow elite or class – for example, the protection of their rights to personal freedom and property – create an explosive situation for the whole of society. Renunciation of this kind of legal privilege is a difficult reform to implement, but not impossible. Many societies have managed it, from Britain and Japan to Peru and Chile. In many countries the process is taking place today, but in Russia it somehow cannot even get started. In our situation, given our oddly colonial history, the transition to inclusivity would need simultaneously to incorporate a degree of 'decolonization'. But let us not get ahead of ourselves.

— 6 —

THE LOCK ON THE DOOR

The Priority of Security

The collapse of monarchy in the West

The kings and queens of England ran out of luck. Unlike the Russian tsars, they did not succeed in remaining the principal owners of property in their country. Increasing numbers of property owners, large and small, appeared in England and, as time went by, they encumbered their monarchs with increasing numbers of conditions. From the thirteenth century onwards, monarchs periodically found themselves obliged to sign agreements imposed on them by their subjects. The Magna Carta came about in just that way, although it was only a temporary concession and the struggle continued for hundreds of years after it. Whether it was the golden age of agriculture, the upsurge of trade with overseas colonies or the vigorous development of the land market, the beneficiaries were always the few.

At the beginning of the seventeenth century, almost everything in the country – clothes, belts, buttons, pins, butter, fish, salt, pepper, coal – was produced and sold by monopolies. There were over 700 of these and they were an excellent way of topping up the exchequer. These over 700 favoured individuals or groups, however, who paid the king for their privileges, blocked access to wealth for thousands of others. The group of the successful and wealthy was too small. The number of those discontented with the privileges of the elite grew, and the malcontents had a strong and active representative: a parliament with people sitting in it who aspired to make money through manufacturing and trade. They did not like the monopolies, they did not like the way the king made free with property rights, and they did not like the arbitrary way taxes could be increased. They failed to reach agreement peacefully; disputes were followed by civil war and, towards the end of the seventeenth century, the Glorious Revolution, which proved crucial for turning England into a modern state.

Parliament and those who wanted the power of the king curtailed benefited from another circumstance. By the seventeenth century, after Henry VIII had broken off relations with the Vatican in the previous century and dissolved the monasteries, the lands of the country's largest landowner, the Church, were redistributed. England suddenly had a lot of new landowners, new economic players with a political agenda of their own. A time came when their combined forces were alarmingly powerful: the united citizenry was capable of raising a greater army than the Crown, and proceeded to do so during the civil war of the 1640s. James Harrington, a thinker who was a contemporary of these events, was the first to see a link between the distribution of property and political power. He believed the monarchy could remain absolute only if the king owned at least two-thirds of England's land. After successive redistributions, the kings of England were well short of that. Indeed, after the Restoration, the monarch owned a mere tenth of the land of his island kingdom (see also information on changes of land ownership in England in chapter 4).[1]

Success in the East

Russia's rulers managed these changes much better: they prevented them. Recognizing the threat to themselves sooner than their English counterparts did, they did everything they could to subjugate existing players who had ambitions, and to rule out the possibility of others emerging.

The danger of new landowners with interests of their own was constantly arising because the state of Muscovy was growing through annexation of new territory. New lands meant new subjects and new landowners. People with different cultural values, these new subjects could represent a threat to the unity of the state. The rulers of Muscovy were aware of that and kept things firmly under control. The greater Moscow grew, the less tolerant its rulers became of independence. The redistribution of land in Russia followed a pattern diametrically opposed to that of Western Europe.

In the days when the feudal lords in Europe were keeping their vassals under strict subordination, there was no such strictness on the part of Russian princes: their boyars enjoyed a degree of freedom unheard of among Western nobles. They could move from the service of one prince to that of another while retaining their fiefdoms. Serving under contract elsewhere, a free noble was deemed to be satisfying his service requirements 'in law and tribute over land and water' relating to his land. This relationship is reflected in a condition common to all princely contracts: 'boyars and servants shall be free to choose which of us they will serve'.[2]

The trends were in opposite directions: while Western landowners were tied, Russian landowners were comparatively free, but when landowners in the West started posing a formidable threat to monarchs, Russia's princes vigorously set about centralizing control and transforming ownership of land into tenure conditional upon service. The grand princes demanded ever greater loyalty in return for ever less security.[3]

Ivan III ('the Great', r. 1462–1505), the 'gatherer of the Rus lands', did not only capture and annex new territories, he changed the character of land ownership. After his subjugation of Novgorod, in order to safeguard his position against unruly Novgorodians, Prince Ivan allocated them land in new places, but not on a hereditary basis, only for their lifetime, thus making them wholly dependent on him. He applied the same rules to Muscovites he moved on to the Novgorod lands.[4] It was expansion through subordination.

Ivan IV ('the Terrible', r. 1547–84) continued his grandfather's policy of increasing his subjects' dependency on the tsar. Grants of land to new people were usually only for life rather than as patrimonies. Even that remained conditional on the rendering of service. Ivan developed the conditional nature of land tenure: an estate could continue in the possession of the person to whom it was granted after his death only if he had a son capable of rendering service. If there was no such son, the land reverted to the treasury.[5]

Gradually, the problem of the old patrimonial princes (of Yaroslavl, Suzdal, Tver and others) and the boyars was resolved. Initially, Ivan legislated to limit the right of some of the princes to sell patrimonies, to transfer them to monasteries or to give them as a dowry for daughters, but later applied the restrictions to all of them. He commanded that the lands of any who died childless should revert to the sovereign. If any broke the law on selling, he ordered that their land should 'be taken for the monarch without payment'. Those who left no sons were allowed to bequeath their patrimony only to brothers and nephews who would be capable of rendering service. Land could not be bequeathed to daughters or sisters, and only the tsar could decide how much was to be left in the lifetime possession of a widow. After her death, the patrimony would again revert to the sovereign.[6]

Ivan the Terrible's division of the country into *oprichnina* land and *zemshchina* land (ruled by the Boyar Council) was a further mechanism for resolving the problem of excessive independence. Territories which had constituted the old landed principalities were seized for rule by the *oprichnina* (later renamed the tsar's court). One of the key tasks of the *oprichnina* was thus to break the customary patrimonial tenure. The traditional states within the state with their aristocratic suzerains were to be done away with, and with them their ancient privileges and rights, including the right to retain an army of several thousand men which the princes could place at the service of the grand prince. It was an attack against the old order instigated by the monarch himself. 'The *oprichnina* moved masses of service people from one piece of land to another. Princely and monastery land was taken for distribution to those serving the tsar, and the patrimony of the prince himself was confiscated by the monarch. There was a radical revision and general reshuffling of property rights.'[7]

This uprooting was not, however, confined only to such major landowners as appanage princes and those with patrimonial lands. Ivan the Terrible divided those serving him into the 'proximate' and the 'remote' without regard to their social origins or wealth. The *oprichnina* terror was directed not only against mutinous appanage nobles but also against independently minded service people considered to have treasonable sympathies with Lithuania. The confiscation of land from anyone who was not 'proximate', who did not prove their readiness to serve the will of the tsar, did in a literal sense cut the ground from under the feet of all opposition. Some one thousand nobles and 'boyars' children' were driven off lands taken into the *oprichnina*. The majority of those who fled abroad were, according to historian Daniil Alshits, less than wealthy service people.[8]

These new rules not only accomplished the strategic task of establishing control over potential rivals, but also boosted Ivan's coffers. They did, however, have a downside. The appearance of so many dependent people created a lot of work for the tsar and his far from numerous administrative team. There was suddenly much more 'hands-on control', as might be said today. The tsar now had to concern himself with the problems of all his new service people; in a literal sense he had to act as the guardian of his subjects and worry about how their elderly parents, children, wives and widows were to be cared for. If a landowner was having trouble making ends meet, he would appeal to the tsar for extra parcels of land for his estate. Against the trend, from time to time land would be awarded as a hereditary patrimony. There was nothing systematic in all this, as there still is not to this day: the nature of property ownership depended on the whim of the tsar.

In spite of all his inconsistencies, Ivan the Terrible was pursuing one goal throughout his reign: tying the ownership of property ever more firmly to the rendering of service. The new territories conquered and the land redistribution within the *oprichnina* area contributed to just that end. Land should not simply be owned by someone, it should not be 'freed from service dues'.

Control as the top priority

If, at the beginning of the fifteenth century, two-thirds of the land belonged to Russia's boyars, princes and the Church, and only one-third to the grand prince, by the mid-sixteenth century the proportions were reversed: the nobles and the Church now owned one-third and it was the grand prince, now renamed the tsar, who owned two-thirds. By the end of Ivan the Terrible's reign, there were only two significant landowners in Russia: the tsar and the Church.[9]

Its contingency on service had become the main feature of the right to own property in the Russian state. It was clear that, sooner or later, the fate of other kinds of ownership, such as the free tenure of their land by the peasantry and the property belonging to the Church, would be decided in the state's favour.

In the case of ecclesiastical land, a consciousness of the divine nature of its ultimate owner was a major obstacle, and it was only in 1764 that the Empress Catherine II (Catherine the Great) felt strong enough to act decisively and issue a manifesto secularizing the Church's lands. The state gained an increase in its annual income three times greater than the amount it agreed to spend on maintaining the Church.[10]

The issue of the peasants' land was on a larger scale and more complex. The peasantry's fate, like that of the boyar nobility, evolved in a direction quite contrary to that of the West. Every state needs to maintain troops and be able to feed them, but whereas some states met those needs by gradually emancipating the population, in the eastern part of Europe the population was gradually subjugated.

In the West, the Black Death, which swept across Europe in the mid-fourteenth century, caused a massive scarcity of labour that 'shook the foundations of the feudal order' and allowed labourers to demand higher wages.[11] Tenant farmers and farm labourers were able slowly to free themselves of obligations to landlords. Monarchs tried to restrain this: England's Edward III in the Statute of Labourers of 1351 aimed to fix wages at pre-plague levels and forbade 'enticement', whereby one lord attempted to poach scarce peasants from another.

Ultimately, these attempts to restore the serf-like status of labourers proved futile and only led to rioting. Wat Tyler led the Peasants' Revolt in 1381, which captured most of London. The revolt was suppressed and Tyler executed, but there were no further attempts to enforce laws on fixed wages and the ban on migration. Feudal labour service dwindled and was replaced by what looked increasingly like inclusive market relationships.

Meanwhile, in the east of Europe, landowners were strengthening their dominance over the workforce. In Poland, Hungary and the eastern part of Germany, labourers became increasingly dependent: the amount of time they had to work for their feudal masters increased during the sixteenth century from a few days a year to two or three days a week.[12]

This process of a second enserfment occurred in Russia, too. In the sixteenth century, as Russia's territory increased in size, the room for liberty was shrinking proportionately, and not only for service people but also for peasants. While in Western Europe this was a time when tied peasants were becoming yeoman farmers or free labourers, in Russia free people were being driven into serfdom.

Some historians attribute this second enserfment of Russian peasants to the increasing demand for East European grain in the West, but a Russian landowner, unlike, for example, one in the Baltic provinces, had virtually no ability to export his produce. Until Black Sea ports became accessible in the mid-eighteenth century, Russia's main agricultural exports were hemp and flax, which the English bought in Arkhangelsk. Significantly, the process of enserfment was not occurring around Arkhangelsk but in central Russia, which had no access to the sea. Vasiliy Klyuchevsky showed that the closer one came to Moscow, the greater was the proportion of peasants who were serfs.[13] It was as if Moscow created servitude and serfdom.

One thing the economic situation in Eastern and Western Europe had in common was a shortage of workers. 'No other factor contributed so much to the enserfment of the peasants as the universal shortage of manpower.'[14] If, however, landowners in the West failed to retain power over labourers, those in the East did so very successfully.

The rulers in Moscow managed to introduce a vertical command structure whose aim was rapid exploitation of resources such as fur, land and human beings. There was a clear logic, dictated by circumstances, to their actions. At the time, this was probably the fastest route to national prosperity and territorial expansion. The Muscovites played their game, and played it better than many others.

It is not only Russian historians who readily admit this. '[T]he Muscovite state focused its energies on strictly limited objectives.' These were 'the preservation of military and political order – or, more precisely, the avoidance of political chaos'.[15]

The Russian ruling family and boyar elite saw their task as 'knitting together an expansive, poor, sparsely populated region', whose residents had also to be mobilized 'for constant defense against a host of aggressive neighbors'. The methods Moscow had discovered in the fourteenth to sixteenth centuries proved effective and resolved four problems faced by every emergent kingdom: 'the problem of faction, the problem of wealth, the problem of mobilization, and the problem of conflict resolution'.[16]

While Europeans were constantly plagued by attempts by nobles to share power with the ruling family, Moscow's monarchs succeeded in getting a mandate for one dynasty to rule and dedicate itself wholly to building an empire. Whereas in Europe various social groups were constantly questioning the legitimacy of monarchies, the Muscovites faced no comparable problems. The grand prince was the supreme arbiter over others with power. Already by the end of Ivan III's reign there is no evidence of political opposition to the institution of autocracy.

After many years of bloody strife, the elite came to the conclusion that society must accept the indisputable power of a single dynasty. Establishing political stability was the first major achievement of the Muscovite state. The second was creating a mechanism for controlling resources. If European monarchs had to engage in complex negotiations with various strata of society to obtain funds for the Crown, the Muscovites were able to dispense with this.

The third achievement was the readiness (under duress) of the nobility to serve. On occasions when money was in short supply, it was an advantage to have people at your disposal who could simply be ordered to serve, and had no option but to do so if they wanted to hold on to their lands. '[N]ot only did the Russians survive, they prospered, creating in the span of a bit over a century an empire that stretched from Archangelsk to Kiev and from Smolensk to Kamchatka,' writes Marshall Poe, emphasizing the durability of the institutional solutions he is describing.

These decisions were taken in specific historical circumstances, but persisted far longer than necessary. 'By almost any standard,' Poe continues, 'Muscovite political culture proved to be quite durable, lasting in its pristine form for almost two centuries and, according to the opinions of some continuity theorists, well into modern times under one guise or another.'[17]

These were undeniable achievements that benefited the nascent state. Looking back over five centuries of Russian history, it is impossible not to acknowledge the magnitude of its military power and the scale of its territorial expansion. If we were to take as the principal criteria of a state's success the surface area of the earth over which it ruled and the number of years for which it its domination lasted, Russia has no equal in the world. Of course, states can have other achievements, but for the present we are considering space and time, which, unlike freedom and well-being, are easy to measure.

Rein Taagepera, an Estonian statistician and political scientist, calculated and compared in the 1980s how many square kilometres had been controlled by particular empires and for how long. If Muscovy, the Russian Empire and the Soviet Union are regarded as a single state, its score immediately before the collapse of the USSR was 65 million 'square kilometre-years'. Its nearest rival, the British Empire, scores only 45 million, and the Roman Empire 30 million. On the basis of statistical evidence from all empires, Taagepera predicted (and this was at the end of the 1980s) that the Russian Empire in its basic configuration, albeit possibly after losing certain territories, might be expected to survive for approximately another 400 years.[18]

Russia's rulers coped well with the challenges facing them while the state was emerging; they resolved only too well, if rather hamfistedly, the problem of governability. Ever since, their successors have taken the view that this is how they should always behave, irrespective of the historical circumstances. A major role in disseminating that belief has been played by the Church, which sanctified feudal autocracy. The very conflicts between an autocrat, his retinue and the Church, which the rulers of Muscovy were so successful in averting, were the matrix in Europe for individual social groups to develop their autonomy, leading to the formation of a negotiated relationship between society and the monarch.

The principle that security (or controllability) must be the top priority crushed all other objectives, including the development of trade and manufacturing, and this had major consequences. Stable development had to be sacrificed for the sake of territorial gains, for which no price was too high. That is what lies behind the readiness, and the ability, to dominate both the nobility and the peasantry. It lies behind the readiness to abolish those rights of individuals that might stand in the way of efficient extraction of resources, foremost among which was the right to own property.[19]

An aspect of this process was the destruction by Ivan the Terrible of the republican institutions that emerged in Novgorod and Pskov. We should not, of course, idealize the Veche 'democracy', but ought just to remember that it was a different institutional path from that of Moscow. In the unitary state that the Muscovites were constructing, property rights and other institutions in the struggle for interests that did not coincide with those of the state were a hindrance and a sign of defiance. For centuries Russians sought, by compulsory mobilization of resources, to ensure their country's ability to wage war. This sapped its strength and restricted opportunities for development and intensive growth.[20]

It was at this time that the figure of the supreme ruler was established, not only at the top of the administrative pyramid, but also at the top of the food chain: more precisely, at the head of Russia's principal dining table, located in the Kremlin.

The tsar's retinue were remunerated at court, but also received 'palace rations': meat, fish, wine, malt and hay. On feast days, the boyars might be handed a more substantial gift in the form of a fur coat or a length of costly fabric. If a feast day passed without such a gift from the tsar, that was seen as a warning that access to privileged rations could be terminated, and suggested an urgent need to negotiate with a well-placed official if favour was not to be withdrawn completely, leading to demotion from food to fodder.

The Petersburg period of Russian history can be seen as a protracted but deliberate exploration of a path different from that of Muscovy. It saw the appearance of a regular, structured civil service, army, police force, the transformation of service-based ownership to a fully fledged right to own private property, a sophisticated judicial system, reform of local government, emancipation of the serfs and the first steps to extend property rights to the most numerous class in the empire, the peasants. This experiment lasted 200 years and, tragically, was never completed. It was a systematic movement towards greater autonomy of citizens, of organizations and institutions. It was a movement away from relations based on status to relations built on consent.

In terms of personal initiative and emancipation, the Soviet regime was a force not for modernization but for restoring archaic ways. 'As they settled more comfortably into the Kremlin, the Bolsheviks inherited a mindset dating back to when power in that place was at its apogee, in the sixteenth and seventeenth centuries,' Tamara

Kondratieva writes.[21] The new regime re-created an ancient system of relations on a new level, and this happened almost automatically. The Kremlin could not but become the main source of food and other goods for its citizens, for the simple reason that the new regime destroyed the Petersburg institutions, first and foremost the market economy and private property, which had allowed people to take responsibility for their own welfare. Accordingly, the regime found itself instantly obliged to feed a famine-stricken country and provide people with accommodation.

A further paradox was that, in place of the 'Petersburg state', which had been unable to bear the burden of multiple simultaneous threats, not least the burden of its own size, there came a new 'Muscovite state' that saw even more threats confronting it. From the moment the Bolsheviks seized power, security was the top priority for the Soviet government. The Bolsheviks were politically uncompromising. For Lenin, even a minimal deviation from the ideological creed was cause for implacable hostility. The victorious sect refused to work with other sects that were ideologically close to it, let alone with any that opposed it.

Any institution that might protect the interests of other, non-Bolshevik forces – a parliament, other parties, non-governmental organizations, business firms and even publishing houses – was immediately seen as a threat. Any activity unsanctioned by the government was a threat.

Worrying about material well-being also became a threat. Soviet Russia turned into a state where asceticism was obligatory. Only a select few were permitted to enjoy, in secret, material well-being sanctioned and directly supported by the state. In Russian history, the demand for security had always prevailed over demands for material well-being, and in the Soviet state that predominance was reinforced ideologically and by legislation.

Security as a threat

The struggle against various threats, internal and external, has been a priority for the Russian state during all the centuries it has existed. Any state has to confront threats, and indeed that is how states take shape. The real question is how to reconcile security with development.

Russia is a state where economic development comes second to the need to 'neutralize threats', sociologist Simon Kordonsky suggests. Ministries and agencies see it as their mission in life to maximize the number of threats and exaggerate the dangers they pose, because that determines how much funding they can expect.[22]

> A torrent of unverifiable information about potential or actual threats not only wells up through the hierarchies of government, but also gushes by way of the media and social networks into the national news, which is inundated with information about the problems of particular individuals, communal and natural disasters, the catastrophic state of towns and regions, the state of culture, health, education, social security, the organization of the armed forces and their ability to counter attacks by foreign or domestic adversaries.[23]

This fuels the regime with threats. It lives and replicates itself, terrifying its citizens and itself. It makes money, spends and raises it in order to battle for security. Ensuring security is thus still the fundamental goal of the Russian government, only we have to qualify that by remarking that, to a large extent, the threats the state keeps talking about are made up. What is worse, as so many of the threats in the news are false, inflated to cadge money out of the budget, we have little idea what real threats Russian society is facing. We end up with, on the one hand, intimidated and mistrustful citizens and, on the other, a guaranteed brake on social reform.

Any reform represents change, and change brings new threats, which provide a new opportunity for enterprising administrators to get their hands on additional resources. Attempts to modernize the state only lead to modernization of the range of threats on offer. This explains why the actual result of privatization was to consolidate control over oil and gas resources. That is why the actual result of political liberalization has been a tightening of the political screws on independent players, be they non-profit organizations, human rights activists, opposition politicians, or ethnic or sexual minorities.

One part of the government has only to come up with a plan of reform for another part to present itself to the ruler with a list of new threats that this might supposedly introduce. Some tell him how dangerous the diffusion of state assets is, others how dangerous human rights campaigners are. Yet others warn of the collapse of civilization that would result from tolerance of minorities, support for the wrong sort of cinema industry, introduction of a standardized state examination, and so on and so forth. There is good money, indeed there are fortunes, to be made out of an ability to spin a good horror story to the listener-in-chief about our threat-laden future. In reality, this is not too difficult in an environment already permeated by distrust of the outside world. You just add a few details and statistics to the hoary old chestnuts about the perfidy of American foreign policy and the subverting of states and, before you know it, your budget and responsibilities have been pleasingly increased. This is swiftly followed by new villas in Europe and opportunities to study at the world's best universities. In this somewhat roundabout manner, at least a small part of Russia's budget is spent on top-class education.

The chasm between official rhetoric and the regime's actual deeds is, therefore, not so much evidence of schizophrenia in the mind of one particular individual as testimony to the relative success of certain pedlars of doom over others. Those who argue that Russia will slide into the abyss if its ruler does not establish a good investment climate are manifestly losing out to those who claim the country will slide into the abyss as a result of gay marriage, the doings of non-governmental organizations, and revolution in Kiev.

There is endless harping on about the threat of revolution. The security agencies worked out long ago how to play it up to enlarge their powers. They are allowed to burst into citizens' apartments, confiscate whatever they choose, conduct thousands of interrogations and carry out dozens of arrests on a kind of 'shoot first and ask questions later' basis. Officially there is no state of emergency, but unofficially there is.

The crises Russian politicians are so skilled at engineering dramatically increase public support for 'emergency' measures by the regime.[24] That, however, has a long history. In the Russian system of governance, emergency legislation is never far away. Indeed, the first Soviet law enforcement organization was the Cheka, the All-Russian Extraordinary Commission for Combating Counter-Revolution, Speculation and Sabotage. Its mission was to protect the revolution, and later the regime, rather than the rights of citizens. The Chekists were the 'combat wing of the Party', not of society. For as long as the Moscow regime continues, the only question is who is standing in for the Communist Party, not whether Russian society is prepared to accept emergency measures. Of course it is, because it has never had time to grow out of them, and because the system serves up one threat after another that urgently needs to be addressed.

An undeclared state of emergency has long hung over Russia's economy and politics; all that changes is how extensive or intensive it is. There is no telling where the next threat will come from, so the country needs a list of strategically essential enterprises. It does not matter that Russia needs investments: policy is guided by the fear of some vague threat. First, it forces the government to promise to bring back direct election of governors, but then the law is framed in such a way that they might as well not have bothered. Fear dominates the business climate. In this context it is impossible to plan for the long term. The sense of needing to keep your suitcase packed has become a daily reality for businessmen, except that the suitcase was long ago replaced by property abroad, and having passports and visas at the ready.

In this way, the aspiration to security is itself a threat. It is a threat that obliges people, if they want a guarantee that they will be able to assert their right to life, liberty and property, to do so outside the borders of Russia, a country where the powers of the security specialists are unconstrained by transparent rules.

There is really no need to repeat that security is a public good, the foundation on which the modern state has been built, and for the provision of which it is answerable to its citizens. There is no question of ceasing to consider it one of the most important public goods. We may compare the situation to a door: some people focus on how well it opens and closes and their priority is being able to enter and leave. For others, however, and this is the case in Russia, the sole concern is for the quality of the lock, which means priority goes to the keys and those who guard them.

— 7 —

LABOURERS

Moral Economics and the Art of Survival

The plough, the scythe and the axe

Peasant farmers are the class most lacking rights, and at the same time the most dangerous for the regime. They are the main source of the state's prosperity, and at the same time a powder keg for society and the state. None of the various incarnations of the Russian regime have had an easy relationship with them.

Looking back two, three or four generations, the majority of Russians find they have peasant roots. We have not been town dwellers so long as to have lost touch completely with our forebears. Should we look to this inheritance for an explanation of our current situation? To serfdom, the peasant commune with its egalitarian periodical 'repartitioning' of land? To the collective farms and forced labour camps? Have we really inherited a levelling-down culture of subordination and dependency, averse to innovation? To what extent does Russia still bear 'the stigma of the yoke of slavery'?[1]

For most of its recorded history, Russia's peasants had no doubt they had a right to the land, we are told by Vasilii Yeliashevich, a civil lawyer at the beginning of the twentieth century who finished his survey of the history of property rights in Russia in emigration. The most ancient documents testify to the fact that the peasants themselves believed 'the land belongs to the grand prince but we possess it'. Yeliashevich notes the existence from the outset of two parallel rights to the same land: the rights of the peasant and the patrimonial rights of the prince. This conflict, never clarified in law, has cropped up in various forms and at various times in Russian history, and at the time of the 1917 Revolution it remained unresolved.

A peasant acquired title to the land when he settled on and began working it. It can be called a labour right because the amount of land was measured in terms of capacity for labour. Possession of it, or, as the peasant expression has it, its 'due toil', was defined as continuing for 'as long as the plough, the scythe and the axe do toil upon it'. The 'due toil' also determined the obligations imposed on the peasant. Land could be acquired from another lord, but importantly the right to it ended if work stopped. The peasant retained his right for as long as he paid in kind and in labour. Selling land was seen as a readiness to withdraw from working it.[2]

For a peasant, freedom meant the right to leave freely. He always wanted the option to move on, and for most of Russia's history he had it. Indeed, the right to move on was a key regulator of the legal and economic status of peasants. The peasants themselves considered it an ancient and inalienable right, which is why the process of enserfment was so slow and arduous, and the memory of their ancient right to freedom of movement was lodged in the peasants' consciousness for centuries.

When Peter III and Catherine the Great made the nobles almost free (only almost, because a mere few, extremely prosperous, landowners were able to enjoy the fruits of their freedom) by breaking the link between land ownership and service, the peasants concluded that, since the nobles were now exempt from service, so were they. Rumours circulated among them that there were two manifestos, but the second, proclaiming freedom from service for the peasants, was being withheld from them by their masters. This was a long-running saga: for the entire period of enserfment, peasants were certain that the landowners were withholding the news of the royal favour shown to them. The peasants remembered that their being tied to the land had resulted from the needs of the state, rather than from the fact of their belonging to one particular landowner. The peasants, and especially state-owned serfs, considered themselves free citizens who paid taxes and had rights.

> The peasants' belief was all the more natural given that, despite the changes made by Peter the Great (and some which preceded his reign) to the legal status of state peasants towards levelling down their condition to that of serfs (the only difference being that it was the state that should be considered their master), it remained their firm belief (and this to some extent remained the case in the legislation) that they were free men who had property rights over the land they farmed and that their obligations towards the state were not as a landowner but as a state in our modern understanding: that is, as a public authority having

the right to levy taxes, to impose various state obligations, but not as a body with any sort of rights of ownership over them.[3]

The position of enserfed peasants was even more complicated. There was never any official talk of introducing the right of landowners or other legal entities to 'own' peasants. For centuries, the authorities operated only with the aid of temporary restrictions, initially seasonal, the famous Yuriev (St George's) Day, which in Russia fell after the bringing in of the harvest and the onset of winter, when peasants were allowed to move away from their present master, and later annual. Ivan the Terrible made a temporary measure permanent, and also declared 'reserved' years during which no moving away was permitted at all. Later tsars introduced equally pusillanimous half-measures, sometimes appearing to grant complete freedom of movement only to cancel it, trying at one and the same time not to anger the nobility and not to sow disaffection among the peasants. Freedom of movement was finally done away with after the Time of Troubles (1598–1613), when it was decided that the state could solve its economic problems only by tying the peasants to the land.[4]

What made enserfment particularly odious was the fact that rights and opportunities were taken away surreptitiously, by things unsaid and by outright cheating. There never was an official, logically and legally defined institution called serfdom in Russia. The dominant position of the landowning class came about from reign to reign by means of *ad hoc* prohibitions and decrees. Peasants were able to enter into economic relations with other classes long before they were granted the legal right to do so: they bought windmills and pasturage, even entire villages, using nobles to register the ownership.

Moreover, when the legal possibility arrived, peasants readily entered contractual relationships with each other and with other classes and were prepared to defend their interests. This can be seen from the work of a US researcher, Tracy Dennison, who analysed the archives of one of the Sheremetiev estates, the village of Voshchazhnikovo in Yaroslavl province. On this estate, the Sheremetievs effectively created a state under the rule of law within the state for their peasants. The peasants could register a deal with a notary or bring a lawsuit, and the patrimonial authorities acted as bailiffs, implementing the rulings of the court.

The patrimonial archive preserves hundreds of contracts agreed by peasants. Without resort to the *mir* (commune), patriarchal traditions and family ties, the Sheremetiev serfs went to see the notary. When they had access to legal procedures, the peasants were only too glad to make use of them, which gives the lie to some supposedly innate peasant inclination to collectivism and lawlessness.[5]

The only trouble was that the institutions available to them were not real. They were either domestic institutions set up by enlightened landlords, which had no legal standing with the state, or shady, private deals which were also outside the law. There was a great gulf between the truth and what the law recognized as the truth. 'No matter how robust and strong particular peasant holdings were, the legal system of serfdom had a disastrous effect even on them, exposing all their acquisitions to arbitary injustice, making them unable to count on the law to protect their rights,' writes Andrey Teslya.[6]

Legal ambiguity is typical of an estate-based society. In Russia, every class had rights, but the classes did not have equal weight and influence. The interests of the nobility were better protected than those of others, but there was ultimately no clarity about their situation either. To fully satisfy their aspirations, the nobility needed to be openly given the peasants as private property. Attempts to draft a legal framework for serfdom were made from the reign of Peter the Great, but the authorities continued to fudge the issue, fearing that bringing legal clarity to it might cause the country to explode in new peasant wars.[7]

The question of whether to retain or abolish serfdom confronted every nineteenth-century Russian monarch. Possible solutions to this unresolvable issue were informally and secretly discussed but did not and could not lead to action. The first laws indicating movement towards emancipation were adopted less than twenty years after Catherine the Great's Charter to the Nobility (1785, see below). Catherine even planned to issue a charter to the state peasants but did not see the matter through, aware that any legislative act in this area might destroy the fragile equilibrium between the government and the rest of the population.

There was understanding from the outset of the need to escape from this trap, but fear of change paralysed politicians at the crucial moment. Alexander I's 1801 decree allowed all members of the free classes to own unsettled land, which was particularly important for the merchant class. Two years later a decree on free tillers of the soil, issued in another connection, described for the first time the legal status of peasants who were being released from serfdom.

They could be released only on the initiative of their landowner, and few of those had any wish to free them. During the reigns of both Alexander I and Nicholas I, lavish grants of land, together with peasants, continued to be made. In effect, state peasants were being enserfed at the same time as the other serfs were being transferred to the status of state peasants. The balance was, nevertheless, moving overall in the direction of emancipation: from the beginning of the nineteenth century until the abolition of serfdom in 1861, the proportion of serfs in the peasant population gradually decreased. As of 1857, the proportion of privately owned peasants in the empire was 42%; of government peasants, 52%; and of patrimonial peasants owned by the royal family, 6%.[8]

Nicholas I, like his brother Alexander, knew that emancipation of the peasants was necessary, but was also certain that the reform would tear the country apart: 'There is no doubt that serfdom in its present form in Russia is an evil, sensitive and obvious to all, but to touch it at this time would be an even greater disaster.'[9]

The peasant reform is a classic example of a political measure everybody recognizes as essential, but which is put off because society is considered not yet ready for it. A conservative regime is afraid to disturb the balance between those in favour and those against, mistakenly supposing that the existing social equilibrium is the only one possible. If a government sees its unalterable priority as being an orderly society and political stability, that is an indication that the ruler is afraid to challenge certain interests and, as a result, allows himself only measures that will affect no substantial interests, and accordingly will change nothing.

It was in this vein that Nicholas I acted. In the latter half of the 1830s, the tsar agreed to regularize the status of state peasants, formally recognize village society as the collective owner of communal lands and introduce a degree of self-government. In the 1840s, a legislative act was drawn up establishing new rules for peasants to be freed from serfdom, but the 1842 Decree on Obligated Peasants was adopted in such an emasculated form that the peasants noticed almost no impact.

Moral economics

It did, however, have some impact, only not on the peasants. The decree caught the attention of a Prussian law expert, Baron August von Haxthausen, who was interested in the institution of the village commune. Von Haxthausen published a favourable article about the decree and the Russian envoy to Berlin reported it to the minister of state property, Pavel Kiselyov, who reported it to the emperor, who ordered that von Haxthausen be invited to visit Russia and even given a substantial grant of 1,500 rubles to study the land question. The Prussian jurist's expedition was brief and limited in scope. He stayed in Russia for less than a year in 1843, travelling several thousand kilometres and spending much of his time on the road. The official accompanying von Haxthausen was instructed to discreetly 'remove all things which might give this foreigner cause to come to incorrect or inappropriate conclusions'. The visitor was taken particularly to regions where Kiselyov had reformed state-owned villages in 1837. The essence of the reform was to establish a pyramid of departments with responsibility for the peasants, a bureaucratization of management that was entirely progressive for the time, in tandem with official consolidation of the commune's responsibility for the use of the land and accountability. By and large what von Haxthausen observed were the results of Kiselyov's reform.[10]

The visitor did, in any case, already know what he wanted to find. Von Haxthausen had a preconception of the 'Slavic communal heritage', signs of which he believed he had detected in the rural areas of his own country that bordered Slavic lands. The Prussian romantic was sure that the commune, or peasant *mir*, was the main cultural characteristic of the Slavs. He speculated that the Slavs, unlike the peoples of Western Europe, had preserved this primal 'republican' institution. The baron was persuaded that he had discovered a special mentality due to which harmony reigned in the commune, all differences were resolved collectively without recourse to the courts or formalities of the law, and private property, social inequality and other failings of capitalist society were completely absent.[11] On the basis of his researches and reflections, von Haxthausen wrote a three-volume work about life and land relationships in Russia which had a huge impact on discussion within Russia about the country's present and future.

Thanks to von Haxthausen, Alexander Herzen saw the peasant's communal *mir* as 'a bastion which has proved impregnable throughout the ages', an inspiration for social revolution and the promise of a great future for Russia.[12] Very soon, the idea that the Russian people had from time immemorial rejected the Western institution of private ownership of land became an article of faith with the intellectual elite. It certainly was for Leo Tolstoy, who noted in his diary in 1865, 'Russia's historical mission in the world is to introduce the concept of public ownership of land. . . . This idea has a future. The Russian revolution can be based only on that.'[13]

Slavophile Alexey Khomyakov claimed that he was the first person to discover the Russian commune. Khomyakov and von Haxthausen did meet, and their conversation may well have influenced the Prussian jurist. Nevertheless, whoever was the discoverer, the Slavophiles, Herzen and Tolstoy were all convinced that the commune dated from the ancient past and that its roots were Slavic. The articles in which Boris Chicherin, a liberal, assured his contemporaries that the commune was an instrument for fiscal management, and a relatively late tsarist innovation to boot, did nothing to halt the spread of a lofty myth of the innate communal leanings of Russians.[14]

The reality is that communality is neither uniquely Russian nor a Romantic invention, but something inherently human and in every respect a perfectly down-to-earth phenomenon. There is not the slightest doubt that the practice of periodical redistribution of land holdings, just like the practice of jointly managing communal property, was and is to be found in agrarian societies across the globe. Many anthropologists believe that in groups of hunter-gatherers, where human nature was largely formed, moderate forms of redistribution gave a group the edge over other groups that did not practise it.[15]

Collective forms of organization in agrarian societies are a manifestation of what James Scott calls a 'subsistence ethic'.[16] For a peasant, a bad harvest is a direct threat to his life. One way to deal with risks is to share them equally. Accordingly, relationships arose in peasant communities that enabled them to survive hard times.

Over the centuries, communes split into two types: hereditary and redistributive, in which the area of land allocated to a family was subject to regular review. The redistribution could be carried out in a number of ways, but its main purpose was to ensure a stable correlation between the amount of land and a family's capacity for labour.[17]

Common ownership of pasturage and periodic reallocation of arable land are survival strategies that were common at one time to French, Russian and Italian peasants. They are widespread in some developing societies to this day. The point of these practices is to provide all the members of a community, the strong and weak alike, with a minimum subsistence level proportionate to the resources available. Scott popularized the term 'moral economy', coined in the 1920s by the Russian scholar of the peasant economy Alexander Chayanov. Its overriding aim was survival of the community.[18]

In Europe, the village commune appeared in the late Middle Ages as a collective body overseeing the reallocation of land, the use of communally owned resources for the public and the maintenance of public order, but by the beginning of the nineteenth century it was already in decline.[19]

The commune in Russia became redistributive comparatively late.

One explanation of this is that the redistributions arose in response to a poll tax introduced by Peter the Great and first levied in 1724.[20] Historians posit a link between the tax and redistribution because there is no evidence of it before the introduction of the tax, but it is also possible that redistribution was a response to population growth and the accompanying land shortages. Be that as it may, we can say with a high degree of probability that in Russia redistribution dates from the middle of the eighteenth century.[21]

Owing to a dearth of data, we know little about the situation in the eighteenth century, but thanks to the subsequent rapid development of a culture of bookkeeping, we know that by the beginning of the nineteenth century the commune was being actively used in Russia by those managing estates and by the state itself as a taxation and administrative unit. Its existence was legally recognized, at first for state-owned villages but after the 1861 reform also for those formerly in the possession of landlords.

Landowners could decide whether they wanted the poll tax to correspond to the proportional distribution of land. Historian Stephen Hoch, who has studied the hearth inventories and credit and debit records for the first half of the nineteenth century of the village of Petrovskoye in Tambov province (which belonged to the princes Gagarin), found that those managing the estate did just that: they insisted that the commune should distribute the land in proportion to the number of labourers in a family. The same system was operated in the communes of state and appanage peasants. It is no exaggeration to say that this practice offers no more evidence of a primal predisposition in favour of egalitarianism among Russian peasants than does a factory owner's equal allocation of machines to factory floor space.[22]

What did a commune do? It distributed strips of land, decided on expenditure from the communal budget and addressed petitions and complaints to its estate's administrative office. The commune monitored the breaking up of families, decided who was to be sent as conscripts to the army, and was responsible for care of communal land, which provided essential grain stocks if the harvest was poor. It allocated labouring duties. The commune also served as a legal entity in all relations with the local government, collecting and paying taxes and other levies and giving the requisite bribes. It could be called upon to repair roads and bridges and, in time of war, to provide transport, food and accommodation for troops.[23]

The poor peasants, the middle peasants and the richer 'kulak' peasants were, as a rule, stages in the development of families rather than fixed social categories, as Soviet ideologues tried to claim. A patriarchal community seeks to redistribute wealth from those who are younger to those who are older. Such a transfer is possible only in larger families. Large families were encouraged by the system: estate managers, or heads of families themselves with the support of the managers, hampered the breaking away of young families from old households. The result was a dominant stratum of peasants where leadership went with age. Households that averaged eight to ten individuals and consisted, as a rule, of three generations could provide both uninterrupted labour for the landowner and a dignified old age for the '*bolshak*', the patriarch. The interests of the elder peasants on most of the important issues coincided with those of the owners of estates.[24]

Military service was a convenient way of getting rid of the poorest households and problematical members of the commune. Families that did not conform to the standard pattern of the patriarchal three-generation household were practically unprotected from economic ruin if the head of the family was laid low by illness or accident. It was in the interests of the commune and of the estate manager to send such peasants off to military service: it reduced the number of recruits taken from larger, 'successful' families, and reduced the number of families in need of support. It was also a way of reducing economic inequality. Other peasants who might find themselves packed off to the army were those who were lazy, light-fingered, the sons of people caught stealing, those with criminal convictions, widowers, cripples, those responsible for fires and those who got on the wrong side of the manager.[25]

Compulsory labour was allocated on the basis of a '*tyaglo*', a labour unit consisting of a husband and wife, and those responsible for ensuring it was done were overseers and task allocators who were themselves peasants. Laziness was punished not by the manager but by another peasant senior in age or position. Taxes were calculated per capita but the commune as a whole was responsible for ensuring they were paid, so trying to avoid work or evading your taxes was a risky business. It would be your fellow peasants who would be the first to punish you, even to the point of shaving your head and dispatching you to the army. If a peasant was caught stealing, any other peasant who knew about the incident but did not report it was also held responsible. A young peasant who wanted to set up a new household would have to go against the interests of his own father. That was the ingenuity of the system. Enforcement costs were carried by the commune itself: the interests of the collective and the regime coincided.

This system could not exist without coercion. The old men and managers were constantly faced with resistance from the younger generations. In the above-mentioned village of Petrovskoye, in 1826–8 at least 79% of the grown men were flogged, and 24% of those were flogged on more than one occasion. In a population of 1,305 souls, male and female, there were 714 floggings.[26]

A manager had two very different tasks: to prevent breaches of the peace and to motivate the peasants to work. The means of achieving both were, however, the same: the use of violence. Judging by the punishments selected and their relative severity, maintaining public order had a higher priority than increasing output. This is an important conclusion: the task of providing revenue for the landlord came second to maintaining order. Public order was more important than economic logic: security came first. This is the other side of the 'morality' in the moral economy.

The commune versus the private farmer

If the tsarist government did not put the problem in these terms, it was undoubtedly aware of it, but left addressing it too late. The succession of reforms and changes in legislation that began in 1861 and continued until the collapse of tsarism were all designed to make the rural economy more efficient.

It proved impossible to move society easily and swiftly from a communal economy to one based on individual initiative. The changes were very painful, for which both the reformers and the objective difficulty of the task were to blame. The reformers introduced changes without abandoning the privileges of the nobility and were, accordingly, trying to modernize society and the economy while preserving their archaic domination and the archaic institution of the commune. The resulting oppressive conditions attached to the emancipation of the serfs compelled many peasants to cling to the commune.

The government tried to abolish the old subsistence programme without providing a new, workable development programme to replace it. Private property could have been the foundation stone of such a programme, but that was not done because few considered it desirable or an acceptable solution. The introduction of private land ownership led to a rapid reduction in the size of holdings, and brought with it an obligation to pay for the land for many years into the future. The price of land, meanwhile, rose steeply, by 750%

between 1861 and 1901 (or, according to some, by anything from 1,000 to 1,300%). Olga Sukhova comments that 'The real reduction in the size of holdings, the heavy burden of redemption payments, and oppressive conditions attached to renting did not conduce to establishing social harmony.'[27]

Additionally, a direct result of retaining the commune in Russia was a surplus of labour, which, by the beginning of the twentieth century, amounted to anything between 5 and 33 million workers. The availability of such a huge army of hired hands was one of the reasons wages were low, not only in the countryside but also in the towns.[28]

It has to be admitted that the task really was very difficult: society simply cannot be changed so rapidly. The fairness of the commune became a prism through which the peasants, at least in Central Russia, looked at the world. The idea of equalizing all land holdings along the lines of the commune was not consigned to the past, but took root in the national psyche, and seemed to many (though not all) to be the pattern for an ideal future. Alexander Engelgardt enthused in one of his 'letters from the country',

> A redistributing of the land occurs in the communes after a certain period of time, an *evening out* among the members of the commune . . . during the universal redistribution there will be an *evening out* among communes. Here the question is . . . of . . . evening out of *all the land*, both the landowners' and the peasants'. Peasants who have purchased land as property or, as they say, for eternity, also talked about this, just like all the other peasants, and did not doubt at all that these 'lands which are bound to them by law' can be taken away from the 'legal owners' and given to others.[29]

The ancient concepts of entitlement to land through labour and service to the tsar rather than to the landowner were firmly lodged in the peasant consciousness. The landowner's property resulted from the peasant labour invested in it, which had not been paid for. The great redistribution of the land the peasants dreamed of was seen only as changing them from labourers for their landlord into labourers for the state. Even Pugachov had no ambitions beyond that, and a hundred years after his rebellion, immediately before the 1861 reform, the peasants still had no expectation of more. They expected to be freed with all their land and to live like state serfs, liable for the same dues as they were, but exclusively to the state's treasury.

What was revolutionary about Pyotr Stolypin's agrarian reforms after the 1905 Revolution was that, unlike all previous reforms, they encouraged not communal but private ownership. To contemporaries such as Alexander Alexandrovich Chuprov, the change of direction was very evident. 'Just two years before the reform began, the "ruling class" was inclined to encourage further development of communes, not to ban them. How are we to explain this unexpected change?' Chuprov was a statistician and economist who in 1912 had written an article on the Russian commune for the British *Economic Journal*, edited at that time by John Maynard Keynes.[30] 'Two events occurred that caused the landowning gentry, which the government was trying to protect, to take against the commune and begin to fear it: the 1905–6 peasant uprising, and the agrarian reform proposed by the first Duma,' Chuprov continued.[31]

The Socialist Revolutionaries and the Trudoviks, who saw themselves as representatives of the peasantry, demanded a total redistribution, without compensation, of all private agricultural land in favour of the peasants. The Constitutional Democrats proposed increasing the peasants' land holdings at the expense of land owned by the state, patrimonial princes and monasteries, and also to compulsorily purchase the land of private owners and give it without charge to the peasantry.

Given the situation, the rule that security must always come first now called not for preservation of the status quo in society, but for the creation of new institutional obstacles to the 'great redistribution' that society as a whole was favouring. The authorities believed that extending private property rights to as large a proportion of the population as possible would diffuse and divide what the prime minister, Pyotr Stolypin, described as the 'combustible material', that is, the peasantry.

All the most influential political forces in Russian society viewed the institution of private property negatively. Its only fully committed supporters were conservative associations of the nobility and the government itself. 'The principle of the inalienability and inviolability of property is, throughout the world and at every level of development of civic life, the cornerstone of national well-being and social development, a fundamental pillar of the state without which its very existence is impossible,' declared Ivan Goremykin, chairman of the Council of Ministers of the First State Duma. His speech, with its clear echoing of Enlightenment notions that, a hundred years previously, would have been considered revolutionary, sounded in the early twentieth century like no more than an attempt to scrape together an extra argument in defence of a doomed despotic regime.[32]

How realistic was it to attempt to introduce a profound institutional shift in favour of a culture of private property in such political circumstances and, essentially, as a firefighting measure? The very question anticipates tragedy.

The reforms were nevertheless introduced. The First Duma, which sat in the spring of 1906, was dissolved in the summer and by autumn a decree was issued detailing Stolypin's reforms. These gave every holder of a share of communal land the right to consolidate it as private property (Decree of 9 November 1906, 'Supplementation of Certain Provisions of Current Law Relating to Peasant Land Tenure and Use'). A peasant could submit a 'demand' to the commune, which was obliged to issue a suitable order, a '*prigovor*', within a month. If no decision was reached, the peasant could apply to the head of the district council, the *Zemstvo*. If that produced no result, he could apply to the district assembly and, in exceptional cases, to the provincial government.[33]

The decree also sought to deal with the problem of strip farming. The peasant could demand that the commune assembly grant him the land due to him in a single location. If it proved impossible to reach agreement, financial compensation could be claimed from the commune, the sum to be determined by the subdistrict (*volost'*) court. The amount of compensation awarded was not always acceptable to the applicant, but in that case he just had to put up with the scattered strips he had been farming previously.

Subsequent legislation amended the procedure for converting communally held land into private property and oversight of the progress of changing the property arrangements, but the logic of the reforms survived: individual farms were to replace communes. It proved a slow and difficult process.

The authorities did their best to promote private ownership. To mark the 300th anniversary of the Romanov dynasty, a number of private farms were presented with awards, and descriptions of these 'pioneers of new forms of working the land' were published. The propaganda had minimal effect: supporters of the commune hated the owners of privatized land and vice versa. A majority of the farms (93%) separated out against the wishes of their commune. After the 1906 decree, there was a kind of politicization of the countryside: 'Them as believe the government, think farms are better and them as are against it think the communes are.'[34]

Evidence gathered by researchers during the Stolypin reforms indicates,

Those leaving are most hated by the commune for siding with the government. . . . The ministers and all the big people in authority are the largest landowners, idly enjoying several thousand *desyatinas* [hectares] of land, and leavers are fools for settling for only 4 or 5 *desyatinas* a head.

While those against the commune argued,

> The commune gets in the way of everything. Firstly, the communal estates are wretched. Secondly, if anyone decides to plant an orchard the peasants look down on him and uproot all the trees; if he makes a vegetable plot they plunder it. The commune and the hope of getting awarded extra land have spoiled the peasant and turned him into a savage.

Peasants did, nevertheless, leave the commune and consolidated their land into private property. In the Volga region, for example, Samara province led in consolidation of land ownership, and by 1916 almost 30% of the peasants there were 'leavers'.[35]

In the eight years of the reforms, 36.7% of households notified their withdrawal from the communes. Only the First World War prevented extending the reforms to a majority of the peasantry.[36]

The reforms instigated a clash of two fundamentally different social systems and the outcome was decided by the revolution. Demands for the confiscation of all privately owned land were louder than those in favour of the slow and bureaucratic process of consolidating private land ownership. After the revolution, supporters of the communes began persecuting the private farmers and the leavers were forced back into the communes. Those who owned their land were labelled supporters of the tsarist government, which was seen as having trampled on what was just.

We can date the victory of the 'commune revolution', or, more precisely, reaction, from spring 1918, when a new nationwide redistribution of land began and all forms of land use other than communal were terminated. The moral economy took its revenge.[37]

Dictatorship of the collective

We have seen that under the commune system social stability took priority over economic effectiveness. There were not enough birches, so to speak, with which to beat its members into troubling about the quality of their work. All the effort was directed towards maintaining public order, and it was needed: the moral economy had no trouble coexisting with double standards. If the top priority was survival of the family, then breaking the law to ensure that was no sin: 'Need

113

knows no law,' was the saying. What the agencies of law enforcement might consider illegal could be seen as 'permissible in the circumstances' by the peasant *mir*. Oleg Vronsky notes:

> Attuned for centuries to ensuring collective survival, the commune formed in its members a sense of justice conducive to that overarching objective: steal, if that was in the interests of your household and did not jeopardize the economic interests of the commune; do not pay debts for which the commune was not jointly liable; kill, if a horse thief was a threat to the commune's herd.

On the other hand, members of the commune fleeing legal or administrative justice were guaranteed the support of the mir: their fellow villagers looked after their own.[38]

The peasants in the village of Petrovskoye regarded birching for theft or poor work (which accounted for 78% of all misdemeanours) as a fact of life. The estate manager simply could not have maintained even a minimum of order, faced with constant insubordination and theft of everything from firewood to livestock, without using birching right, left and centre. The peasants reacted in their own way. The punishment registers show that they responded to this regime with sabotage and apathy, punctuated with shortlived outbursts of violence.

Historians have noted a similar reaction on the part of American slaves. They did not accept the legitimacy of the power exerted by their overseers, which did nothing for their sense of personal responsibility or inclination to put their backs into their work.[39] Apathy, sabotage, giving the appearance of working hard rather than actually doing it – these traditional forms of passive resistance to coercion invariably accompany the imposition of forced labour.[40]

People behave analogously in all environments characterized by institutionalization: prisons, mental hospitals, concentration camps, on plantations, and in the army if they are conscripts. These are places where private life is reduced to a minimum. They are designed to provide their denizens with the essentials, however defined, but those people have nothing, or virtually nothing, of their own. Everything is either communal or belongs to someone else. The occupants of such institutions – prisons, hospitals, monasteries or landowners' estates – are in very similar personal situations, their existence strictly regulated, all their actions repeated day after day and season after season. Their horizon is bounded by their own restricted community and they are cut off from the outside world.

The response to coercion and a lack of positive encouragement is rarely dedicated hard work. Rather, such conditions give rise to a particular work ethic which we know only too well from the classics of Russian literature: not only from Saltykov-Shchedrin, but also from such writers as Alexander Solzhenitsyn. Despite the profound political revolution, 'survival ethics', or, if you will, a peculiar version of the moral economy, outlived the property of landlords and revived in the collective farms, prisons and concentration camps of the USSR. Here is an excerpt from *One Day in the Life of Ivan Denisovich*:

> 'Listen here, eight fifty-four! Just give it a once-over, don't make it too wet, and get the hell out of here!' . . .
> Shukhov made a quick job of it.
> There are two ends to a stick, and there's more than one way of working. If it's for human beings – make sure and do it properly. If it's for the big man – just make it look good. Any other way we'd all have turned our toes up long ago, that's for sure.[41]

The prison camp foremen, overseers and task allocators come straight out of the routines of serfdom. On the estates in tsarist times, the overseers and task allocators were other peasants, while in the camps they are other prisoners, invested with a modicum of power over their fellows. Their worst punishment would be to lose their position; their worst, daily, misfortune is the hatred of their fellows. They have no escape: if you go easy on your own kind, if you let them steal or shirk, you'll get it in the neck yourself from the estate manager/camp commandant, and also from your fellows. The household on which the commune relied, and the work gang on which the labour camp relied, had plenty in common. The mechanism of coercion was the same too.

> Why, you may wonder, will a *zek* put up with ten years of back-breaking work in a camp? Why not say no and dawdle through the day? The night's his own.
> It can't be done, though. The work gang was invented to take care of that. It isn't like a work gang outside, where Ivan Ivanovich and Pyotr Petrovich get each a wage of his own. In the camps things are arranged so that the *zek* is kept up to the mark not by his bosses but by the others in his gang. Either everybody gets a bonus or else they all die together. Am I supposed to starve because a louse like you won't work? Come on, you rotten bastard, put your back into it![42]

It is the same indirect coercion: each individual has his task, but the team bears joint responsibility; everyone is in it together. It is an arrangement that means you can't shirk on the job completely, but it's also senseless to do it well. Make a show of putting in the effort but do not do it, not out of apathy or laziness, and certainly not because that is a national characteristic. There is nothing national about either the coercion or the response to it. Both on an estate of a wealthy landowner and in a Soviet forced labour camp, economizing on effort and opportunism is an entirely international human survival strategy. The commonest behaviour of those languishing in coercive situations in America, or Africa, or anywhere else is lassitude. If it were anything more dynamic, 'we'd all have turned our toes up long ago'. When threatened violence from the regime has materialized, when the bloodshed and arrests are already happening, a society can see it is going to be bullied for an indefinite period of time. At this point it adopts a passive survival strategy: no resistance, no fight, no altercation, just a quiet reorientation towards doing what is in your own self-interest – discreet, low-profile opportunism. In such a situation, group loyalty is usually minimal, and organized joint action is rare.[43] That is how it was on the estate of any average landowner, how it was in the Soviet Gulag and, more generally, in numerous Soviet institutions.

Historian Yelena Osokina suggests that James Scott is mistaken in describing this strategy as 'everyday resistance'. 'The aim of resistance is to change the existing system; the aim of everyday insubordination is *adaptation* to living under the system. The aim of everyday insubordination is to find ways round, while the aim of resistance is a struggle to defeat the current system.'[44] Let us again turn to Solzhenitsyn: 'He knew from what free workers said – drivers and bulldozer operators on construction sites – that the straight and narrow was barred to ordinary people but they didn't let it get them down, they took a roundabout way and survived somehow.'[45]

The problems encountered by citizens of the new Soviet state – hunger, chronic shortages of goods, a lack of decent accommodation or even minimal amenities – called more for survival skills than for an appetite for revolutionary struggle. The population did not aim to destroy the system but to develop resistance to its numerous ills. Accordingly, Osokina suggests, what is observed in the Soviet Union is not resistance in a conventional sense, but in the sense of an active social immune system.[46]

Perhaps, as we look back, we would like to see a heroic confrontation between an inhuman system and its citizens, but for the vast majority it was just a desperate battle for survival. Active conflict is not the first thing that comes to mind when people are finding life so grim. The main thing is to try to survive, to conform and, as far as possible, take advantage of the situation. Social conformism is the natural state of a person even in thoroughly abnormal conditions, and the desire to improve society has to be acquired as the result of work on oneself. 'Human beings are rule-following animals by nature; they are born to conform to the social norms they see around them, and they entrench those rules with often transcendent meaning and value,' Francis Fukuyama writes in his book *The Origins of Political Order*.[47]

Russian intellectuals in the late eighteenth and early nineteenth centuries accepted private property with understanding and hope as a basis for personal independence and economic development. In less than a century, however, everything had been turned upside down and, as we shall see, property came to be perceived as quite the opposite: a basis for oppression of the individual and an obstacle to economic development.

— 8 —

MASTERS

The Tragedy of Domination

Owners and rulers

Ivan Pnin, who died in 1805 at the age of thirty-two, might have become the Russian Locke or Mill if he had lived longer. He was the illegitimate son of Field Marshal Prince Nikolai Vasilievich Repnin, hence the surname Pnin (truncated surnames were given to children born out of wedlock), but although illegitimate he was educated like the son of a grandee, studying at the boarding school for the nobility at Moscow University and in the Artillery Cadet Corps in St Petersburg, before going on to serve in the artillery.

In the late 1790s, Pnin, already retired from the service, became friendly with Alexander Bestuzhev, the father of future Decembrists, and in 1798 they jointly published the *St Petersburg Journal*, a high-brow monthly that was very progressive for its time. The publication was a veiled polemic on the part of the future Alexander I with his father, Tsar Paul I, financed by the young grand duke, who was himself the freethinking pupil of a Swiss tutor, Frédéric-César de La Harpe. Nowhere was the name of its august publisher indicated but, because everybody always knew everything, Pnin and Bestuzhev were immune from harassment by the censorship. The young men allowed themselves to comment on the most controversial issues of the time and published translations of the contemporary fashionable political economists James Denham Steuart and the Marquis de Condorcet. The editors saw themselves as an intellectual powerhouse in which the political programme of the future reign was being fashioned.

In a pamphlet, *An Essay on Enlightenment in Respect of Russia*, written after Alexander I had already become tsar, Pnin summarizes their main conclusions: in order to be a good subject, a person must be a citizen, and the way for him to become a citizen is by owning property. 'The greater confidence a citizen has in his own security and property, the more judicious, active, felicitous and hence useful and devoted will he be to his state.'

Pnin was conscious of the difference between written and unwritten rules: 'Where there is no property, all ordinances exist merely on paper.' He was certain that a ruler must operate not with threats but with positive incentives.

> Russia has had many owners but few rulers. . . . To rule means to respect justice, to preserve the law, to encourage diligence, reward virtue, to disseminate enlightenment, strengthen the Church, to reconcile the impulse to gain honour with the impulse to advance utility and, in a word, to foster the common good. . . .
>
> Property! Where you are absent there can be no justice. . . . In what incomprehensible way shall the edifice of society endure where it has not that sound foundation, where the rights of society are trampled underfoot, where justice is known only by name and where it is more readily obtained through money or patronage than through honouring the law? There all is veiled in obscurity, all depends only on chance. In a single moment the social edifice is gone. In a single moment its ruins proclaim the nation is in turmoil.

Pnin was passionate in calling for the right to private property, and other rights of free people, to be restored to the peasants, because only thus could the long-term prosperity of the country be assured. The peasants once had rights, but they had gradually been stripped of them through the unscrupulous behaviour of landowners and those in power. 'To right this wrong and return his dignity to the farmer is within the power of the government,' Pnin concluded.[1]

Alexander read the pamphlet and rewarded its author, but even so it was banned by the censor. It was the same story with the standard-bearing *St Petersburg Journal*: the grand duke, without a word, simply ceased to support it. The reformist ideas discussed over tea in the Privy Council, an informal group of the tsar's progressively minded young friends, suffered the same fate.

Pnin's ideas remained just paper architecture. Highly germane to their time, they never made it into the mainstream of political thought. He was one of the first of a select, naïve breed of intellectuals who found themselves sidelined by the authorities and apart from the traditions of the Russian intelligentsia, most of whom were left-wing, often extreme, and saw their mission as being to struggle against tyranny. Official thinking tried to stay as reactionary as possible in order not to show weakness, while oppositional thinking strove to be as radical as possible, the better to nettle the autocracy. Moderation is always an irrelevance in that kind of game.

But it was there: 'an opposition of common sense', a 'moral opposition' consisting not only of writers and philosophers, and it always had supporters at the very pinnacle of power. Both Catherine the Great with her Enlightenment enthusiasms and her grandson Alexander I were entirely familiar with the ideal of reorganizing the state under the rule of law. Needless to say, they could not openly reveal their favouring of such ideas, but they did in their different ways try to implement them.

'Let not the nobility be dispossessed of their estates without due process of law'

The right of nobles to own property independently of the whims of the Crown were confirmed by Catherine the Great in 1785.

Her Letters Patent gave the nobility rights and freedoms that would have horrified the founders of the Moscow state.[2] The sacrosanct nature of landowners' property played an enormous role in Russian culture, providing the material underpinning for the independence of several generations of educated and thinking people.

Just fifty years before Catherine's Letters Patent, an attempt by the nobility to wrest a Russian Magna Carta from the monarch went down to humiliating defeat. One of the court factions attempted to impose 'conditions' on the future Empress Anna, which included reference to life, liberty and property. Locke had seen the whole point of the state as being the preservation of 'Lives, Liberties and Estates' (see chapter 4). What was written in these conditions was, 'Let not the nobility be dispossessed of their lives, estates and honour without due process of law,' but the empress, once she had power in her hands, fearlessly tore up their conditions.

What had been so easily done by the Empress Anna was more than Catherine could allow herself in the second half of the same century. She knew her situation was more precarious. She had seized power by force; she suppressed the Pugachov rebellion and used police methods to bring down Alexander Radishchev and Nikolai Novikov, the most brilliant figureheads of the nascent intelligentsia. Catherine closely followed the revolutionary events in America and Europe. In her correspondence with French philosophers, the empress readily talked about liberty, but was always fully conscious of the boundary between polite conversation and political reality. Nevertheless, she showed that one can do more than just talk about such things. The state, it transpired, needed private landowners, and talk of honour, liberty and estates was heard from the highest in the land. We read in the Letters Patent on the rights, liberties and privileges of the Russian nobility:

> 'Without due process of law let not the nobility be dispossessed of their honour. Without due process of law let not the nobility be dispossessed of life. Without due process of law let not the nobility be dispossessed of their estates. ... We confer in perpetuity on the families of the hereditary Russian nobility liberty and freedom.[3]

Similar words were being heard at this time in America and France. Much was being said and written worldwide about the impermissibility of depriving a person of his life and property without due process. The crucial difference was, however, that in America and France those doing the talking were intellectuals and revolutionaries, while in Russia it was a woman endowed with absolute power. Russia's 'bill of rights' was an initiative handed down by the monarch. Rights won in struggle by a society and rights handed down from above in an already existing state are very different things; all the more so if that state is estate-based and it is the dominant social group that is seeking to safeguard its privileges.

In the Russian situation the conferring of the right of ownership was not only a step in a process of modernization but also a step intended to strengthen the social order. Russia's 'Declaration of Rights' did, on the one hand, lead to a slight increase in the number of free citizens able to participate in public life, but on the other it strengthened the power held by some Russians over others. The letters were addressed only to one class. In emancipating the nobles, the empress reinforced unconditionally the dependent status of the peasants. The Letters Patent granted to certain select citizens the right to preside over the destiny of a large proportion (some 40%) of the Russian population.

The introduction of private property actually proved an obstacle to the emancipation of the peasants. To make them free without land would be unjust and dangerous, while to take land from the landlords would be illegal. The peasants, we recall, were tied to the land, not to the landlord, but now they found themselves in fact, if not in law, the property of the landlords. This snare was to hold back for decades the long-overdue decision to abolish serfdom, which inevitably coloured how people in Russia felt about the institution of private property. The attitude towards property of the property owners themselves,

121

the best educated and freest section of society, became emotional and simplistic:

> Half our rural population is much more disadvantaged than in the West. In the villages we encounter morose, gloomy people cheerlessly drinking far too much green wine, their exuberant Slavic temperament crushed, their hearts plainly burdened by a great wrong. That wrong, that misfortune, is their status as serfs. . . . How is anyone to explain to other people that half the population of a vast nation, people strong in body and mind, has been given into slavery by their own government, without a war, without a revolution, by means of a number of police measures, a number of secret agreements never openly expressed or published as law?[4]

Herzen is describing here the Russia of Nicholas I, but Nicholas, who is usually considered the conservative antithesis of liberal Alexander I, was in fact faithfully continuing his brother's policies. The government had no intention of abolishing the nobility's rights, so the peasants were destined to remain a subordinate class dominated by the nobles.

The tsarist regime imagined that, by endowing the nobility with land and all the privileges that went with it for generations to come, they were laying the foundations of political stability. The nobles were to take on the role of stewardship (*encomienda*) of the masses, as described in chapter 5 above. Millions of peasants were placed at their disposal, and it was for them to ensure in return that their wards did not rebel and even, if possible, did some work. This right of stewardship over Russia's citizens has continued in various forms ever since, including some that proved very painful and wasteful. Russia's monarchs maintained the lavish lifestyles of the elite from one generation to the next. An economy that has yet to see the beginning of industrial growth can rightly be called 'Malthusian': that is, an economy in which an increasing number of consumers are making claims on a limited amount of resources. For one to become richer, another must become poorer. '[S]trong property rights simply reinforce the existing distribution of resources,' Francis Fukuyama writes in his book *The Origins of Political Order*. 'The actual distribution of wealth is more likely to represent chance starting conditions or the property holder's access to political power than productivity or hard work.'[5] The new legal order, arising in a pre-industrial economy, was exploited by the Russian elite not to develop their own lands, not to create wealth, but to preserve their dominant position, and they had the full support of the government.

In 1823, Yegor (Georg Ludwig) Kankrin was appointed minister of finance. One of the reasons for appointing him was Alexander I's desire to remove the previous minister, Dmitry Guriev, who has won a place in history as the man who invented Guriev semolina, but who could have been the man who laid the foundations for an efficient financial system in Russia. Guriev, who was close to Mikhail Speransky, adviser to Alexander I and often referred to as 'the father of Russian liberalism', was planning to close the Credit Bank, which was the successor to banks of the nobility and a source of cheap loans (more akin to subsidies) to nobles. He was planning to develop the Commercial Bank, a credit institution that would provide funds for industrial enterprises irrespective of the customer's official rank. This could have been a breakthrough. At the Credit Bank the title and rank of the creditor counted for more than his creditworthiness. Moreover, Guriev, like everyone else in the tsar's entourage, knew the nobles spent their agricultural credits not on developing their farming but to cover operating costs and import luxury goods.[6]

In public, everyone supported the plan for financing industry but, needless to say, the palace elite did not want to lose a source of easy money. It was Kankrin's mission to restore a reliable means of supporting their extravagant lifestyle. The new minister resumed issuing loans, which Guriev had stopped, claiming that providing credit to the nobility was 'unavoidable', while making loans to develop industry was too risky. As collateral for loans, only 'census souls', that is, peasants, were accepted, which meant that loans were available only to estate owners.[7]

Kankrin killed two birds with one stone. By transferring a proportion of funds out of the Commercial Bank into the Credit Bank, he reduced the resources for lending to industry while continuing to extend privileges to the elite. The banks of the nobility, and later the Credit Bank – in contrast, for example, to the Bank of England, which was created to stimulate trade – saw their aim as being to inhibit the uncontrolled growth of industry and help the nobility to keep up a wholly unjustified level of expenditure. Infrastructure development was also hobbled: Kankrin was opposed to railways, which, in his opinion, only 'encourage frequent, needless travel, thereby increasing the inconstancy of spirit of our age'.[8]

The government was well aware of what rapid economic growth would lead to: rapid urbanization, the appearance of large-scale production and depersonalized market relations. These developments were seen as a hazard rather than a blessing, and accordingly growth was not encouraged but held back. The government did not, for example, introduce corporate forms of business, fearing that its spread would contribute to accelerated economic development. Kankrin declared that where new corporations were being established 'the government should proceed with utmost caution': 'It is better to reject ten less than positive companies than allow one that is detrimental to the public and to government itself.'[9] The government tried to slow the growth of production by limiting the number of factories that could be built in close proximity to each other, in order to avoid concentrations of workers and consequent unrest.[10]

Maintaining public order took precedence over commercial development. The management methods employed on Russian estates were, as we saw in chapter 7, entirely consonant with that view. The authorities did not see efficient management as the primary mission of the nobility or, in later years, of the merchant class. Their main role was to act as effective gendarmes of society, as social classes responsible for ensuring good order in the section of the population entrusted to their care.

The Russian Empire gave nobles the option of mortgaging their estates without worrying overmuch whether it ever got its money back. Unredeemed mortgages were transformed into foreign loans and inflation. In 1856, some two-thirds of privately owned male Russian peasants had been mortgaged, but we know of only a few dozen cases of actual repossession of land for unpaid debts.[11]

The indebtedness of Russian nobles was legendary. They were constantly appealing to the tsars for money, and that despite the extremely favourable credit terms they enjoyed. As we have seen, loans were issued on the basis of social status rather than credit history, which in the case of most Russian nobles was appalling. They were not above exploiting their official position to keep themselves in funds.

John Quincy Adams, a future president of the United States, spent five years in St Petersburg as ambassador (and two years before that as a translator). He witnessed the war of 1812 against Napoleon and was well acquainted with Russian high society. Here is how the material aspect of the life of the nobility looked to this American guest:

> The tone of the society surrounding us is set almost entirely by people whose expenditure exceeds their income. The state's servants all live well beyond their salaries and many are notorious for never paying their debts. An even greater number of them are known for supplementing the balance of their budget by means which would be considered disgraceful in our country.[12]

124

This, of course, is no revelation. Today's Russians learned all about it at school. It provides the subject matter of half of Russian literature, including present-day writing, and was the staple of Russian polemical journalism. The response of regimes, however, to public knowledge of the fact that the Russian elite are morally corrupt has, paradoxically, always been to continue to encourage embezzlement and the squandering of resources. Connivance, and often direct incitement to thievery and financial mismanagement, have not been regarded as anything immoral.

Only a few individuals showed any interest in managing their estates, increasing output and making a profit. Most of the denizens of Russia's pre-revolutionary Olympus considered it beneath them to attempt to increase revenues in this mundane manner. They did not as a rule, consider it beneath them to feed at the trough of their official position and take bribes. Perhaps the right to own securely did not last long enough to bring economic benefits. How much can you do in 130 years?[13] Could the nobility have become an independent historical force in such a short time?

They distinguished themselves mainly in the field of literature, because the economic and political spheres were exclusively dedicated to promoting stability and public order and that was not open to debate. Perhaps this unbreachable exclusion from real economics is one reason why their educated elite espoused radical political beliefs. Herzen, Tolstoy and Turgenev were formed in a country where the government all but openly admitted its aim was to hold back development. The irony is that the tsarist government was trying to halt the march of time for their, the nobility's, benefit, in order to preserve their way of life.

The birth of free people

This way of life gave birth to a great literature and became the main subject it depicted and criticized. The late eighteenth and early nineteenth centuries saw the rise of great literature and journalism for many reasons. It cannot be wholly attributed to material circumstances, but neither can they be ignored. A significant number of educated people were granted freedom and an income that did not call for much exertion, and a certain number of those people realized themselves as creative artists.

In my work as an editor, I am constantly on the lookout for knowledgeable people who write well and can express their opinions freely.

There are some who do not want to speak out, for fear of problems or persecution. There are highly educated and well-informed people who would like to speak out publicly, but cannot because they are bound by their responsibilities or considerations of secrecy. The more weight a person's opinion would have for society, the more likely it is that there will be circumstances preventing them from speaking openly. Then, of course, there are people who are only too willing to speak out but may not have anything interesting to say!

The combination of competence and freedom tends to result from a happy concatenation of circumstances. These are people who have earned their freedom either through commercial or creative success, such as popular articles or books, or blogs on the Internet. In Russia, there are few autonomous institutions, positions that would vouchsafe freedom of expression. In other societies, such institutions might be a major newspaper, a church pulpit, public societies or chairs in universities where contracts are for life. People with tenure of one kind or another have often become the voice of their age, the creators of books, discoveries and inventions.

It was 'tenure' that the Russian nobility received at the end of the eighteenth century. Catherine acted out of political expediency. She needed a class of people who were loyal to her, but the unintended consequence was the emergence of a whole class of free people. For centuries, those who might be called the Russian aristocracy were, in fact, servants of the state with special privileges. In that capacity, they were totally beholden to the monarch. There had been no immunity to arbitrary confiscation of land in Russia since patrimonial land tenure was suppressed, right up until the reign of Peter III and then of Catherine.[14]

Present-day historians advise caution when considering the institution of private property that Catherine introduced. We need to remember that the first land survey of the European part of Russia was completed only in 1840.[15] That, however, is only part of the issue. Catherine's reform was less a liberation of the nobles than a change in the approach to compelling them to serve the state. As a result of Peter the Great's reforms, minor and middling nobles had been forced to spend most of their lives far away from their estates on onerous government service. Now they were no longer being forced to serve but incentivized to do so. Service, especially civilian service, was much needed by the state. The professional bureaucracy in Russia in the eighteenth and nineteenth centuries was weak and little developed. Nothing comparable with the French elite colleges for the state's finest existed in Russia, so that scions of the nobility were needed to supplement the less than numerous bureaucracy. This had the advantage of simultaneously reducing tensions within the nobility and improving the situation in the state administration and army by attracting people motivated to serve there.[16]

And there were people so motivated, because the vast majority of the nobility simply could not afford the leisured life of a rentier; in reality, the liberation was such for only a small proportion of them. The overwhelming majority owned tiny estates. Only a very few, 1 to 3% of the total, had estates with hundreds of serfs who could provide an existence on independent means.

The changes were, nevertheless, profound and structural, and, unlike in the West, where the institution of private ownership developed over a long period, they were abrupt. If before, the fate of an individual and his property was in the hands of the tsar, now it was taken out of that kind of hands-on control. One relatively small group, which considered itself a separate class, was guaranteed a degree of independence no other group enjoyed, but even that proved to be a substantial change.

The combination of an unearned income, the opportunity of obtaining an education at home or in Europe, of travelling, of choosing an occupation one cared about, and of expressing in print whatever opinion they chose (if not in Russia, then abroad) without fear of having their property confiscated proved amazingly productive for Russian culture. Never in the country's history had there been so many well-educated people, financially independent and under no obligation to account for themselves to anyone. They took little interest in their estates and used their time for reflection and creativity. A private fortune was the source of their livelihood, but simultaneously something they subjected to intense and often merciless scrutiny.

Alexander Herzen was one such free citizen-philosopher, and he was also a political émigré who succeeded in getting his assets out of Russia. It is a curious fact that Herzen beat a path to the West not only for Russian free-thinking but also for Russian capital.

Traduced and sacred law

Alexander Herzen, the illegitimate son of a landowner called Ivan Yakovlev, in 1846 inherited one-third of his father's estate, 106,000 silver rubles plus bonds and promissory notes. After the death of his mother, Louise Haag, Herzen also received her part of the inheritance, another 106,000 silver rubles and securities. The total capital of mother and son was estimated at 300,000 silver rubles. In addition, Herzen received some 10,000 silver rubles in income from his estates in Kostroma and two buildings in Moscow that he rented out when he left Russia. As a result, when the Herzen family arrived abroad after expatriating everything it was possible to get out of Russia, they had around 1 million French francs at their disposal. Herzen mentions in a letter that he is renting a spacious apartment in the centre of Paris for 8,000 francs a year.[17] For comparison, an associate professor at St Petersburg or Moscow University was paid an annual salary in the mid-nineteenth century of 3,500 rubles, and a full academician at the St Petersburg Academy of Sciences was paid 5,000 rubles. A skilled worker earned between 150 and 200 rubles per annum.[18]

Herzen's capital was sufficient to interest the head of the Paris branch of the Rothschild banking house, which for the rest of his life was his financial adviser. Under the guidance of James Rothschild, Herzen made his first, very successful, investments in the late 1840s. He bought a house in Paris, No. 14, rue d'Amsterdam, for 135,000 francs, acquired US government bonds to the tune of $50,000, and bonds of other countries for smaller amounts.[19]

Rothschild also helped Herzen get his mother's assets out of Russia. The intricate plot of this story was played out against the backdrop of revolutionary events in France. As a subject of the Russian Empire, Herzen was ordered to return to Russia from a Europe shaken by anti-governmental rallies. He refused, whereupon the Russian government froze the accounts of Louise Haag which held her share of the legacy from Yakovlev. Herzen devised a ruse, asserting that he owed his mother between 100,000 and 120,000 rubles, and that the Rothschilds had paid this to his mother against the security of his (sequestrated) estate. As the bank's archives show, the ministers of foreign affairs, of internal affairs, and of justice were involved, as were the chief of police and Nicholas I personally. A part was played by the newly strengthened property rights in Russia, but more important was the desire of the Russian government not to spoil its credit status in Europe.[20]

We will refrain from judging what sort of light this shows Herzen in – an ardent campaigner against slavery and author of a pamphlet denouncing serfdom titled *Baptized Property*. He at least acted rationally, which was a rarity among the Russian nobility. Moreover, property as a concept and property as the basis of private life were two completely different issues for the émigré revolutionary. The aspiration for a utopia to be built on the foundation of an idealized Russian commune in some distant future was a goal in which he believed and for which he campaigned. The property owned by an individual called Alexander Herzen made it possible for his views to be disseminated and for him to try to sway others by publishing books and journals. It was merely a means, even if it came by courtesy of the 'enemy':

> It would be foolish and affected in our time of financial disorder to neglect one's fortune. Money means independence and power; it is a weapon and nobody discards a weapon during a war, even if it has come from the enemy, even if it is rusty. The slavery of poverty is a terrible thing. I have studied it in all its forms, having lived for years with people who fled with only the clothes on their backs from political shipwrecks. That is why I found it just and necessary to take measures to snatch what I could out of the bear-like paws of the Russian government.[21]

Herzen set himself a lofty ideal and saw it as separate from the base means of attaining it. The ability to turn a blind eye to the means of achieving their ends proved later to be highly typical of the Russian revolutionary intelligentsia, and was a stance subsequently adopted by the Soviet leaders. Herzen evidently saw no problem in the fact that his intellectual and investment practices diverged strikingly. Here is how Derek Offord, a present-day specialist on Russian culture, puts it after studying Herzen's correspondence with his bankers in the Rothschilds' archive:

> It might therefore be said that by investing in the stock of governments that the Rothschilds supported Herzen the investor was making a personal contribution, however small, to the preservation of the stable European order which the Rothschilds, as financiers, valued and helped to maintain by means of their political influence but which Herzen, as a revolutionary, supposedly hoped to undermine. A socialist might also have been expected to baulk at an investment in Virginia, a slave-owning state of the ante-bellum southern confederacy.[22]

To be fair, we should note that, remaining in emigration, Herzen ceased to be the owner of 'baptized property' in Russia. Not even a Rothschild was able to quash the sequestration imposed by the tsarist government on his estate in Kostroma.

Another doughty opponent of property, Leo Tolstoy, was also unable to resolve the contradiction between his lofty spiritual goals and material resources. In the 1880s, Tolstoy adopted a firmly negative view of private property and began living the principles he preached. This was no simple matter for a father of eight children. 'My mother not only did not share my father's negative attitude to property but, on the contrary, continued to believe that the richer she and her children were, the better,' Tolstoy's eldest son, Sergey, wrote.[23] Reacting to Tolstoy's attempt to give away his property, his wife Sofia Andreyevna threatened 'to have him placed under guardianship for improvidence resulting from mental disorder'. Tolstoy then proposed making over to her his houses, estates, land and all his other property, but that she also objected to. 'Why, if you consider all this to be evil, do you want to encumber me with it?' Tolstoy had no option but to settle for half-measures, one of which was to transfer to his wife the rights to all his writings. Sofia Andreyevna prepared the first edition of his collected works in 1885. The last, twelfth, volume consisted of new works, including those parts of *What Then Must We Do?* that the censor would allow to be published. There was immense interest in Tolstoy's new writing, but the twelfth volume could be bought only as part of the entire collection. Sofia Andreyevna refused to let it be sold separately, which caused attacks in the press on the supposed avarice of the 'repentant count'.[24]

The irony of Count Tolstoy's situation was that everybody needed him to be rich. It was not only his family that needed his money. People came to him from all over the country, and most often what they asked for was not spiritual advice, as he would have liked, but material assistance. The bulk of letters and personal requests to him were appeals for money, and it made no difference that on several occasions he wrote to the newspapers reminding people that he had renounced property and relinquished the rights to his works.

Russia's leisured class failed to develop into a force in either economics or politics, but it was destined to become a force in literature and philosophy. Property contributed not to the economy but to culture. In Europe the nineteenth century was a time of tempestuous economic and, in parallel, civic growth. Citizens fought tenaciously and ultimately successfully to extend their participation in affairs of state. In Russia, in contrast, the achievements were Gogol's *Dead Souls* (1842), Turgenev's *A Sportsman's Sketches* (1852) and *Fathers and Sons* (1862), Tolstoy's *War and Peace* (1867), Saltykov-Shchedrin's *The History of a Town* (1870) and *The Golovlyov Family* (1880). All these were written by property-owning aristocrats. The inner freedom that gave the impulse to the creative freedom of the pre-revolutionary period proved stronger than the censorship, stronger than the laws of economics and society. Russian literature won a leading position in world culture and continues to exert its influence on other cultures. A monarchic political system that valued class-based stability above the ideal of national development was something the writers criticized. Private property, as a component of that system, did not become synonymous with citizenship, law and participation in public affairs; it did not gain a good reputation either as an ideal or as an institution. For some, it was a legal means of retaining their dominance, for others, such as Tolstoy in *Strider: The Story of a Horse* (1864), it was evidence of the profoundly unjust nature of the social order.

> The words '*my* horse' applied to me, a live horse, seemed to me as strange as to say 'my land', 'my air', or 'my water'.
> But those words had an enormous effect on me. I thought of them constantly and only after long and varied relations with men did I at last understand the meaning they attach to these strange words, which indicate that men are guided in life not by deeds but by words. They like not so much to do or abstain from doing anything, as to be able to apply conventional words to different objects. Such words, considered very important among them, are *my* and *mine*, which they apply to various things, creatures or objects: even to land, people, and horses. They have agreed that of any given thing only one person may use the word *mine*, and he who in this game of theirs may use that conventional word about the greatest number of things is considered the happiest. Why this is so I do not know, but it is so.[25]

The attempt to share

To the west of the Russian border, the political game consisted of extending effective property rights and equality before the law to a growing number of people, purely in order to retain power. In Russia, the game involved staking everything on a small group of the 'best people', who were accorded all the benefits and safeguards and who, it was hoped, would help to keep their patrons in power. These people had liberty, education, property and impunity. They were allowed to make money, to create and to travel, but their relationship with society at large was, in legal terms, unclear and, in human terms, estranged.

One Russian was the owner of another Russian: property owners and their property spoke the same language and attended the same church. The division was along estate lines, but ran so deep that sensitive educated Russians who belonged to the ruling class, no matter how it might choose to define itself, felt like foreigners in their own country. That feeling has been alive in Russian journalism and literature since the time of Pyotr Chaadaev, who wrote in 1836:

> We live in our houses as if we are stationed there; in our families we have the outlook of foreigners; in our cities we are similar to nomads,

we are worse than nomads. . . . Our remembrances do not go deeper than yesterday; we are foreign to ourselves. . . . Our experiences disappear as we are moving ahead. This is a natural consequence of a culture that is entirely borrowed and imitated.

Also in 1836, Gogol described St Petersburg as 'something similar to a European colony in America'. In 1845 the Slavophile Alexey Khomyakov wrote that in Russia, the Enlightenment assumed 'a colonial character'.[26]

Russian property owners were the main critics of the regime and, at the same time, themselves were the regime, making their own way of life the foundation of national politics. This was largely the reason reforms were not introduced until long overdue. Who relishes reforming themselves? The changes came too late to be effective. Neither the belated development of infrastructure and industry, nor the peasant reform, nor the attempt to convert the property of the commune into private property, undertaken on the eve of the empire's collapse, were able to create an extensive class of people capable of defending their private interests in political bargaining with the monarchy. What were the elite nobility guilty of? These people did not consciously defend their power and property; they were simply in a situation where they did not have to share either.

The paradox of private property in Russia is not that it was insufficiently 'private' but that, from the reign of Catherine the Great until the revolution of October 1917, it was too private. The legal ambiguity of the traditional peasant understanding of the situation ('The land belongs to the grand prince but we possess it'), in which the patrimonial right of the tsar did not conflict with the labour rights of the peasant, had, thanks to Catherine, become a thing of the past. The land, and with it the rivers, lakes and forests, had been privatized.

In this, as with the enserfment of the peasants, the political process in Russia was going in the opposite direction to that of Europe. In France, ownership of natural resources symbolized the feudal privileges of the *ancien régime* which had been done away with by the French Revolution. In Germany, the ability of private individuals to dispose of natural resources as they pleased was gradually reduced during the nineteenth century in the interests of prudent management and optimal use of forests and rivers. As a result of these restrictions, in the course of the nineteenth century, natural resources in Europe came increasingly into public ownership. In Russia, in contrast, the introduction of private property by Catherine led to enclosure of forests, rivers and mineral wealth. Peter the Great

132

had introduced 'mining freedom' throughout the empire, giving the state the freedom to extract mineral wealth wherever it chose, but Catherine had decided that the freedom to own territory absolutely would be a better incentive to commercial activity. Where Peter had allocated management of the forests to the Admiralty (the main user of timber in the country), Catherine handed over ownership to the landowners.[27]

Catherine's openhandedness also caused difficulties over the use of water resources. Private owners ignored their legal obligation to remove structures, such as water mills, that impeded navigation, and were extremely reluctant to respect the right of boat owners to haul barges along rivers, ignoring a law prescribing a 20-metre-wide public towpath. If a boat sank, landowners would, despite the government's efforts to enforce the rules of navigation, extort payment from merchants recovering their wares from the 'private' river. In 1900, Count Illarion Vorontsov-Dashkov tried to block the construction of hydroelectric power stations on the Dnieper, claiming that a deed of gift granted by the Empress Catherine to one of his ancestors gave his descendants private ownership of a section of the river.[28]

Oddly enough, something that Russian law found extremely difficult to deal with was the issue of the state's right to compulsorily acquire ownership of property. We consider the institution of private property to have been weak in Russia, but at the height of the St Petersburg period this was the state's Achilles' heel in disputes with property owners. There were, of course, instances of compulsory acquisition of land for the construction of roads and bridges, but there was no standard procedure for doing so, partly because of the traditionally blurred boundaries of property ownership and partly because of the legal lack of clarity over the status of the state and society.

After the Napoleonic Wars, a substantial part of Europe remained under the sway of the 1804 Napoleonic Code of civil law. This proclaimed the absolute nature of property ownership, but did not extend it to such resources as rivers, lakes and roads, which were designated as falling within the realm of communal or public property. European law distinguished between *domaine privé*, *domaine public* and *domaine de l'État*. Russian law had no problem defining what was state property and what was private property, but could not define what was meant by public property. This was hardly surprising: what could be owned by the people in an autocratic empire? In France, the right to manage resources on behalf of the people was based on the notion of a '*nation politique*', an idea profoundly alien to the Russian

133

autocracy. It was also difficult to define the status of the state: was it a bureaucratic machine with the tsar at its head or a community of citizens ruled by the monarch? Could such a community own property? The concept that ownership was a right guaranteed by the monarch obstructed development of a law of public property.[29]

The attitude of educated Russian society to private property, largely influenced by changing moods in Europe, moved from rapturous at the end of the eighteenth century, to reserved and then to negative. In the absence of a political solution for developing the public domain, philanthropy in the European spirit came to be seen as a sign of good breeding. The idea of sharing 'nicely' became widespread.

In the late 1910s, after the death of his brother in a duel, the young Prince Felix Yusupov became the sole heir of a vast fortune and began aspiring to the role of a patron of the arts.

> I longed to turn Arkhangelskoïe into an art-centre and build close to it a number of houses for painters, musicians, writers and craftsmen in the same style as the main building. They should have an academy, a school of music and a theatre. . . . We owned houses in St Petersburg and Moscow which we never lived in; these I intended to turn into hospitals, clinics and homes for old people. The Moïka house and Ivan the Terrible's palace would become museums, where the finest specimens from our collections would be exhibited. I further planned to build sanatora [sic] on our Crimean and Caucasian estates. I meant to reserve a room or two for my personal use in all these different places. I would present the land to the peasants, the factories and workshops would be converted into joint stock companies.[30]

These lofty plans were not well received by his parents. They reminded their young son that he was the sole heir of the Yusupov family, that he must marry and prepare himself to become a pillar of society in the old sense, that is, to remain a privileged property owner. In other words, he must continue to be a conquistador in his own country. 'When I realized that I could never convince my mother, and that these discussions upset her, I gave them up,' Yusupov concludes in memoirs written in exile, after nearly all the plans he mentioned had already been carried out by the Soviet regime. A modern scholar suggests that the prince may have thought these up with the benefit of hindsight.[31]

Thinking back to Ivan Pnin, whom we discussed earlier in this chapter, we may conclude that the Russian elite consciously preferred the role of property owners to that of rulers. It was not a one-off choice but was confirmed repeatedly in different eras under different rulers.[32]

The fact that in our culture property did not result from the development of common law or a liberal tradition but was conferred on Russia's upper class from above is a very important circumstance. 'The peculiarity of Russia is that the first person to advocate the idea of private property in the political and intellectual spheres was the ruler of the Russian Empire,' comments Ekaterina Pravilova. 'As far as we can tell, the empress saw property more as a gift than a responsibility, more as a privilege than a natural right.'[33]

We know that at the same time as she granted the nobility the right to private property, Catherine II also coined the Russian word for property, *'sobstvennost''*, for them. But what we are looking at is not a right wrested from the monarch after hard bargaining or conflict, but an act of delegation. The right to own private property that she conferred was in effect a privatization of the power of the state at local level. At the same time as cutting the state treasury's expenditure and the liabilities of the central government, she handed over to private owners something she could not in any case rule.[34]

In the West, defending property rights has historically been the foundation for protecting civil and political rights more generally. Both these areas of law were much of a muchness. In Russia, however, property and civil rights were quite separate: property rights were defended by the government, while civil rights were defended by people fighting the government. The very concept of private property was seen as linked to the fate of the tsarist state, which, in the eyes of the oppositionally minded segment of society, was the root of the general lawlessness.[35]

The autocracy and private property, existing within a system of estate-based rights and communal land ownership, were conjoined at a very deep level. There was no creative tension between them capable of generating that 'third force', a public, a community of citizens.

Private property was a project of the tsarist regime. None of the political forces popular on the eve of revolution could offer an alternative project with a coherent place in its ideology for private property. Repudiation of the autocracy in 1917 did not lead to the formation of a republican system in Russia: a new regime just began work on its own new project.

ARCHITECTURE, HAPPINESS
AND ORDER

The project we live in

Buildings designate space. Like landmarks, they are usually situated in the most prominent positions: on a hill, by a lake, in the bend of a river. Buildings in a city are the city itself. We do not know what a city would look like without them. They are the environment in which we live. We walk or travel along the lines of streets, past buildings; we look up and examine them. Inside the buildings, we move the way an architect has decided we should. We follow the plan he has designed, with doors, a corridor, a room. We climb stairs at a particular angle, or circle up a spiral staircase. We take off vertically in a lift. The internal design affects how we behave, helping or hindering us. The interior space creates flows, pushing us out of some rooms and causing us to congregate in others. But what if there is no external environment? I, for example, had none, because it consisted of apartment blocks identical to those in the adjacent 'microregion' and simply did not lodge in my young memory. I remember everything inside and nothing outside, except for the pond near our block, because that was the local sight. We took the bus to look at buildings in the city centre as if we were going to a museum. You could walk around the city, but not live in it. (I could not imagine anyone living in Kropotkin Street.) Where we were you could live, but there was no point in walking around: all you needed was to find your way back to your own entrance and disappear into it. I could not take seriously the attempt to plant a flowerbed by the entrance, and just felt sorry for the flowers in their little concrete recess. I wanted to scoot past them and the old lady sitting at the entrance and be inside. For me, as

I suppose for many others who grew up in a high-rise, what mattered was the interior.

It was, of course, very plain. The architect, or more exactly the engineer, who drafted the design had limited resources, so no spiral staircases or bay windows for us. We lived in a cell exactly like the cells of everyone around us. I found it perfectly natural that my best friend's apartment, where I spent almost as much time as I did at home, was the same as ours: exactly the same, to the extent that the hallstand was the same, the lights were the same, the bookshelves were in the same place and the books on them were pretty much the same.

This life, which had no external environment, was something my grandparents found wonderful. I remember their tales about moving into our nine-storey block. The apartment was an improvement on a room in a communal apartment or a hut. A big improvement. It also brought good news: you would not have people prying on you; you could go to the toilet when you needed to; you could wash in your own, private bathroom. You had emerged from a world without privacy, where everything was public, into a home of your own. You could hide in it, even it was only a cell put together out of panels prefabricated in a housebuilding factory. It was, in any case, the only solution on offer.

> The law of Economy necessarily governs our actions and our conceptions.
>
> The problem of the house is a problem of the era. Social equilibrium depends on it today. The first obligation of architecture, in an era of renewal, is to bring about a revision of values, a revision of the constitutive elements of the house.
>
> Mass production is based on analysis and experimentation. Heavy industry should turn its attention to building and standardize the elements of the house.
>
> We must create a mass-production state of mind.
>
> A state of mind for building mass-production housing.
>
> A state of mind for living in mass-production housing.
>
> A state of mind for conceiving mass-production housing.
>
> If we wrest from our hearts and minds static conceptions of the house and envision the question from a critical and objective point of view, we will come to the house-tool, the mass-production house that is healthy (morally, too) and beautiful from the aesthetic of the work tools that go with our existence.[1]

Le Corbusier wrote that in the 1920s. It was he who pitted architects against engineers. He wrote that architects had forgotten the original purpose of a house; they had got carried away with decoration and were about to be taken down a peg or two. There would soon be nothing for them to do: '*We have no more money* to pile up historical keepsakes.'[2] Engineers, on the other hand, were on the rise and would be taking over the reins of human residential accommodation. Le Corbusier could, of course, have had no idea just how firmly the engineers would take over the reins of housebuilding in far-off Russia. He could have had no idea that during his lifetime, in the 1960s, thanks to the industrialization of residential building conducted by Nikita Khrushchev, a whole society would be brought up in houses that were an industrial product.

We were that society. The mighty law of Economy, translated into the language of decrees issued by the CPSU Central Committee, condemned the 'extensive spread of ostentatious architecture' and proclaimed a Party line focused on economy and efficiency. The five-storey apartment block was born, built with precast concrete panels, with apartments of minimal size, with no cellar, assembled like Meccano, mortar-free, on site, in a matter of twelve working days. The K-7 prefabricated building project was designed by Vitaliy Lagutenko and based on the work of a French engineer, Raymond Camus. The Soviet Government even paid Camus' company for a licence for the first system for mass production of concrete building components, but it was then redesigned by Soviet engineers.[3] Later there were nine-storey buildings, such as the one I grew up in, put together from rough-surfaced grey panels. Later still came sixteeen-storey blocks and all the other house-tools, beautiful in the way that functional tools are beautiful, and integral to our lives.

Did it evoke the desire to live in such a house, as Le Corbusier hoped? Of course it did, because for most of us this was home. For the majority of people today this is the only chance they have of creating at least a small space of their own, even if it is one cell in a large building. For exterior environment we can still, as we did as children, take a trip to the city centre or, better still, to other cities or other countries, look at the environment there and even, for a time, tarry in it. An old house in an old European town can indeed feel like a keepsake: you just wish you could pick it up and bring it home with you.

There is no need to explain further what kind of house you would like to bring home with you and what kind you would leave where it is. I, like many people who live in faceless buildings, have a particular attitude towards architecture. That is probably why today we find the rational, egalitarian architecture of the twentieth-century avant-garde so difficult to appreciate. Most of the houses built in the short-lived era of constructivism in the latter half of the 1920s and the early 1930s are in need of cultural rehabilitation, so that today's school pupils can tell the difference between the models created by the avant-garde and the simplified prefabricated panels mass-produced during the Soviet and post-Soviet eras. The austere approach to form, the functionality, the growth of the architectural design from the interior out rather than from the façade in, which became the foundation and the language of world architecture in the twentieth century, means almost nothing to us. The functionality and elegance of constructivism were squeezed out by building on an industrial scale. Unlike most of their colleagues abroad, our architects were given an opportunity to create an entire environment, to build up square kilometres with housing to their own designs, but the law of Economy proved relentless. The resulting environment seemed to be no environment at all.

The famous communal housing built by Moses Ginzburg for the staff of the People's Commissariat of Finance is in every architecture textbook, but the people who moved in refused to change their lives to fit the architecture. The Soviet Union's financial officials did not start living in accordance with the design, taking their meals and relaxing collectively and only sleeping in their 'dwelling units'. The communal spaces designed for relaxation were partitioned into rooms, and the residents found themselves cooking meals in their living units. They did not like the building.

The residents would come to like it in time, the designers were certain. It was just a bit futuristic. 'The unacceptability of these buildings in practice was usually put down to the time not yet being ripe. The assumption was that society would eventually mature until it was ready for the way of life posited in the housing communes.'[4] The reality was, however, that, like most fantasists, it was the designers who were behind the times. To the extent that genuine communes had been created, they were an attempt by workers to resist a hostile social environment. Surrounded by enemies, workers who supported Soviet power had little option but to come together in practical communes during the civil war.[5] These communities, viewed in the light of utopian concepts from the past, gave architects the idea of creating commune houses. With the apparent victory of socialism, however, what the proletarians, now the masters of their own country, needed was not defensive communes but comfortable urban housing. They could only dream on.

Stalin's orders

Stalin's residential blocks attract attention and can be found pleasing, with their many oddities and excesses, their towers, statuary and gigantic arches. The architects of these buildings were ready to defy the human scale and nature by erecting spacious Italian loggias, suited to a hot climate and bright sunlight, in the centre of Moscow. 'This culture seemed to belong a few degrees to the south of the sixtieth parallel, to at least Mediterranean latitudes.'[6] The buildings seemed to be telling Soviet citizens as they emerged from their hostel accommodation and were walking around the centre of the capital, 'This is accommodation for special people. Engineers erect housing for plebeians, architects design accommodation for patricians. The people living here are superior to the rest. Even the climate in their houses is unlike ours: they have Mediterranean sun, while we have a sky heavy with thunderclouds and perpetual coldness.'

The Stalinist style arose when The Leader envisaged, and conveyed to his subordinates, a new mission for architecture. With the outlines of the new social order in place, it was time to defend and consolidate it. The secret police, forced labour, 'non-governmental' societies created from above were all tools of control and coercion. What was also needed was a positive programme and, in particular, a pleasing aesthetic. Hence all the cinematography, all the literature, and the lifestyle of the new aristocracy: the grandiose buildings topped with pillars of the Stalinist order, symbolic of Stalinist stability. These high-rise buildings, imperiously proclaiming the impregnability of the Soviet hierarchy, were built to be enviable.

The word 'order' acquired other meanings in Soviet parlance. An order for an apartment (accompanied, of course, with registration as a resident of Moscow) was a kind of title to property in a country where there was no property. It was an obvious return to Ivan the Terrible's practice of granting property in return for service. Apartments in the new Stalinist skyscrapers with their towers and pillars were conferred by the Soviet state on high-flyers, on the famous and, of course, on the leaders themselves.

An order could, however, also refer to an arrest warrant. There were cases (and the fate of those moved into the supremely prestigious House on the Embankment is the most famous) when, shortly after an individual received an order for an apartment, there followed an order for his or her arrest. The state could issue someone with a

140

licence to have a private life in return for loyal service, but it reserved the right to judge whether the service really was as loyal as it seemed. If it was deemed wanting, entitlement to a private life was terminated and the former beneficiary was then entitled only to a very public life in a labour camp. That is what orders could do.

In Russia, splendid, desirable accommodation in a good location has not only an architectural but also a moral dimension. This has nothing to do with religious trends or ideologies that repudiate private property; it has nothing to do with Rousseau, who believed that civilization with its passion for borders had corrupted mankind. It is again all about property linked to service.

In the autumn of 1933 Osip Mandelstam received his first and only private accommodation, an apartment in a writers' cooperative building in Nashchokin Street. He was not to be accorded this settled life for long: in May 1934, he was arrested in his new apartment, the order following hot on the heels of the order for accommodation. It is popularly believed that the main reason for his arrest was a poem about Stalin ('Our lives no longer feel ground under them . . .'), but when he was being interrogated, he was also questioned about a poem directly associated with his apartment in Nashchokin Street: 'The apartment's dumb as paper . . .'

> Damned walls as thin as paper
> And nowhere left to run,
> And I'm obliged to caper
> To entertain some one.
>
> My reading's books for rations
> I'm lectured by a hack
> And threaten with my ditties
> Some hapless ex-kulak.
>
> A literary draughtsman,
> A bard of fake and quake
> Some organizer ought to be
> Impaled upon this stake.
>
> Some principled informer
> For whom the purge is bliss,
> His family's bread-winner,
> Deserves a flat like this.[7]

Nadezhda Mandelstam recalls that the appearance of this poem was prompted by a brief conversation with Boris Pasternak.

He had looked in to see how we were getting on in our new apartment in Furmanov Street. As he was leaving, he lingered for quite a time in the entrance, saying how wonderful it was: 'Now you have an apartment, you'll be able to write poetry,' he said as he finally went out.

'Did you hear what he said?' M. asked me. He was furious. He couldn't stand it when people blamed their inability to work on external circumstances, such as bad living conditions or lack of money. It was his profound conviction that nothing should prevent an artist from doing what he had to do, and, conversely, that material comfort was not in itself a stimulus to work – though he wasn't against comfort as such and would not himself have turned up his nose at it. At that time, as we saw all around us, there was furious competition among the writers for the good things of life, among which the greatest prize of all was an apartment. A little later, country villas were also handed out 'for services rendered'. Pasternak's words touched M. to the quick: he cursed the apartment and said it should go to one of those it was intended for: 'the worthy traitors, the portrait-painters', and all the other time-servers.[8]

There is no Tolstoyan, or indeed any other philosophical, rejection of property as such. Mandelstam was enraged by being reminded of subjugation of creativity to service to the regime. Pasternak had good-naturedly, and probably without the least subtext, been talking about more settled domestic circumstances and having a comfortable place to work, but what Mandelstam heard was a reminder that housing could not be bought but was conferred for, at best, capering 'to entertain some one' and, at worst, betrayal and pusillanimously faking your writing. 'This curse he pronounced on our apartment does not mean that he thought it better to be homeless – he was simply expressing his horror at the price one was expected to pay. We got nothing – apartments, villas or money – without paying the price.'[9]

That special price, not denominated in currency and demanded by the state in return for entirely basic domestic amenities, was an integral part of the way Soviet life was contrived. The profound inhumanity of the Soviet regime was not only that it murdered and maimed people physically, but that it crippled them morally. That goal was not written down anywhere in the Party's programme, but the Party leaders effectively pursued a policy of moral humiliation of educated and spiritually independent members of society. Compromise and surrender of intellectual honesty in science and the arts were encouraged by the award of goodies, apartments, food and money. A refusal to compromise, intellectual honesty, independent-mindedness were punished by sanctions, arrest and death.

The very presence of this monstrous choice obliges us to view Soviet life in a particular way. There was a high price to be paid in those times for any show of independence, any refusal to march in line. Those who paid it are heroes and we must honour them. In Stalin's time, the dilemma of whether or not to cooperate with the regime was very cruel, but in later years, too, the choice was not easy. All that changed was the size of the risk. Prizes were awarded for playing along in life (although that was not guaranteed), the same all-encompassing 'palace rations'. For not playing along you could lose not just the extra rations but also your career and life. The decision whether to be stopped from accomplishing anything in your homeland or to emigrate (in the Brezhnev period, when emigration became possible) was, in many cases, a tragic and noble choice. We will never know the names of all those who did not sign up to deals and were prevented from realizing their potential. They renounced compromise but were deprived of the opportunity of their own voice ever being heard again.

To survive, to realize yourself creatively and as a human being without soiling yourself with betrayal or other ignominy, was probably the highest form of virtuosity in those times, and very few people managed it. The enviable, elite apartment blocks were occupied by people who had sold out their principles and themselves. Some might envy their prosperity, but others might be horrified by the thought of what or whom they had trampled underfoot in order to secure their place in the 'elite'.

The buildings put up in the Stalin period, especially the Stalinist skyscrapers, have a charm I find it difficult to explain even to myself. Perhaps it is simply an aesthetic appeal, the possession of character at a time when individuality and expressiveness were the exception. At the beginning of this chapter, we mentioned that living in the standard high-rise blocks built by Soviet engineers seemed to have no external environment. This in itself encouraged self-absorption, a focus on the family hidden away in its prefabricated cell.

External appeal perhaps also arises from the fact that these buildings have been lived in for a considerable time. Appeal cannot be generated by architecture alone: environment and history also have a part to play. In this case, however, the history is tragic and, in contrast to pre-revolutionary history, which is now virtually out of living memory, that is well understood by most people living today. Elite apartment blocks are monuments not only to architectural bombast but also to enslavement elevated to the status of something glorious. Servility and betrayal are embodied in those towers and wrought-iron railings.

In the 1960s and 1970s, discreet, but also superior, accommodation began to be built for those in the upper echelons of the regime. Everything about it was laden with significance: the renunciation of elaborate decoration, the spaciousness, the 'Western' design, utility rooms, even fireplaces and underground garages. The ceiling height could reflect your place in the hierarchy: there is a well-known block in Granatny Street in Moscow where one of the storeys, built specifically for Brezhnev, has higher ceilings than all the others. That is barely detectable unless you are actually looking for it: the extraordinary amenities of the housing for the nomenklatura class of the bureaucracy, unlike the trappings of the Stalinist Imperial style, were not intended to be glaringly obvious.

Those fancy towers, the design, those extra-high ceilings are the icing on the unfreedom that goes with all conditional property, held on sufferance, premised on service. If a house is given for work, services or achievements, it can equally well be taken away. As far as property relations are concerned, under the Bolsheviks the government effectively rolled back the reforms of the previous 150 years by abolishing at the time of the revolution every element of property rights that had taken root. Land, housing and other goods were transformed from private property into items held conditionally, subject to approval by the regime.

As they eliminated property rights, the authorities also eliminated individuals capable of acting independently of the regime. The Soviet leaders probably went further in their destruction of independence than even Ivan the Terrible. In practice, all goods became privileges or, to move back further towards the Middle Ages, benefices. All well-being was rationed. And that is how architecture became part of the grand project in which Soviet people lived.

Khrushchev's social revolution

Soviet building to this day puts its stamp on the character of most Russian cities. Buildings are eloquent, if only because they are always in plain view and always in the same place we saw them in yesterday. They last longer than people and bear their message impassively and insistently. Sometimes what people really want can become an obsession. 'The buildings we admire are ultimately those which, in a variety of ways, extol values we consider worthwhile,' says Alain de Botton in *The Architecture of Happiness*. 'We should know to ask at once what people would have to lack in order to see an object as beautiful and can come to understand the tenor of their deprivation even if we cannot muster enthusiasm for their choice.'[10]

It is not too hard to understand the choice many of us make. Architecture in countries where the regime is more dominant than the market and property rights, where orders from above are more dominant than contracts, is always particularly eloquent. That is why we in Russia understand architecture instantly and instinctively. The high, the unique, the elite is out of reach: you have to serve to get it, or pay whatever price is demanded. It is the fact of being elite that creates value, whatever it is that at a given moment is deemed elite: an apartment in a Stalinist skyscraper, a fortress-like brick mansion or a sterile minimalist home; while what is entirely faceless is not architecture but an item manufactured by the egalitarian engineers. The latter are simply architects who have been obliged to devise residential accommodation as cheaply as possible.

In order to properly appreciate simplicity, you need already to be well acquainted with complexity and sumptuousness. The distilled forms of modernist architecture, the surfaces of unfaced concrete can be appreciated only by people who have tired of complex spaces, strident façades and cluttered architectural ornamentation. Those actually immersed in the Soviet reality of that time when architects and engineers were at loggerheads knew nothing of complexity or ornamentation, as a rule had no home of their own, and were only too grateful to the Soviet regime for the blocks of prefabricated housing it gave them.

Most Soviet people, having no alternative, lived in a world devised by engineers who were starved of funds. When Nikita Khrushchev became leader of the Communist Party and the Soviet Union, the housing situation was appalling. The amount built in the pre-war and post-war years was statistically insignificant and was, in any case, dwarfed by the scale of wartime destruction. About one-third of the total housing stock of the USSR was destroyed during the war, leaving 25 million people without a roof over their heads.[11] Building residential accommodation was both a passion of Khruschev's and one of his most important political projects. In his memoirs, he constantly returns to this theme: 'People were suffering, living like bedbugs in every nook and cranny, several people to the same room, many families to a single apartment.'[12] When he describes his visits abroad, he talks enthusiastically about the way of life of his counterparts. The Danish prime minister, for example, lived in a cooperatively built two-storey house. 'His accommodation was on two floors. This Western housing system is the most convenient for a family. As a

145

rule the kitchen and dining room are downstairs and the bedrooms are upstairs, and there is a small garden just outside the windows,' Khrushchev writes. 'A good, simple family without pretensions, well-off but without luxury, which I liked even more. I liked the house itself and the way it was furnished. I admit I thought to myself we should adopt that way of life, rather than us leaders living in quite different conditions, which was just not right.'[13]

Private, individual building was the response to the housing problem in the immediate post-war period. Before any coherent policy emerged, people simply built houses for themselves. In terms of floor space, individual housebuilding exceeded that of the state right up until 1961.[14] This could have become an important change of direction. Private housebuilding could theoretically have been given the state's blessing. In March 1945, there was an exhibition at the Architects' Club on 'Rapid Construction in the United States', which was closely examined by Soviet architects. Officials scrutinized the building of individual houses and couriers hared off to the UK, Finland and Switzerland.

A decree of 1957 indicated that a decision had been taken to follow a different, industrial, path. Soviet people were to be given individual accommodation but of an industrial type. To implement the solution a change would be needed from architecture to construction, from individual efforts to industrial procedures, from the Stalinist Imperial style to engineering. The result was residential building at phenomenal speed. 'The 1957 housing decree was one of the most important signals of the Khrushchev era. It gave the green light for an unprecedented building boom on the largest scale by a wide margin in Europe,' writes British historian Mark Smith. In December 1963, Khrushchev claimed at a plenary session of the Central Committee of the Communist Party that in ten years, more than 100 million people had seen their living conditions improved. On other occasions he gave the figure as 75 million.[15] Other calculations, over the longer period of 1953 to 1970, suggest a doubling of the USSR's residential floor space. Over that period, in town and country, the Soviet government and Soviet citizens built 38.2 million apartments and individual houses. More than 140 million people moved into new accommodation.[16]

This was a real revolution, technical and social, but it was a revolution riven with contradictions. The five-storey apartment blocks that became known as *khrushchoby*, 'Khrushchev slums', saved the country from homelessness, and the fact that millions of people received a place of their own was one of the major achievements of the Khrushchev Thaw. The Twentieth Party Congress, at which Stalin's personality cult was debunked, took place in 1956 and Khrushchev emerged victorious in the Kremlin power struggle only in 1957. He immediately embarked on a massive building programme. Soviet architects and designers were extremely limited in what they could offer the citizenry. This resulted not from the focus on economy or even from the lack of new technology, but from the practices and regulations governing distribution of residential floor space. On the one hand, there were minimum standards, sanitary norms, originally introduced back in the times of the Bolsheviks. These were initially 8, from the 1970s, 9, and in some towns 12 m² of floor space per person. The real densities were never that generous, amounting on average to only half the stipulated area. On the other hand, since the Stalin period it had been a priority that one apartment should be for one family. Soviet architects might design an admirable apartment with several bedrooms, a dining room, study, a hallway and cloakroom, but the reality was that it would become a communal apartment (unless it was a special one for a member of the nomenklatura). The problem was that if only one family occupied it, its members would have more floor space than the norms allowed: the acute housing shortage had transformed minimum areas into maximums.

The size of apartments and the number of rooms had to be reduced because they were breaking the rules. ('Putting families of three to five individuals into individual apartments is possible only if the design is calculated on the basis of a 6 m² norm per person,' the architect Pavel Blokhin warned in 1944.[17]) But even that did not solve the problem. Architects were obliged to reduce not only the overall size of the apartment but also the corridors, bathrooms and kitchens. This was a further unintended consequence of the simultaneous operation of norms of floor space and a policy of providing individual homes. Reducing the area of apartments meant they could be separate but increased the cost of construction, because the more infrastructure there was in a building relative to its residential floor space, the more expensive each square metre became. This led inevitably to the reduction of ancillary areas: the entrance hall and corridor were done away with, the bathroom and toilet were combined, and communicating rooms appeared. The latter not only helped to eliminate communal sharing, but also meant the corridor could be dispensed with.[18]

Rooms with specific purposes, the dining room, sitting room, study and bedroom, disappeared from architectural plans. Each room now had two or more roles. Bathrooms and toilets were placed next to the kitchen to save on infrastructure. This entailed mixing together hitherto separate zones within the home. Separating the domestic space into public, private and service areas disappeared and led to the kind of space in which many of us still live, a space designed not so much around its occupants as around the rules and practices of how accommodation was allocated.[19]

Every lucky new owner of a private apartment also got a personal kitchen, small, inevitably, but not shared, and these small kitchens became one of the main debating arenas for the contest between capitalism and communism.

In 1950, those responsible for implementing the Marshall Plan displayed an American house at an industrial fair in West Berlin. It was a six-room house produced to a standard design and furnished with the latest in modern furniture. It had a kitchen fitted out with all the latest gadgetry, and this was the exhibition's great sensation. Thousands of East Germans (the Berlin Wall had not yet been built) came to see it. In 1959, the Americans successfully repeated their trick at an exhibition of US industrial products in Moscow. Debates between Richard Nixon, the future president of the United States, and Nikita Khrushchev took place partly in the kitchen of this standard-design American home. Khrushchev had to argue the merits of the Soviet system against a background of unheard-of wonders: a refrigerator, a washing machine and a dishwasher, built into a futuristic fitted kitchen. He tried to laugh the situation off: 'Don't you yet have a machine to put the food in your mouth and chew it for you?' This spacious house crammed with home appliances had quite an impact on everyone who managed to get into the exhibition in Sokolniki Park.

Soviet planners and designers could not give people a convenient, well-equipped kitchen, but the separateness of an individual apartment and the falling away of government interference in the personal sphere had one more unexpected result. The kitchen was to prove the birthplace of the Soviet public sphere, just as the English coffee house and the French salons in the seventeenth and eighteenth centuries had been (according to Habermas) the birthplace of the 'bourgeois' public sphere.

That time, the late 1950s–early 1960s, saw the first introduction of much that was to prove fundamental to the lifestyle of the next half-century. A policy of mass housebuilding was adopted, with resettlement of people in Russian cities continuing to this day. The interest Khrushchev and his officials took in building individual houses in conformity with British, Swiss and American models had no chance of leading on to a programme of mass private housebuilding. The rituals of the Cold War required that this approach should be condemned. A shortage of resources also led to limitation of individual housebuilding: the maximum permissible size of a home for a single family was laid down by the regime in a special directive. Such were the origins of the prefabricated urban landscape. All resources were concentrated on prefabricated panel houses, just as, under Stalin, all resources had been concentrated on building blast furnaces and power stations. Even the ubiquitous power and heating station pipes that service whole communities and have become such a visual feature of most Russian cities are a consequence of decisions taken back then.

Without them it would have been impossible to light and heat all those millions of square metres of housing. Panel-built houses and communal pipes are to this day the unifying factor of the urban landscape, linking the entire country, from Kaliningrad to Magadan, from Orenburg to Murmansk.

Houses last longer than people, and if, fifty years ago, they were built to avert a catastrophe, today they are being built by inertia, as if they are something inevitable. A long-overdue decision to resolve an emergency turned into an unchallengeable orthodoxy extending over decades. It is an example of how a zigzag on the way to a great goal can turn into a major highway. Addiction to the path chosen can set in very rapidly, like a rut in a field. Shaking off the addiction, just like getting out of the rut, becomes increasingly difficult. Mass-produced high-rise blocks were an excellent solution for the Soviet state because the Soviet economy was well adapted to producing goods in large volumes where 'wholesale' quantities were more important than quality. Cost considerations dictated the size of rooms, the height of ceilings, the number of storeys (five because the rules said that was the maximum permissible without a lift) and the appearance of communicating rooms. A room was not defined by its function as 'the bedroom' or 'the living room'. Its function generally varied with the time of day: at night the sofa became a bed. To this day the size of apartments in Russia is stated in terms of rooms rather than bedrooms.

It might have been expected that with the advent of the free market all this would have changed. Demand should have influenced supply, houses should have changed as the way of life changed. It became evident, however, that in a market economy, housebuilding factories were a profitable asset. Their directors realized that the factories could be privatized and make money if they just carried on producing the same old panels, if slightly modernized. At all events, it was far quicker and cheaper than building individual homes. This is just one of many instances of technology overruling revolutions.

After the collapse of the USSR, the residential blocks devised by Soviet engineers and planners became real estate, and areas built up with high-rises came to be seen in post-Soviet eyes as 'less desirable'. That division of areas is only reinforced by the fact that when the old five-storey prefabricated apartment blocks are demolished they are replaced by new prefabricated blocks. As Andrey Kaftanov wrote just before the recent start of the five-storey block demolition programme:

> If we demolish all the five-storey buildings and replace them with new blocks, we will end up with exactly the same thing we have been trying to get rid of, namely, a 'new estate'. There will be nothing desirable about it because K-7 series blocks will be replaced by P-44 series blocks. That will not be a town, it will be a new generation overflow suburb.[20]

Today's quality of life, posited on the notion of a private urban apartment, is something very recent. If we take as the criterion of minimal habitability an apartment with at least two separate rooms, a kitchen of at least 8 m^2 and all necessary utilities, we find that for most people this bastion of private life has been attainable only in the last two or three decades. Until the 1970s, only 10% of the apartments being built met that standard. During the 1970s, the proportion rose to 23%, and in the 1980s it was 60%. On the eve of the collapse of the Soviet Union, only about 30% of adult citizens were living in 'habitable' apartments.[21]

Khrushchev's revolution proved longer lasting than Stalin's, in that it defined the lifestyle of the country in terms of kitchen, apartment and microregion. If Stalin's social engineering went down to total defeat – building a society to a single plan failed – Khrushchev's physical engineering has left us a massive high-rise legacy.

One unplanned achievement of his period was that the first steps were taken towards a more secure right of residential ownership. The sheer number of apartments awarded to citizens led to greater autonomy of the individual: it was not possible to keep tens of millions of people under surveillance. It became extremely rare for an order awarding an apartment to be followed by an order for arrest. The tenant of an apartment was beginning to look more like an owner. Mark Smith reminds us that property rights differ in different periods and in different cultures. There is a combination of elements of ownership: the right to enjoy, possess, have at your disposal, rebuild, sell or alter. Soviet property rights were imperfect, but they were still a combination of rights that could fit within the logic of Europe. Under Khrushchev, more of those elements were included, although it is only in the post-Soviet period that they have been written down and consolidated.[22]

Something else that was consolidated was the melancholy formula that architecture was for patricians while plebeians got engineering. The stratification can be traced back to ancient Rome, where, by the time of the late republic, social inequality was evident both in life-styles and in the nature of accommodation. Only a select few could afford an individual house, a *domus*. A detached house was a sign of high social and material status. The house was the heir to the country villa, modified to city needs. It was an area with an atrium courtyard and a garden courtyard, tucked away inside the property behind windowless walls. Houses for the middle class and the poor – the *insulae* – were a purely urban invention. These were multi-storey buildings of up to seven floors, with small rooms that were rented out.

Roman poetry and correspondence are full of complaints about the terrible living conditions in the *insulae* – the overcrowding, insanitariness, dangers and high rents. Cicero writes to Atticus that two of his taverns are falling apart and that not only people but even the mice have fled. Plutarch calls fires and collapsing buildings 'fellow inhabitants of Rome'. Imagine how insanitary this kind of accommodation must have been: without an adequate supply of water – who was going to carry it up to the top floor? – it could not be kept properly clean, and got covered in soot and polluted by the fumes from braziers and lamps. To cap it all, the rent was very high: Juvenal writes that in a rural area you could buy a house with a garden for the same money you had to pay in Rome for a dark nook fit only for a dog.[23]

In the past two thousand years, has anything at all changed in how people live? Well, where once Rome was the only big city, there are now, regrettably, thousands of them. But then again, felicitously, life without an environment, without architecture, is no longer the inevitable lot of the majority. In Russia, the function of a real house, one you can retire to from the city, is most often served by a dacha (a vast topic that deserves a discussion to itself).[24]

Every culture has its own answers to the issue of the home, and one way of measuring progress is to look at the proportion of people able to afford what in the past was a luxury reserved for patricians and kings, namely the ability to arrange the place they live in to their own liking.

If someone of average means can take a loan, build a house in any style and create a space that corresponds to the environment they would ideally like to live in, then progress exists. The more people who can afford their personal utopia, the better the society. A society where everyone lives in identical housing and public spaces are monopolized by the state is suffering from a deficient public

151

sphere. A society in which elite status is highly prized is suffering from a surfeit of private life and stratification. A house of one's own offers an escape from both extremes to one's own idea of the ideal life. That is why, if we examine private homes, we will see not only a contest between wallets but also an exhibition of ideals of happiness.[25]

Happiness and order

In a broader sense, however, housing and the environment of which it is a part are a display of order, a physical reflection of the rules of living in the community that have evolved in these parts. Living in our cell-like apartments, in a bubble of private life but excluded from public life, we have arrived at the polar opposite of the ancient Greek *polis*. The *polis* was a public city. The outward appearance of a private house and its design were unimportant to the ancient Greeks because they spent so little of their time at home. The houses in the city-states of the classical period were so simple that, if today we were transported to the residential quarter of Athens in the fifth century BC, we would be hard pressed to believe that this was that famous city. The house was neither something in which you invested money nor something you took a pride in, because it was not the centre of gravity. The centre of gravity was the forum, the arena of public life. The mild climate and a keen interest in the state's affairs impelled houseowners out into the street early in the morning. An ostentatiously expensive house was considered a sign of poor taste: resources and effort went into construction of public buildings and temples, not into private homes.

With the passage of time, houses became increasingly comfortable and luxurious. Alcibiades, who lived in the fifth century BC, caused widespread outrage when he adorned the walls of his house with murals. Demosthenes, who lived almost a hundred years later, complained that in his time such extravagance had become commonplace and private homes were beginning to excel public buildings in their grandeur.[26]

> Believe me, that was a happy age, before the days of architects. . . . For they were not preparing a roof for a future banquet-ball; for no such use did they carry the pinetrees or the firs along the trembling streets with a long row of drays - merely to fasten thereon panelled ceilings heavy with gold. Forked poles erected at either end propped up their houses. With close-packed branches and with leaves heaped up and laid sloping they contrived a drainage for even the heaviest rains. Beneath

such dwellings, they lived, but they lived in peace. A thatched roof once covered free men; under marble and gold dwells slavery.[27]

The notion that the private sphere should be restricted in favour of serving the common good, that restraint and simplicity should be a deliberate choice, deserves thinking about. The very possibility of consciously introducing moderation in thought, culture and everyday life is something the ancient Greeks discovered.

'Nothing beyond measure,' said the sage Pittacus. 'Moderation is best' is attributed to the sage Cleobulus. Moderation has a special place among the virtues most important to the Greeks. Here is how Mikhail Gasparov explains it:

> Intelligence is the knowledge of what is good and what is bad; courage is the knowledge of which good acts should be done and which should not; justice is the knowledge of who should have good deeds done for them and who should not. The sense of moderation is knowing how long good deeds should be done for and when it is time to stop. Courage is a virtue for war, justice for peace; intelligence is virtue of the mind, moderation is virtue of the heart. Of intelligence, understanding and goodwill are born; of courage, constancy and composure; of justice, level-headedness and kindness; of moderation, clear-headedness and orderliness.[28]

The path has been long to what today we find the natural pre-dominance of the private in everyday life, in the economy, in our social relationships. Not only luxurious private residences, but even the art of the individualized portrait depicting the characteristics of a particular person, were unknown in ancient Greece.

The private entered culture only gradually, supplanting and eclipsing the ideal, and then the tendency proved unstoppable. The art of building, the urge to adorn the home with mosaics, paintings and marble statues, grew steadily stronger as private life became increasingly differentiated and the gap between rich and poor became more pronounced. Ultimately, the perfect relationship between public and private life remained as a cultural ideal, finding physical expression in architecture at its best, and this was perhaps its most important mission. It is illuminating that 'order' was one of the first ways of classifying different forms of architecture.

In life, consistency and order are always in short supply, both in the human environment and within people themselves. Accordingly, individuals try very hard to create them and establish rules and limits. Architecture is the visible manifestation of this insatiable craving for order. At the same time, ideas of what constitutes order change from one period to the next, and from one building to another, even if they are adjacent.

A building is the representation of a perfectly ordered world. Russian church architecture embodies an elegant concept of a hierarchy of beings in heaven and earth. That ideal of order has outlived the Soviet era, when churches were used as warehouses, hostels and swimming pools. Whatever mayhem may have been going on inside them, the form of the church continued to bear witness to its message. It might be stripped of its icons, its walls might be peeling, but it remained clear what was the place of earthly things and what was the province of heaven.

A concept of order is evidenced by a peasant hut, a wooden hostel for workers, a communal apartment, a Stalinist skyscraper, a Khrushchev five-storey block, a luxurious building for those staffing the CPSU Central Committee, and a palace on the Black Sea said to have been built for Putin. The Villa Rotunda designed by Andrea Palladio also testifies to an ideal of order, as do Frank Lloyd Wright's Fallingwater, and even a caravan, a fisherman's shack and the tent of a nomad. People living in a house may not, however, feel at ease in the environment in which they find themselves, and then they will try to do something about it, to break free of their palace, their hut or their prefabricated apartment block. In deciding where they should move to, they can fall back on concepts of order and happiness that have been tried out in the past. The ideal of order to which the Soviet buildings around us testify is, however, highly idiosyncratic. As this is the environment in which Russians live, let us take a look at it, the better to understand it.

Russian order

Stalin's order is not wholly a thing of the past, neither in terms of aesthetics nor as a piece of paper. Order in the architectural sense lives on because buildings have long lives. Demand for accommodation in old nomenklatura buildings is still there, although it is gradually being eroded by the new 'elite' aesthetics, which either imitates Stalinist aesthetics (like the residential region, with its distinctively 'ruling business class' name of Dominion, behind Moscow State University on the Vorobiov Hills), or tries to be emphatically minimalist and similar to the modern style (like Moscow's Golden Mile in the streets between Ostozhenka and Kropotkin Embankment). There is no longer the 'only option' of engineer-designed residential accommodation: there are also architect-designed buildings. The Putin era has not, however, spawned an aesthetics of its own: we cannot identify anything resembling a Putin Style. At all events, the era had not created its own grand style by the mid-2010s. The abundance of high-end and just plain expensive housing built in a neo-Stalinist style does not seem to be an intentional aesthetic project; it is simply a rut we have yet to get out of. In the absence of any other grand style, if you want to sell property for a lot of money, an obvious option is to build a replica skyscraper or another of Ivan Zholtovsky's Stalinist palazzos.

The order, in those other senses of a sign of favour or an arrest warrant, has not, of course, lost its currency. Elite apartments are rarely available for no reason: there is a price to be paid, but in monetary terms it is usually below the market value. In the pre-Putin period, especially in Moscow while Mayor Yury Luzhkov was in office, members of the political elite and those servicing it could acquire apartments from the municipal government at bargain basement prices. This was a gesture of goodwill on the part of the state, based on an unwritten contract with Moscow. It was the city's way of paying back the liberties it enjoyed. The practice of shielding high-ranking officials from harsh market realities continues to this day. During the 2013 election campaign in Moscow, it became known that Sergey Sobyanin, who had replaced Luzhkov as mayor, had been allowed to privatize his official apartment for far less than the market price. In 2013, the price for this apartment of just over 300 m^2 was approximately $5.3 million. The opposition politician Alexey Navalny estimates that this was six times more than the bureaucrat's family income for the next ten years.[29]

Some purchasers pay the full market price for such apartments, but even so not everyone will satisfy the criteria for the right to live next to a Sobyanin or businessmen and officials known to be close to the president. In Moscow, there is an apartment block known as the Putin's Pals' Club at No. 3, Shvedsky Tupik. Journalists from *Forbes* and the Bloomberg agency discovered Igor Sechin (Rosneft'), Andrey Kostin (Foreign Trade Bank), Sergey Lavrov (foreign minister) and Alexey Kudrin (ex-finance minister) all living there. In order to rub shoulders with such select citizens, you would need tens of millions of dollars in the bank. A duplex penthouse with 1,000 m^2 would have set you back $50 million in 2013. There are cheaper apartments in the block: not many, but they do come on the market.[30]

For the best homes in the best locations in Moscow and the suburbs you need to pay 'supermoney'. Here the order is symbolic, and issued not for the living space itself, as in Soviet times, but for the ability to make that supermoney without which this kind of property cannot be bought. People who know the value of money have no need of such property, but buying property that is manifestly overpriced is a kind of fee for the access to wealth, a return of a proportion of your funds to the kitty. This is an odd kind of Putinesque order, a pass admitting you to the milieu of top officialdom and businessmen, which is needed by people who have made money and now feel the need to show they belong to the new aristocracy.

The practice may be destined to grow. Russian millionaires and billionaires are going to be invited ever more insistently to make their investments in Russia. There have been official statements to the effect that, in the course of a new wave of privatization, tranches of shares in Russian companies will have to be sold on Russian trading floors. Calls for major offshore capitalists to come back and invest in Russian assets have been backed up by a law prohibiting officials from holding foreign bank accounts.[31]

Thus in the post-Soviet 'Russian' order there are both pre-revolutionary and Stalin-era elements and, more generally, Soviet aspects. In post-Soviet housing, as in Soviet, cost is more important than aesthetics. The only difference is that today the cost should be as high as possible rather than, as in the days of mass-production housebuilding, as low as possible. Housing is an asset. For most citizens its primary role is as their only capital: capital in a country whose citizens have historically been deprived of any capital at all.[32]

Price and liquidity are more important here than amenities, infrastructure and the architectural qualities of the building. This 'order' has nothing to do with aesthetics. The place of grand style has been taken over in its value system by the high cost per square metre. This means that the style of the 2000s and the first half of the 2010s is set to be less enduring than that of the Stalin era, because what can destroy it is not physical deterioration but just a crisis in the housing market.

— 10 —

THE HALFWAY HOUSE

Favour from the tsar

As already mentioned, in 1970 my grandfather was awarded a three-room apartment in Belyaevo. I like to think of it as the same parcel of land he could have expected if there had never been a revolution. If there had been no collectivization, my grandfather would have had a splendid house on the high bank of the River Oka. There would have been a large family living there. In that imagined life in which there had been no collectivization, no forcing of people into the towns, there would have been many children in the family. (In his actual, Soviet life my grandfather had only one son, my father.) That imagined family would, however, probably have been keen to send the children to study in the town. My grandfather would have had to save up or take out a loan for their education in some provincial bank. In that eventuality, my father would have stood a chance of becoming a first-generation town dweller, or perhaps I would have been the first.

Well, in the real USSR, my grandfather got an apartment in the city, in the country's capital, no less, a few years before retirement. Can that be seen as a manifestation of a higher justice? The fact of the matter is that many former peasants, my grandfather's peers, never lived to see the day when apartments were being given out. They perished in the years of collectivization and war, lost everything and got nothing in return. In that sense my grandfather was fortunate: he survived and, at fifty-five years of age, got a home of his own.

The massive building of apartment blocks in the Khrushchev and Brezhnev years was a social revolution that affected the way of life, education and structure of families. It was a social phenomenon

157

commensurable with collectivization and was, in some sense, a reversal of it. If what took place in 1929 and the 1930s was a vast destruction of rights, confiscation of property and destruction of value, the events of the 1960s–1980s saw the introduction of a huge number of new rights and the creation of property and value.

As the 1920s ended and the 1930s began, the greater part of the country's population, the rural population, were deprived of their land, their property and their link with the place where their ancestors had lived. During the war, many of those who had moved to the towns lost everything all over again. According to one estimate, in the 1,710 cities, towns and villages occupied by the enemy, some half of the housing stock was destroyed. In total, in the course of the war over 1 million houses were destroyed.[1] We noted in the previous chapter that the war left some 25 million Soviet citizens homeless.

The state created by the Bolsheviks repudiated the market economy and proclaimed its right to avail itself of all property on behalf of the people. After the Second World War, that state had on its hands the largest homeless population in Europe. What was needed now was not to reallocate property but to create it, without the benefit of private developers. Building and distributing homes was what the state owed the population, and having a place to live was now their right. The truth of the matter was that they had not chosen to surrender their land to the collective farm and go to live in communal huts in the towns. This was not just a matter of their constitutional 'right to accommodation' (which was, in fact, included in the Soviet Constitution only in 1977), but something more serious: the right to trust a state that had taken so much of their strength and energy and that was now due to repay the debt.

The state began doing so: from the 1960s to the 1980s the former peasants and their children, now town dwellers, were allocated apartments in tower blocks. These apartments were analogous to the parcels of land which, in different historical circumstances, they might have been allocated in a peasant commune, only now this great commune was operated by the state. It gradually released the former peasants from their communal apartments and huts and awarded them some modest floor space in panel-built houses in numerous new suburbs.

The housing shortage had been a major problem of the system: in the 1950s the Soviet regime had been in power for forty years, yet people were living in even more overcrowded conditions than before the revolution. Ideologically this was a tricky topic. The return of private life to a socialist society was in need of explanation. Perhaps through the medium of fiction? Private life and accommodation are the main theme of Ilya Ehrenburg's *The Thaw*, which, published in 1954, gave its name to the entire era. In *The Thaw* the issues of separate accommodation and the quality of private life are treated as equal in importance to the demands of industrial production, and that, indeed, is where the thaw is occurring. One of the major characters in the novella is Zhuravlyov, a factory director with a Stalinist management style who insists that output takes priority over everything else. He decides to invest resources allocated for housing in production instead and comes to grief, because times have changed. The director loses even his wife's respect and ends up with neither his wife nor his job.

> Last summer, the Secretary of the Town Committee had told him in front of her that the dilapidated hovels and hutments of the workers were a disgrace; the building fund had been approved a year ago, and what had it been used for? 'The new precision casting bay', said Ivan unruffled, 'was an absolute necessity. Without it we could never have fulfilled the quota, we'd have disgraced ourselves, there's no doubt about it. Weren't you the first to clap us on the back because our output was sixteen per cent above the target? As for the houses, don't worry, they'll outlast us all. I've seen worse in Moscow.'
>   'Nothing upsets him,' Lena thought. 'He has one answer to everything – "We'll get by." He's selfish all through.'[2]

Authors, scriptwriters, filmmakers, architects, engineers, designers and interior designers were all brought into the campaign to bring about a cultural breakthrough in favour of private life. Architects drew new buildings, designers created new furniture, and the 'engineers of human souls' encroached on forbidden topics in their writing.

Khrushchev might have had little understanding of modern art, but in his own way he was a considerable radical. He wanted to do away with the system of privilege, to move from the distribution of benefits on the basis of loyalty, to the communist principle of giving to each according to his or her needs. This was no longer an impossible aspiration. It became increasingly rare for people to have to live in their share of an old building. Under Khrushchev, only 5–10% of new accommodation was for communal occupation in large apartments old and new. All the other millions of square metres were new, small apartments, cramped but private. Housing output surged in 1957 to 3 million apartments, peaked in 1959, and fell away slightly thereafter, reaching a plateau at 2.2 million apartments per annum. For the first time in Soviet history, the regime was distributing new housing rather than just dividing up the existing stock.[3]

159

The state did not, however, succeed in deciding the matter based only on need, which would have established a working communist institution. Historian Steven Harris, in a study of the allocation of housing in the Soviet Union based on his work in the Leningrad archives, quotes an executive committee official as saying, 'We can't let it end up that hairdressers are getting housing first, and the workers are left at the end of the queue.'[4] The general waiting list, which anybody who lived in the USSR remembers only too well, was in reality, especially when it came to housing, neither general nor a genuine waiting list.

The state failed to create a national waiting list by taking over all powers to allocate accommodation from enterprises and institutions. Factories and organizations did everything they could to hold on to 'their' stock of housing, because that was their trump card for attracting the best workers. In addition, the transfer of waiting lists from the factories to the soviets involved changes in who got priority, string-pulling and corruption reared their ugly heads, and citizens tended to see the factory lists as having been fair and the government-managed lists as worse. Diverting the blame when housing was not allocated seemed to take up no less time than actually allocating the available accommodation. The outcome was that the government-managed queue proved to be less a pioneering communist institution than a complicated socio-political phenomenon. One had to have earned a place on it through service, patience, begging or, ideally, to have attained such heights in the Soviet hierarchy as to be able to jump the queue completely. Members of the nomenklatura were too important to join the ordinary queue, but even for them there were more exclusive queues. Everybody else's chances were dependent on their position in the Party-state system, the status their profession enjoyed in the social hierarchy, their personal attainments, age, how long they had resided in the city (native Leningrader, native Muscovite, etc.), state awards, criminal record, and so on.

Getting a place on the waiting list or being excluded from it become a crucial barometer of the relationship between an individual and the state. We need to remember that Soviet citizens considered that they had a right to housing. That right became fundamental to how people viewed their citizenship. The hope of obtaining their own square metres of floor space, separate from those of other residents, and thereby acquiring some privacy, made possible some rewriting in the post-Stalin years of the unwritten contract between the state and the citizen.[5]

Fear gradually ceased to be the mortar binding society together, but with it there also disappeared what had been the principal stimulus to working selflessly: mobilization of the population in the face of deadly threats. Of course, the ritual ideological background of the Cold War gave traction to the external threat theme, but it had lost its earlier force. In addition, thanks to Khrushchev, the state renounced terror as an instrument for forcing people to work. A positive incentive was needed, and the promise of privacy in a separate apartment provided it. We need to remember, though, that Soviet society still attained privacy through fear. It was a society born of fear, and it was fear that was behind the longing to have your own little apartment to hide away in.

The totalitarian Soviet state could not completely escape the stratification created by the nomenklatura system of distribution, but it was partly successful in depoliticizing the allocation of housing, that is, in making a start on allocating it according to need rather than proximity to power. The very scale of the distribution made society far more inclusive; as we have said, during the rules of Khrushchev and Brezhnev as many as 140 million citizens moved into new apartments.

Needless to say, the floor space was not distributed evenly or among everyone. Needless to say, the 'parcels' of the Party elite were substantially greater than the average. Nevertheless, overall, bearing in mind the heavily evened-out income differentials compared with incomes in free-market countries, in the 1960s to 1980s Russian society was much more egalitarian than it is today. Estimates based on Soviet and American research in 1991 indicate that the coefficient of variation of per capita living space in the United States was twice that in the USSR. Incidentally, at that time the Gini coefficient, the most commonly used measure of inequality, was considerably higher in the US (0.41) than in the USSR (0.29). We are today, in this respect at least, much closer to each other, with the US on 0.45 and Russia on 0.42.[6]

Jane Zavisca, a US academic, notes that the Russian respondents in her surveys in the mid-2000s spoke of their acquisition of apartments using the passive voice in a context unusual for Americans (but entirely familiar to Russians): 'We were given an apartment,' 'We were allocated an apartment.' Young people often spoke along the same lines when they asked rhetorically, 'Who is going to give us an apartment now?' Despite the significant rise in the indicators of inequality, Zavisca remarks, Russians tend on the whole to regard the ownership of accommodation as a universal right.[7] Echoes of the post-war social contract are thus to be heard to this day.

Only slightly tongue-in-cheek, we can say that the post-war social contract and its gradual implementation over the ensuing decades were that same 'favour from the tsar' (see chapter 7) as the peasants were awaiting in the nineteenth century, except that instead of land what was being distributed now was floor space. Apartments, like the land of the commune, were subject to periodical redistribution: the children in a family grew up and wanted to fly the nest. If possible, the apartment would be exchanged: the son's share in his parents' apartment would be combined with his bride's share in the apartment of her parents, and there was your new taxation unit and new parcel of land. That, of course, was a best case scenario. If the young people did not have an apartment, they had to join the queue and wait for the state to release a new allocation. The tie to the land now took the form of obligatory registration of their place of residence, so the analogy with the state peasants of the past is not all that far-fetched. The tsar, in the guise of the Soviet government, had indeed taken the land from the landlords and priests and given it to the toilers, only in the form of apartments, and not very equally, and with a long historical delay.

Property without the market

The battle between the socialist queue and distribution by the market was long. The emergence of market mechanisms was supposed to finally convert private space from a privilege into an ordinary commodity, while simultaneously making it affordable. Can we tell how successful the transition from state allocation of housing to the free market has been?

For example, if the transition was successful, the link between level of income and living conditions should have increased. This, however, has occurred to only a very limited extent. Yes, most of the residential apartments and houses in Russia are now in private ownership, but the distribution of housing continues in many respects to reflect the Soviet queue: the descendants of the Soviet elite are in possession of the old elite apartments, while the descendants of engineers and intellectuals live in prefabricated apartment blocks.

An unduly low percentage of the population can afford to buy a new apartment, although this proportion was growing steadily up to 2014. A significant part of the market is redistribution by exchange of the existing Soviet housing stock. Zavisca calls this 'property without the market'.

If in Soviet Russia there was a housing shortage for administrative reasons, in post-Soviet Russia there is the same situation, but caused by the market. Certainly, over the past twenty years, it has become possible to live a little more expansively in the world's largest country by area than one could in the USSR. If the average living space for a Soviet citizen was one quarter of that in the US, for post-Soviet citizens the figure is one-third.[8] We need to note that this is due not only to an increase in available square metres of floor space, but also to a reduction in the size of the population. The sense of overcrowding persists.

'In tiny Holland or Venice, apartments are bigger than for the ants in Moscow. From outside you see a tiny house, but inside it is spacious. In Russia, it's the other way round,' comments someone who often has to accommodate a large number of people in a small, ordinary Moscow apartment. This is no exaggeration: the average size of apartments in countries very restricted in area, such as Denmark and the Netherlands, is twice the Russian average. In addition, in both Denmark and the Netherlands there are more apartments per 1,000 people than in Russia.[9]

During the 1980s, Russia's housing stock grew by almost a third, in the turbulent 1990s the growth rate halved, and in the booming 2000s it increased by only 14%. If the growth rate continued at the level of the 2000s, Russia would catch up with the provision of housing in Germany in approximately fifty years' time, and with the US in over 100 years, as Mikhail Dmitriev shows in one of his studies. He notes that the growth of incomes in 2012 had ceased to raise the approval rating of the Russian president precisely because the shortage of housing and its failure to match expectations had moved up to first place in the list of dissatisfactions with the regime.[10]

Apart from the quantity, there is also the quality of housing, which is depressing if we look at the data for the whole country, including rural areas. One house in four in Russia has no sanitation, one in three has no hot water, one in five has no mains water supply (data from Rosstat). In Ingushetia, old and unsafe housing accounts for 21% of the available accommodation, in Tuva and Dagestan the proportion is around 19%, and in Yakutia it is 14%.[11]

There have been two crucial changes affecting affordability of housing in the post-Soviet period. The first is that the ratio of housing prices to citizens' income has seriously worsened compared with the former Soviet Union: the cost of a square metre of accommodation has risen much faster than incomes. Secondly, however, the number of people who can afford to buy a home using their own or borrowed money has increased during the post-Soviet period from 10 to

19%. This is entirely to be expected in a previously non-free-market state.

An important factor is that from the outset Russia chose the US approach to developing the housing market (the consultants were American), which relies on an increased uptake of credit among the population rather than encouraging special savings schemes for home-buying on the European model. Analysts are concerned that a mechanical mirroring of American institutions, especially securitization of mortgage loans, where securities are issued using loans as collateral, may prove a time bomb. A future Russian mortgage crisis could be even more damaging than the one that hit America in 2006–7, because Russia will be in a weaker position than the USA to generate a market recovery.[12]

For the time being, however, this is a matter of theory. Before the financial crisis, Russian citizens flocked to take out loans for the purchase of technology and vehicles, not housing. This only aggravated the problem of overcrowding: there was no room in Soviet-era apartments for all the clothes, household appliances and furniture bought in the fat years. The apartments had been designed for a very different level of consumption.

In 2013, only 27% or so of families were in a position to buy a property using their own savings or a mortgage, of whom less than a quarter each year actually did so. This suggests that market institutions in the housing sector are serving only people in the higher income bracket. The other 73% of the population have no affordable option for improving their housing situation.[13]

That being so, people are increasingly solving the housing problem for themselves, recognizing that the traditional Western route of taking out a mortgage is not open to them. This is a typical response in Russia: many take the resolving of difficulties into their own hands, in healthcare, education, and even security. In the case of housing, this is on a particularly large scale. The proportion of housing being built by individuals for themselves is approaching that provided by professional developers: 30 million square metres per annum against 40 million (data for 2013). In terms of floor space (43% of which is being built by individuals), Russia has returned to the level of the 1940s, although we need to take account of the breakdown by region. There is far more building going on in the southern and eastern regions than to the north and west.[14]

Analysts express the affordability of housing in terms of the number of years a family would have to save up for an apartment, assuming that they lived as frugally as monks and put aside all their money towards that major purchase. For example, for the Affordable Housing project (a project for which Dmitry Medvedev was at one time responsible, before his presidency, and which attempts are made periodically to revive), the Institute of Urban Economics calculated a coefficient of housing affordability. This is the ratio of the average market value of a 54 m² apartment to the average annual income of a family of three. The Russian result in 2015 was 4.3 years.[15]

That seems not too bad, considering that in international reports the housing affordability threshold is judged to be three years. If accommodation in a country 'costs' more than three years, it is considered to be unaffordable.[16] But what is the reality behind those 54 m²? That is only 18 m² per person, below the average even by Russian standards. (In the US, the average housing provision is about 65 m² per person.) Moreover, a family of three is less than is required for reproduction of the population. The coefficient of affordability has been designed to make the task seem feasible and for there to be results that can be reported, but in the end what has resulted is an index of unaffordability of accommodation and extinction of the population.

If we use the World Bank's estimates, housing affordability in Russia in 2009 was seven years. For a family in Moscow the figure is about 6.7 years; for Moscow province and St Petersburg it is 7.2 years; in the Belgorod province and the Perm region it is 5.7 and 5.2 years respectively. Using the same estimates, in the same year accommodation in London 'cost' 4.7 years, in Tokyo – 5.6, in Stockholm – 6, and in Amsterdam – 7.8. Accommodation was 'cheaper' than three years (hence notionally affordable) in, for example, Cleveland, Las Vegas, St Louis, and Houston.[17]

It should not, of course, be forgotten that in many countries, including European countries, where unemployment is rising, housing is becoming less affordable. The wave of protests that swept the 'rich' world in 2011–12 was caused, *inter alia*, by this factor. During the occupation of Wall Street and in demonstrations in Israel and Western Europe, there was constant reference to the high cost of living and unaffordability of housing. Other causes were the financial crisis and price rises in some countries, but experts watching the housing markets in the West begin to sound the alarm when the median price of a house or apartment moves beyond five years.[18]

Of course, all affordability indexes are relative. They are heavily dependent on the variables selected and ignore many relevant details. Let us try to view the issue from a different angle. If we look back to the Soviet era, we see that there too the path to owning accommodation was measured in years: years of service or years of waiting in the queue. My grandfather received his 'parcel of land', a three-room apartment in a prefabricated housing block allotted him by his workplace, after some twenty years of working for a large state organization. Moreover, he had led a perfectly relaxed life (see chapter 1), had no savings at all and, of course, had never heard the word 'mortgage'. He was an electrician. Today's migrant electrician is exactly the same sort of newcomer, the same first-generation Muscovite as my grandfather, but in his wildest dreams cannot aspire to a three-room apartment within the city limits.

To be able to do so, he would need to be a firmly established member of the upper middle class. If he paid $2,000 a month, he could buy it with a mortgage in just about the same twenty years. He might, however, have other ideas. For the same money as he would pay for a three-room apartment in the prefabricated Soviet blocks in Belyaevo, with its rusting infrastructure, its traffic jams and characteristic scenery, he could buy an apartment on the shores of the Mediterranean.

In any country where, as in Russia, human activity is highly concentrated in a few gigantic cities, working people have to face up to an extremely unpleasant succession of choices. Will they put up with a long commute to work and continue their career, or find a lower-paid job closer to home? Will they rent an apartment or buy inferior housing and be as dependent as a serf on a bank for twenty to thirty years? Should they stay in their own country or find a way of moving to another, which might mean working only for the future of their children and burying all ambitions for their own development?

The present-day Russian state seems to have it easier than the Soviet rulers had. It does not need to build houses with its own hands and invent slogans about a radiant future. All it needs to do is create the right conditions for development to be profitable for businesses, and ensure that the resultant apartments are more or less affordable for its citizens. As for the future, the citizens can be left to worry about that for themselves. The citizens, however, are greatly hampered in their plans by the fact that housing, by world standards, is not affordable in Russia, particularly in the larger cities. And the larger the city, the greater the transaction costs in the price per square metre: the cost of the procedures for obtaining permissions, connections to communications, and the corruption levy.

Apartments are overpriced also because square metres of residential accommodation, especially in Moscow, are assets. With the laws and regulations changing every day, there are few other safe investments (it is easier to take a factory off you than an apartment). As a result, everyone with money to invest puts it in apartments. These investors have the support of the state, because its officials are themselves investing in apartments and have a vested interest in seeing prices of residential property rise, albeit that makes it unaffordable for ordinary citizens. These officials have a conflict of interest with the state itself.

On top of all that, the financial markets penalize anyone buying an apartment with sky-high interest rates on loans. Taken together, this all adds up to an extremely high price for a private life and a minimum of domestic comfort.

There is, however, one significant difference between Russia today and the Soviet social system at its best, if we take that to be 1987. (The record building output in that year was beaten only in 2014.) In the 1980s, at the peak of prefabricated housebuilding, accommodation built by individuals was very low, amounting only to about 10% of the total. In the post-Soviet years, its share has increased more than fourfold and it looks set to account for half of all residential newbuild. In 2014, 43% of a total of 80 million square metres were built by private individuals.

This is a ratio last seen in the 1940s and early 1950s before the Soviet government launched its programme of massive residential construction.[19]

The increased scale of post-Soviet residential building, still keeping to the old Soviet mass-production templates, will have one important consequence. Investment in old housing and infrastructure is lagging far behind investment in newbuild. Countless new high-rise buildings on yesterday's waste land are becoming a problem. Further building without increasing investment in roads, mains networks and repair of older blocks will have catastrophic consequences for cities and their inhabitants.[20]

The state's decision to distribute the apartments it occupied to all citizens free of charge was universally welcomed, but it cemented the results of the Soviet hierarchical distribution of accommodation. Superior square metres in the best urban areas became the hereditary property of those who had been successful in Soviet conditions. However, the most run-of-the-mill square metres in prefabricated high-rise blocks in the distant suburbs also became private property. Millions of citizens, now having a certain amount of valuable freehold living space to their names, gained access to a new type of relationship. These relationships required far fewer personal network connections and thereby did not proliferate client-like dependencies, including those on the state. The ability to rent and buy housing created the potential for greater independence. In combination with a willingness to work and earn money, owning residential property helped a whole class of new, independent citizens to take shape, many of whom felt they finally were genuine citizens.

A market without property

If the distribution of apartments was rather like collectivization in reverse, the large-scale privatization campaign was an event commensurable with the 1917 revolution. Unimaginably valuable assets were nationalized by the Bolsheviks, and assets on a similar scale were turned into private property in the 1990s. This process restored, and possibly aggravated, the injustice of the situation immediately before the revolution, and that, as we know, was profoundly resented by society and ultimately led to a social explosion.

The situation in today's Russia is, however, somewhat different. The larger and more important an asset is, the more conditional is the right to own it. The Kremlin has built its relationships with property owners so as to discourage them from attempting to act as independent agents, and to ensure that they are ideally docile tools for carrying out its policies. Businessmen do not have to be asked twice to invest in projects the Kremlin favours, to finance election campaigns, to buy up media resources the Kremlin considers it needs to be able to control. 'Contrary to the expectations and dogmas of western political science, big property in post-Soviet Russia has become the tool of an authoritarian regime in its struggle against liberal principles, and in no way a bastion of democracy,' sociologists Vladimir Shlyapentokh and Anna Arutyunyan write in their severe analysis of the situation of big private property in Russia.[21]

It is entirely legitimate to compare these relations with those of feudalism. The fate of major assets often depends on the will of the supreme 'feudal lords'. There are, however, some subtleties. Russian companies have had good reason throughout the post-Soviet period to register themselves abroad. If what we are looking at is feudalism, it has capitalist insurance, but more on that below.

There is no doubt that the acquisition of major assets, and the main threats of losing property, go back to the state. The state, in asserting its claim to the status of ultimate owner, is reliant on widespread public support, and goes to considerable lengths to further strengthen that. Nevertheless, the lack of legitimate property ownership may ultimately damage the stability of the state itself.[22]

The possibility of a new redistribution is never far away, as every entrepreneur and owner well knows. It would come as a surprise to many capitalists in other countries to learn that the source of the threat to business in the 2000s was often the state itself rather than traditional organized crime. 'The real business climate in Russia is formed by perpetrators of illegal takeovers, policemen and judges,' wrote entrepreneur Jana Yakovleva, herself a victim of trumped up charges, who managed to defend herself and create a public society to protect businesses from 'law-enforcement' business predators.[23]

The tragic saga of lawyer Sergey Magnitsky became emblematic. Magnitsky disentangled an elaborate scheme that enabled criminals with accomplices in very senior official positions to steal 5.4 billion rubles from the Russian state budget. Magnitsky thought his work would be appreciated by the state, but instead it took a very different interest in him from what might have been expected. The lawyer was arrested on a charge of tax evasion and held in pre-trial detention for eleven months. In November 2011, he was murdered in prison at the age of thirty-seven.[24]

> Business is more afraid of its own beloved state than of the economic crisis and all its competitors combined. And how could it not be, when what is defined in the Criminal Code as 'causing harm in matters with an economic orientation' is applied against someone whose only crime is to have been in receipt of revenues, and the penalties are such that businessmen can be (and are!) found guilty and sentenced to periods longer than those received by murderers?

These words were written in 2011 by Vladimir Radchenko, the retired first deputy chairman of the Supreme Court, who concluded, 'Continuation of the present criminal law policy brings Russia ever closer to the point of no return: no return to a country run in the interests of its population and of capital.'[25]

Even members of the regime at one time acknowledged that the 'business climate' created in the country was driving people and money out of Russia. The former chairman of the Supreme Arbitration Court, Anton Ivanov, gives an example. There is a building in the centre of Moscow. It was bought fifteen years ago for 1 million rubles. Now it is for sale at 1 billion rubles. According to Russian accounting rules, the difference of 999 million rubles is subject to corporation tax and VAT. That means a total of 38% of that amount, almost 380 million rubles, is payable to the state. Now, if this building belonged to an offshore company and was bought by another offshore company (as does in fact happen), the Russian tax authorities would not even hear about the transaction, let alone get paid the tax. 'You will agree there is something ridiculous about two offshore companies in Cyprus going to court in a dispute about a barber's shop in Moscow. That's the kind of thing we found ourselves dealing with,' said the former chairman of the Arbitration Court.[26] Ridiculous or not, since that interview one or two variables in the equation have changed: offshore property remains, just as it was, a feature of how business is conducted in Russia, but the Supreme Arbitration Court has been abolished and the arbitration courts in general have been lumped into the hierarchy of courts of general jurisdiction.

In Russia today, some three-quarters of industrial output is produced in enterprises which do not officially have Russian owners. They are controlled by their real owners through a chain of companies registered in countries with arrangements that are convenient for those doing business. Capital from offshore companies makes up the lion's share of foreign investments coming into Russia. This is capital of Russian businessmen doing business under foreign jurisdictions, but money flows out of Russia at an even greater rate and in greater volume. Long before the beginnings of the political and economic conflict with the West, Russian businessmen were investing more money abroad than they were returning to their homeland.[27]

It is important to make clear that neither the use of offshore companies nor the expatriation of funds are exclusively Russian problems. Offshore business is global and its services are used by companies and private individuals around the world. Russia, however, is a new and growing economy that desperately needs capital if it is to develop. Our economy is being conducted as if it were an 'old' economy that no longer has a need for money. In recent years, Russia has been the only economy among the countries of the informal BRICS Club, consisting of Brazil, Russia, India, China and South Africa, that has invested more abroad than it has received in foreign investment.[28]

Because the administration of justice in Russia is manipulated, and violent crime can be bought in the marketplace, Russian capital effectively rents the institutions of other countries: it keeps its valuables there and resolves its disputes in foreign courts. This is creating the conditions for supporting a privileged 'elite' divorced from the rest of the country, an elite with its own morality, its own duplicitous ideology and its own set of laws separate from those of the rest of Russian society.

The presence of such a semi-alien elite is a problem not only for Russia. Economists seeking to understand why some countries are better off than others believe that what matters is the rules in accordance with which economics and politics operate (see chapter 5). The elites in countries where economically damaging institutions are present use the coercive powers of the state to accumulate fortunes, redistribute property and create entry barriers for those considered to be outsiders. Such a state ceases to be the ally of society and becomes an instrument for protecting the privileges of the elite. As study of many historical situations has shown, this mechanism is capable of replicating itself even after a change of political regime.[29]

That is what happened in Russia. Despite the fact that more than twenty years have passed since the Soviet system collapsed, Russia feels like a half-completed building site. The markets and market prices are there, but separation of powers, an independent judiciary, independent regulation and the ability to have fair competition laws against monopolies enforced are nowhere to be seen. Of course, it could be argued that this is simply because the reforms are not yet complete.

But it can also be regarded as the finished project. The apparatus of repression passed, virtually unreformed, into the hands of post-Soviet governments, since none of the groups that found themselves in power in the post-Soviet years wanted to give it up. They always needed the security agencies, just as they are, in order to surround themselves with protection.

The secret police and Interior Ministry hindered the establishment in Russia of modern institutions to protect citizens' rights, but the federal government always baulked at reforming them. They feared that, if there was a thoroughgoing changeover of personnel, a curtailing of their powers and an introduction of modern mechanisms for ensuring accountability, the security forces would turn against the Kremlin. Without the security 'specialists' to rely on, the Kremlin was afraid to undertake a root-and-branch modernization. On the other hand, while continuing to rely on the archaic post-Soviet security agencies, it is impossible to carry through a genuine modernization, because the carte blanche given to them makes it impossible to safeguard civil rights, including the right to own property. It is a vicious circle.

The task, then, which it has proved impossible to accomplish either overnight or over many years, is to establish clear rules in the economy and politics that apply to everyone. The Soviet Wonderland we talked about at the very outset (see chapter 1) has turned out to be a tough nut to crack. The legislative aspect of development – the rule of law, including the rights to liberty, property and adequate representation of interests – was excluded by the Communists from their take on modernization. This lack of an entire hemisphere in the social order was not rectified simply by pressing the button of privatization. The social edifice was left only half built.

—11—

TWO OPTIONS: FINISH BUILDING THE HOME, OR EMIGRATE

Property without property rights

Not everybody agrees that the Russian social edifice has been left half built. For many, it is a wholly finished project. The disagreement between those who believe the building has barely started and those who believe all that is needed is a few cosmetic repairs is deep and fundamental. What has, in fact, been left unfinished? A political scientist would say that liberalization of the regime was not accompanied by its democratization. The liberator was not succeeded by a builder of democratic institutions, with the result that the process of transition got stuck halfway. That page of history cannot be seen as having been written nor can the edifice be seen as stable: 'The halfway house does not stand.'[1]

Russia's official ideologists naturally reject this idea as hostile. It is difficult to find a concept more discredited in Russia than 'democratization'. The officially accepted view is that Russia's halfway house is entirely finished right now and that the country has no need whatever of further democratization, especially in accordance with some foreign blueprint. Modern authoritarian systems, Ivan Krastev believes, are in no hurry to transition to anything and are perfectly content to remain in a grey zone between democracy and authoritarianism.[2]

The rulers of autocracies may feel content, but most such systems, as we see from periodical outbreaks of social unrest, are nevertheless unstable, as is the Russian political system. Was it the expectation in the case of Russia that liberalization would lead to democratization? Of course it was. The trouble was, however, that the transition to a more inclusive form of government was highly disadvantageous, even downright dangerous, to the new elite and was, accordingly, put on the back burner.

The authors of the reforms, for whom market liberalization and privatization were a key element, saw their task as being to 'depoliticize' the economy, and by politicization they meant something we have encountered more than once: placing a higher priority on retaining power than promoting development.

In the Soviet Union, the top priority for state-owned enterprises was to maintain public order rather than pursue economic advantage. This was what the reformers wanted to change. 'State-owned enterprises are inefficient because they become the means by which the politician achieves his goals. Overstaffing, artificial maintenance of employment in enterprises, placing of factories in economically inappropriate locations, the regulation of prices of industrial output – all this the politician needs in order to get votes in elections or avoid disturbances.'[3]

This situation has not only not become a thing of the past, but is an entirely characteristic feature of the present day. The state continues to be guided by the principle that security is the top priority, this being understood in an extremely literal manner and including the security of the current ruling group. State-owned enterprises continue to be used primarily to preserve social stability and are viewed only secondarily as economic units.

In effect, security policy is pitted against economic development. The right to own 'big' private property (major assets rather than apartments and buildings) in its Russian incarnation has become a lever to support those very relations of domination it was supposed to dismantle. It was just too much to be asked to give up the levers of power.

Whether the transformation of Russian society has been a success or a failure can be seen in terms of the conundrum of the chicken and the egg. On the one hand, to gain the benefits of privatization it is essential to build free-market institutions; on the other hand, as William Megginson, a leading expert on privatization, and economist Sergey Guriev reflect in a joint publication, it is unclear where the support for such reforms is going to come from before a critical mass of property owners has been achieved.[4] We cannot say that there was a demand for fair rules in some countries in transition while in others there was none. It is simply the case that in some countries playing fair was supported by the government and ultimately proved beneficial, while in others it was not.

In the case of Russia, playing fair did not prove beneficial. In the

1980s, when everyone was completely at sea, citizens instinctively rushed to support democratic government, and elections were something everyone recognized as a manifestation of that. This was in many ways perfectly correct. If you have competitive, free and fair elections – 'that institutional arrangement . . . in which individuals acquire the power to decide by means of a competitive struggle for the people's vote', to use Joseph Schumpeter's definition[5] – you have democracy. That terse definition, however, is laying out minimum requirements in a way that is probably sufficient for Western cultures, but is far too little for Russia. It fails to specify elements of the political system without which elections will be merely a tool of the ruling class: guarantees of rights, including the right to freedom of expression, the right to run for elected office, the right to hold meetings; equal access to the media for candidates; universal access to alternative information; and autonomy of political parties and public societies.[6]

Because these elements were not highlighted, the fledgeling Russian democracy worked well for getting people into office, but very inadequately when it was time to get them out. The group that came to power in the early 1990s chose not to relinquish office. There is another classical definition of democracy (which we owe to Adam Przeworski) specifying that democracy is a system under which politicians and parties can lose power as a result of elections.[7] Russia's leaders agreed to come to power by democratic means, but not to relinquish it in the same way.

Vladimir Gelman reminds us that the new Russian regime began sacrificing political reform to economic reform as early as autumn 1991, when it was decided not to introduce election of heads of regional governments throughout the country. Nobody was in any hurry for that. Citizens who had just lost all their savings, their role and status in society, and had witnessed the destruction of their old way of life had other things to worry about. The European Union, established in 1993 and able to stimulate legal reforms in candidates for admission such as Turkey, was not interested in admitting Russia. As for voluntarily introducing institutional reform that would limit its power, the government showed no inclination. Not many governments do.[8]

Boris Yeltsin dissolved the parliament in September 1993, unable or unwilling to continue debating how government should be structured. The revolt by supporters of parliament that followed was crushed. In effect, the current constitution of Russia, adopted by referendum in 1993, represented victory in Yeltsin's struggle to have his hands 'untied'. Its result was the political system which, in the 2000s, it only remained for Vladimir Putin to lick into shape. The fever of battle, habitually used to justify 'emergency' measures, whether to prevent the return of the Communists in the 1990s, to struggle against foreign agents or, as now, with the entire Western world, has remained the foundation underlying Kremlin policy.

The two sides that confronted each other in 1993 in the conflict between the president and parliament failed to find a way to resolve their differences peacefully. Victory for either side would have meant the absence of political accountability for the winner. Institutions that could serve as arbiters and defenders of the interests of sections of society – the courts, political parties and public societies – could have exercised real influence only if the result had been a draw. A draw would have represented a concord betwen two elites, and perhaps given an impetus to the formation of an independent judiciary, because there would have been a need for a referee both sides could trust. The choice in 1993 was not about who was going to win, but about whether an equilibrium, unprecedented in Russia, could emerge: a balance between equal parties. The victory of one side sent us back to something only too familiar in Russian history: a 'balance' between unequal forces.

Democracy without the rule of law

Was what happened in 1993, and later in 1996 (Yeltsin's 'managed' election for a second term), a betrayal of the democratic revolution of the early 1990s? 'The fathers [of today's protesters] betrayed the very revolution they had accomplished,' Vladimir Pastukhov claims. 'They squandered freedom on privatization and thereby chose for modern Russia the fate it deserves.'[9] Values were indeed sacrificed to interests, but they were not so much democratic as legal values. The issue of fair play ceased to be seen as important.

Democracy so stunned the popular imagination, and in particular the imagination of the opponents of reform, that it overshadowed the far more fundamental question of the prerequisites of democracy. The fact of the matter is that, by and large, if there are no rules unambiguously circumscribing its power, a regime will not act in the public interest, irrespective of whether its power is concentrated in the hands of one individual in the form of a president, or of 'the people' in the form of a parliament.

The most important rules are limitations. Who is in a position to limit a regime? Only someone whose rights, the right to property, for example, are safeguarded. That means a right the regime cannot violate: it literally may not cross the threshold of a home, and certainly may not confiscate property. It means a right that is robust enough to cause a politician to lose power. In other words, a politician does not lose power because of an election: elections are merely a procedure. He loses power because he has lost the game and has to step down if the rights of voters are not to be violated. The power of the law, not the power of the election itself, has to be more powerful than the regime.

The changes in the early 1990s that led to 'liberal' becoming a term of abuse in Russia were nothing to do with liberalism. The fundamental value of the founders of liberalism, we recall, was 'the right to life, liberty and property' (see chapter 4). The proponents of privatization focused on the concept of property and assured everyone that the mere emergence of independent property owners would be enough to make the economy competitive and efficient. They lost sight, however, of the legal right to own property, without which there is no such thing as private property.

We need to understand that, on its own, no institution can be a magic remedy for all Russia's ills: neither democracy, the courts, private property or anything else. 'I make bold to state that private property is not the best or most competitive kind,' says economist Alexander Auzan.

> Neither can I say that of any other kind of property, or of communal access to property. Imagine that you have hanging in your wardrobe a fur coat, a morning suit, a pair of jeans and a swimming costume. If you are asked what kind of clothing is best, you will be unable to answer without asking another question: what are you intending to do? If you are intending to swim, I would not recommend wearing the fur coat or you will suffer the sad fate of Ataman Yermak.[10]

In Russian culture, there has been, and is now, private property. Let us not forget how important it is to today's Russians to own their accommodation; renting is not at all popular. The regime, however, is very hostile to the idea of a fully protected right to property. In this the Russian Orthodox Church is its ally, because it too has little time for the law. Sin may not be an offence in legal terms, and acting in accordance with the law could, in theory, be a sin. This mindset does not accept the notion of 'someone else's property': the right to own property independently of the authorities, outside the all-embracing category of 'ours'. Similarly, for our archaic Russian state, private

177

property would be an affront, 'someone else's property' outside 'ours'.

The introduction in Russia of the free market was primarily an economic reform. It was dealt with by economists, people seen, in accordance with the Soviet logic on which administration of the Russian state is still based, as mere technical experts. These experts were required to assemble, in accordance with their instructions, a new economy in which everything worked the way it does in the West. Incorporating the fundamental component of the Western Meccano set, however, the rule of law, was quite simply outside their remit. The reform was their job, but they were powerless to introduce the key political and legal changes that were essential. They were being employed by the government, and everything associated with the law enforcement system and the law courts in Russia has traditionally been the prerogative of the tsar, firmly under the control of whoever was ruling the country. It is an area into which no economist ever has been, or is now, allowed to stray.[11]

There was only ever a theoretical possibility that the market reforms of the 1990s might be successful. An inclusive system of governance, which presupposes accountability of the regime and its subordination to a legal system common to all, is not conferred from above by the will of the ruler. Leaving aside reforms imposed as a result of military occupation, as occurred, for example, in post-war Germany and Japan, we can say that liberal democracy has never been established as the result of carefully considered concessions made by a benign ruler. As we have already seen, it comes about as the result of conflict and bargaining between different groups in a society.[12]

Law enforcement without the rule of law

Russian society has a special relationship with the law enforcement agencies. It is a long time now since they were our superiors, and we have long been citizens without quotation marks. We are supposed to be equal before the law and the constitution promises us the right to a fair trial, but the reality belies these promises. The legacy of a Cheka (secret police) approach to justice, the legacy of 'socialist legality' for which raison d'état took priority over citizens' rights, makes itself felt to the present day.

Undoubtedly, the law enforcement system as it is at present is perfectly well able to perform many of the functions required of it, but it is not an autonomous institution. It is not, because it is used both by the government and by private players to resolve problems in their favour. Sentencing to order, and countless instances of exploitation of the law, especially the criminal law, to get rid of business competitors and gain control of property, make that only too clear.

Why is our law enforcement sector the way it is? The Russian judicial system, imperfect but improved thanks to Alexander II's reforms, was wrecked by the Bolsheviks. Their decree 'Concerning the Courts', dated 22 November (5 December New Style) 1917, replaced the old courts with tribunals and people's courts. When deciding on the criminality or justifiability of actions, they were guided by laws 'only to the extent that these have not been abolished by the revolution and are not contrary to the revolutionary conscience and revolutionary sense of what is right'. All laws contrary to the decrees and programmes of the Social Democrats and Socialist Revolutionaries were rescinded. The legal profession, criminal investigation department and public prosecution service were abolished, while the police had already been shut down by the Provisional Government.[13]

The Soviet secret police, however, demanded the power to arrest and execute anyone suspected of involvement with counter-revolution, without the necessity of observing any formalities. Martin Latsis, deputy chairman of the All-Russia Extraordinary Commission for Combating Counterrevolution and Sabotage (the Cheka), said in 1919, 'The Cheka is not a law court, it is the combat wing of the Party. It annihilates without trial, or removes people from society into concentration camps. What it says is the law.'[14]

The civil war ended, but the Chekists insisted on the continuing need to retain their emergency powers to keep people's thoughts and deeds under surveillance. There should be a file on every intellectual; the Party should be subject to constant purges. The victorious Party saw White Guardists, Mensheviks and traitors everywhere. In the early 1930s, triumvirate 'troikas' were created by the NKVD (People's Commissariat of Internal Affairs), consisting of the head of the local OGPU (Joint State Political Directorate), the chief of police and the head of the investigation department of the Prosecutor's Office, which could put 'socially harmful elements' behind bars extra-judicially. Other troikas consisting of the chief of the GPU (State Political Directorate), the secretary of the provincial Party committee and the public prosecutor took decisions on expelling 'kulaks', enterprising peasants and their families, to remote areas. Then, in June 1933, a new USSR Prosecutor's Office, independent of the People's Commissariat of Justice, was set up. This combined four functions: investigating crimes; supervising the investigation; supporting the prosecution in court; and supervising the implementation of laws by government agencies. This Stalinist institution was partially dismantled only a few years ago, with the separation of the Investigative Committee from the Prosecutor's Office. As a result, one super-department was split into two departments, which proceeded to conduct a power struggle, although both remained tools of the system.

In parallel, the government expanded the categories of potential criminals and increased the severity of penalties: on 7 August 1932, during the period of a deliberately provoked famine in Ukraine, the Central Executive Committee of the USSR issued a law 'Concerning protection of the property of state enterprises, collective farms and cooperatives and strengthening socialist public ownership'. It was popularly renamed The Five Ears of Corn Law, under which hungry peasants could, for helping themselves to a few ears of corn or potatoes from the fields of a collective farm, be sentenced to death or (if there were extenuating circumstances) to ten years' imprisonment.

In 1937 the Central Committee of the CPSU (b) (Communist Party of the Soviet Union [Bolsheviks]) sanctioned the use of 'physical methods of inducement', i.e., torture, against those accused of crimes against the state. In January 1939 Stalin wrote, 'The Central Committee of the CPSU (b) considers that the method of physical inducement should unquestionably continue to be used, in exceptional cases, in respect of manifest enemies of the people as a wholly correct and expedient method.'[15]

The most serious attempt to 'regularize' the area of law enforcement was, and continues to be, implementation of the so-called 'three strokes' system. This has three basic criteria: quantitative measures (i.e., the number of offences committed, solved or prevented); whether these figures are expected to rise or fall; and how important they are judged to be by a particular law enforcement section.[16] The description sounds perfectly neutral, just a standard sort of reporting system, but the reality is that this is not mere reporting but a quota to be fulfilled. The existence of a 'plan for crime' forces those enforcing the law to conceal or generate crimes because the quantitative measures (the 'strokes') are the main criterion for evaluating their work and deciding whether they should be rewarded or disciplined.

Even the Soviet authorities understood that this approach was deeply flawed. Central Committee directives on the functioning of the police from the 1950s to the 1980s identified the same faults with deplorable regularity: numerous arbitrary arrests, with beating and torture of detainees. The police beat the detainees in order to fulfil their quota of crimes solved.

In post-Soviet Russia, there were, officially, changes to the rules under which the law and order agencies operated. Their functioning is now regulated by laws that proclaim the supremacy of the constitution and the safeguarding of citizens' rights. The Soviet practice of a plan for crime continues, however. In the new circumstances, it remains indispensable because, as Vadim Volkov explains, it tacitly performs the important function of introducing at least minimal discipline among the upholders of the law by associating their private motivations with the formal aims of the administrative apparatus of the state that provides them with resources and authority.[17]

The notion of a plan for crime only seems absurd. If we take the straightforward example of the traffic police, we find that, under the plan, inspectors are issued with standard report forms. They are obliged to report a certain number of violations of each type. What would happen if there was no such plan? The inspectors would not waste their time filling in forms and imposing fines on behalf of the state treasury: they would put the fines straight into their own pockets. Under the present system, they have first to do a minimum amount of work on behalf of the state, and only after that help themselves to bribes. The same principle applies to investigators and the rest of the staff in the system.[18]

At the present time, in terms of the number of those convicted and sentenced to imprisonment, Russia is level pegging with the Soviet Union in the first half of the 1960s, despite the fact that its population has fallen by one-third since then. The increase in inmates of the prison camps in the 1990s to one million can be attributed to the increased crime rate, the imperfections of a Criminal Code that failed to keep up with a changed social and political system, and severity on the part of administrators of justice keen to deter other potential offenders. Even today, however, almost twice as many people are convicted in Russia each year as were sentenced in the RSFSR (Russian Soviet Federative Socialist Republic).[19]

Since July 2002, pre-trial imprisonment has been possible only with a court order. The Criminal Procedure Code and the Law on the Legal Profession prescribe that an arrested person should be given access to a lawyer as swiftly as possible. In December 2003, criminal liability was removed for minor offences. Despite these positive developments, however, the justice system remains predominantly 'prosecution-led'.

What is fundamentally important here is not even the fact that the courts almost invariably convict: the judges, too, are accountable. They, too, are under an obligation to prevent malfunctions, and a higher court acquitting a defendant or quashing a sentence is seen as a malfunction. That is the reason why the real decision about the guilt of an accused person and the real weighing of evidence against him or her takes place before a criminal case is even opened. What the judge gets is cases that are already 'sound'. An unjust justice system is guaranteed by the fact that a person's guilt is determined at the pre-trial stage, when those working in the legal system bear minimal responsibility for their actions and the rights of the suspect are still without safeguards.[20]

A further significant factor, both before and during a trial, is that the resources available to the defence bear no comparison with those of the prosecution. The case file that will be considered by the court has been compiled primarily by the investigator. The collection of evidence by the prosecution is regulated by 103 articles of the Russian Criminal Code, while that of the defence rates only three. A defence lawyer, unlike the investigator, has no right to bring forward expert testimony or to add evidence of the defendant's innocence to the case file. He or she can only apply to do so to the court and the investigation, which can perfectly well refuse. Appealing against such a refusal is a complex and time-consuming business.

The view inherited from our history that 'the security agencies never make mistakes' is typically held not only by investigators and policemen. More than a third of the judges in Russia are ex-prosecutors or ex-policemen: they have passed the qualifying examination but are not free from the inevitable taint of their previous employment. Often they are not interested in considering cases impartially, but continue to see themselves as part of 'the struggle against criminality'. Finally, in the present day, investigators and judges have woken up to the fact that the personal liberty of the accused and the fact that he may have private property at his disposal represent highly liquid commodities in the market for their services.

The reform of the Soviet criminal law institutions has amounted to no more than their adapting themselves to life under market conditions. The defunct ideological and administrative aspects have been replaced by the mechanism of corruption. Officials in the security ministries and judges have partially monetized their powers, and for the most part continue to perform them as if fulfilling the Plan. Moreover, all the law and order institutions remain, exactly as before, 'tsarist', in that they answer only to the president. In this respect they are of one flesh with the Federal Security Bureau, the Federal Protection Service, the Federal Drug Control Service and other security organizations.

The teams in power in Russia, whether reform-minded or conservative, and no matter what they introduced, were keen to retain

182

hands-on control of the country's political and economic processes by retaining control of 'tsarist' ministries and departments. The post-Soviet regimes were eager to keep the institutions of 'extraordinary' coercion in precisely the form in which they had existed under communism: as the 'combat wing of the Party'; as a system for surveillance and repression rather than law enforcement. The Party did not survive, but its combat wing with all its methods of operation did. After the collapse of the USSR, with the Communist Party no longer there to exercise control over them, the security agencies turned into mercenaries and pedlars of 'state' law enforcement.[21]

The government has a lot on its plate: it needs to safeguard property, to establish a taxation system and resolve a variety of administrative problems. Even if we imagine plucking from somewhere the most competent government in the world, it would have to work while sitting at the same table as a tyrannosaur, an unpredictable predator from a different age. On the one hand there will be the laws and regulations, and on the other the 'combat wing', for which all these rules count for nothing. Any political action by the government is *a priori* going to be lame and lopsided.

The open door

Living in a half-built home, a house in which the residents have no guaranteed rights, leads to a situation where people live there only if they can't move anywhere else. Those who can, do. This is a very odd situation and leads to an inexorably self-fulfilling prophecy: we decide there is no future in this place, so we make no attempt to plan our future here; but if we do not plan our future here, there really will be no future.

The task of finishing the building of our home is evidently thought to be such a daunting and long-term project that a substantial proportion of the Russian population is considering emigration.[22] This should not be taken too literally: not 10%, let alone 20%, of the population have or ever will have any prospect of emigrating. The reality is that only a few individuals can actually do it. For most, talk of emigrating is a mixture of the memory in our culture of emigration as it was in the Soviet period, and of dissatisfaction with the quality of life in present-day Russia. But how people think affects what they do, and their surrounding reality is constantly presenting them with new evidence that this is a country without a future.

Even more significant, as a clear signal, is the fact that that the very players who benefit from the current unfinished building works, the lawlessness and lack of consistent rules, are themselves evacuating their families and their own wealth (see the previous chapter). Their behaviour, quite apart from indicating that they have no faith in Russia's future, testifies to a belief that Russian history is fated constantly to repeat itself. In this myth, civic protests by citizens are usually followed by a period of reaction, after which there is a revolution. This may be why the apparent triumph of the political system in the wake of the 2011–12 protests, after all the arrests and the succession of repressive laws, fooled none of the insiders. Capital flight did not stop, but accelerated, because people anticipated that reaction is followed by revolution. When? There is no knowing, but it will surely come: such is the logic of the rutted cart track. The huge sums of money traversing borders and the queue for investment visas to the United Kingdom reflect a very particular reading of Russian history.

An unspoken belief that another nullification is imminent and inevitable (see chapter 1) will always prove a self-fulfilling prophecy. The belief has similarities with the imaginings of sectarians convinced that the end of the world is nigh, who divest themselves of all their worldly possessions and prepare not for an ordinary, earthly future but for their encounter with the Saviour.

In the years preceding the new, harshly anti-Western course adopted by the Kremlin in 2012–14, the traditional Russian pattern of emigration and its political dimension was turned upside down. 'Russia's abroad', an active and politicized section of the émigré community, had long ceased to exist in its old sense. Active civil and political campaigning inside Russia made much better sense.

Business emigrated almost in its entirety. For years assets were registered abroad, business was conducted under the jurisdiction of other countries, and all substantial property owners without exception obtained foreign residence permits.

The families of many officials also emigrated, which confused the situation rather comically. Into the same European cities where once revolutionaries and fugitives from the Soviet regime had lived there now settled the families of Russian governors. On the promenade in Nice, gubernatorial children bumped into the children of tax officials, judicial investigators and the developers of never-built roads. Before the 1917 revolution, books would be secretly smuggled into Russia. In Soviet times, books were smuggled in and manuscripts were smuggled out. Now all that is smuggled in and out is money.[23]

Herzen some 150 years ago pulled off an ingenious wheeze to get part at least of his fortune out of Russia and into Europe (see chapter

8). In the post-Soviet years, thousands of Herzens had, and still have, a whole industry working on their behalf. Officials and security bosses with their estates and enterprises have become caricatures of the fugitives of the past. They have fled from a country in which they call themselves the elite.

In the post-Soviet years, some elements of the liberty before the advent of the Moscow state came back to life. That was the liberty that allowed the boyars to retain the rights to their patrimonies even if they ceased to serve the grand prince.

The only difference was that in the 2000s the 'fiefdoms' had been shifted beyond the borders of the Russian state to where there was a functioning right of property ownership and the majority of citizens were equal before the law.

The economist Albert Hirschman introduced the concepts of 'exit', 'voice' and 'loyalty' into economic and political discourse.[24] Hirschman proposed that the relationship between companies and clients, or between states and citizens, should be viewed from the perspective of these three options: if you are dissatisfied with a product, or disagree with a policy, you can stop buying it, or emigrate (exit); alternatively you can protest (voice). If you are content, or have no ability to mount opposition, your only choice is loyalty. One of Hirschman's conclusions that has relevance for us is his answer to the question of why a poorly governed state may be able to remain poorly governed despite the existence of an alternative. In the case of the state, an alternative is not always a source of competitive pressure. People able to afford to stop using, say, the Russian railway system can drive their own car, or even leave the country entirely and use the railways in France or Spain, but not everybody has that choice. Ivan Krastev believes that precisely this was behind the stability of the regime in Russia in the period before the fiercely anti-Western change of policy in 2013–14. 'The paradox is that the opening of borders, offering the opportunity to live and work abroad, led to a falling off of reformist political campaigning,' he writes.

> Those who were most likely to be offended by the low quality of government in Russia are the very people most likely to be willing and able to emigrate. It was easier for them to emigrate from Russia than attempt to reform it. Why try to turn Russia into Germany, for which a single lifetime might not be enough, when Germany is in any case only a few hours' flying time away?[25]

This is a situation unique in Russian history. In the past, few Russian citizens had any choice between loyalty, exit or voice. There were moments, such as under Stalin, when there was no exit or voice. For many, the choice was between loyalty and non-existence: professional, civil and possibly starkly physical. In Russian history, the choice has generally been only between loyalty and exit. Of course, that has not been the same for everyone. The top echelon of the nobility and the Soviet elite did have a choice, but only a few individuals were ever in that situation.

Least common were opportunities to make your voice heard, but Russians became very adept at exiting. Russian history contains one of the world's greatest collections of exits, departures, disappearances and escapes of every description. There have been major political sensations, like the flight of Prince Andrey Kurbsky during the reign of Ivan the Terrible, the emigration of Alexander Herzen under Nicholas I, and the defection of Rudolf Nureyev from the Soviet Union under Khrushchev. There have been an enormous number of low-profile episodes of escape, emigration, defection of little-known people who are now no more than statistics. Most importantly, in every age there have been discreet 'exits' that never made it into the newspapers or statistics.

Historically, exit has been the Russian path to freedom (we recall the great importance of moving on for the peasants, see chapter 7). The refusal to work in areas in which politicians were taking too much interest, to work in politics at all, the retreat into physical labour, into silence, into oneself, into religion – it is the oldest path and one that millions of Russians have travelled.

Property ownership in Russian culture, unlike in Anglo-American culture, has not historically been tantamount to freedom, and has even been its antithesis, because the right to own was conferred from above and included the right of one class to own another. This is why it has proved so difficult to introduce the rule of law. Consolidating one person's right to own anything seen as valuable has been and will be perceived as consolidating an injustice.

Choosing 'loyalty' is more unforgiving. Those most loyal under the tsars, Communist Party general secretaries, and presidents have been granted access to the exploitation of resources (natural, budgetary or human), usually in the form of a tenure hedged by conditions, but have had to pay for it by compromises with their conscience, by willingness to trample over those closest to them and their colleagues. 'Loyalty' has also demanded human sacrifices in the form of denunciations. Another price paid for 'loyalty' is complete deprivation of 'voice'.

An exception to this were the wealthy nobles in the last century or so of the reign of the Romanov dynasty. Opportunities for self-expression, to make their voices heard – even to the extent of open criticism of the regime (in the second half of the nineteenth century) – became increasingly available and did not entail any loss of access to resources, as we considered in detail in chapter 8. Under the Soviet regime, and even in the post-Soviet period, relations between the monarch and the elite were, in this sense, pre-Catherinian.

In the 2000s, access to resources again came to require unquestioning loyalty, and any attempt to speak out against the regime once more incurred loss of favour. Of course, in the post-Soviet period this restriction typically extends only to a select circle of oligarchs close to the president. Loyalty is ensured not so much by violence as by creating dependency on the source of all benefits and the opportunity to make money. This ancient dispensation applies only to a very few, although it is entirely possible that the principle will be systematically extended. Where it applies, it does so in the fullness of its ancient potency: any attempt to acquire a voice can lead to revocation of the licence to be fed by the hand of the ruler. The opportunity to speak out in public, to own assets and have access to resources, remains conditional. These are not absolute rights but require compliance with the unwritten rules of loyalty to the regime.

The wheel has come full circle. The new Russia tried to throw off dependency and privileges as a relic of the past but has come back to them. Once more the most effective way to prosper economically inside Russia is not to focus on your rights, on profit or independence, but to seek access to privileges. This is an extraordinarily stable constant, but there are, or at least were in 2014, countless new exit opportunities. You can do something else, moving from one city to another, or from one country to another, because the state border is open. For freedom of movement to be available to so many people is unprecedented in Russian history. It is as if every day is St George's Day, when the peasants could move away from their current master.

It is worth noting, nevertheless, that, according to official figures, the number of citizens leaving Russia is falling rather than rising year by year. According to Rosstat, there were just under 100,000 in 2003, and only 33,500 in 2010.[26] These figures tell only part of the story, however, because many Russians who receive a residence permit to live outside Russia keep their Russian passports and are constantly moving between their countries. The statistics, naturally, also tell us nothing about the quality of today's émigrés.

Vladislav Inozemtsev suggests that people living abroad but with Russian connections should not be viewed as an undifferentiated

187

mass but as Russian World I and Russian World II. Russian World I are people who, for the most part, have chosen to live abroad and are beginning to integrate socially into the countries where they find themselves. Russian World II are those who, for the most part, have been unable to leave the new states formed after the breakup of the USSR and have become 'professional Russians' with no wish to integrate into a new life. There are tens and hundreds of thousands of members of Russian World I in Vienna, Berlin, London, Paris and New York. They have highly paid jobs (in the US the average salary of such 'Russians' is 39% above the national average). They are highly educated (in the US there are over 6,000 'Russian' college professors and not fewer than 4,000 in Europe). They control and manage US and European assets worth more than $1 trillion. To all intents and purposes, Inozemtsev comments, Russian World I has created outside Russia an economy and intellectual community entirely commensurable with that in Russia itself.[27]

Looking at the situation in the early 1990s, one might have imagined that the desire for independence to which property gives rise should prove a decisive factor in the new, post-Soviet Russia. In respect of opportunities for the individual, Russian society is indeed freer today than ever. But freedom can be built on a variety of foundations.

Freedom can be founded on a strong bond with the land and a confidence in the future based on rules everybody understands and observes. Freedom can, however, also be based on the lack of a strong bond with the land and the country. Life can be lived in the full awareness that the rules are ambiguous, and with a constant readiness to move on (always assuming that the option of exit is really there), and that is also freedom. To this day the latter situation remains our case: we have the freedom to move on, or to emigrate, or simply to refuse to make any investment in the future.

It was precisely that freedom to exit that the regime was beginning to chip away at in 2012–14 (as this book was being written). Laws have been passed placing restrictions on the property that state officials may own abroad and on their ability to deposit money in foreign bank accounts. There is a new law requiring citizens to declare to the migration service whether they hold a second citizenship or permit to reside in another country; and there are secret rules restricting the right of members of the security ministries and sections of other state organizations to travel abroad. Rules requiring Russian citizens to declare the existence of accounts in foreign banks to the authorities, and to make regular disclosure of statements of these accounts, were introduced in 2015 and 2016.

This may signify that a major political decision has been taken to remove the option of safeguarding property abroad. That decision, supplemented and consolidated by pronouncements about restoring traditional values, may be reflecting an intention to close the borders, thereby removing the previously available option of using foreign institutions to safeguard property rights.

Let us not forget, however, that the traditional Russian freedom to exit is one of the crucial guarantees of the stability of the political system as it has emerged in post-Soviet Russia. The open door is a solution to the problem of the political halfway house we talked about at the beginning of this chapter. What really matters is not so much how many people can slip out of a fenced-in territory and emigrate. It is not so much whether they are leaving temporarily or emigrating permanently. What is crucial is that society knows that this possibility exists, like St George's Day for the peasants in the past.

The open door, or, if you like, the gate in the fence, is a safety valve that allows out the most active, the most discontented, and anyone who needs high-quality services, educational, medical, legal, and so on.

The open door is the solution to the institutional problem. We talked above about the fact that, because the judicial system is open to manipulation in Russia, capital hires institutions in other countries: this safeguards its valuables, the right to bequeath them to heirs, and provides a mechanism for resolving conflicts in a law court if need be. Conditional, unprotected property in Russia is possible only because those who currently 'own' it have been able to secure a double indemnity for their wealth: unwritten guarantees within Russia, and written guarantees backed up by the rule of law abroad.

This dual system, under which physical assets are located in Russia but the property rights to them are guaranteed abroad, has the further aim of decoupling the protection of property rights from the protection of civil and political rights: the one is not to be allowed to provide an avenue to the other. The situation that evolved during the period of the Russian Empire (see chapters 7 and 8) has been replicated using alternative methods in the new Russia.

Thanks to the fact that the legal guarantees of property rights within Russia are a fiction, the political leaders are able to use the assets of 'owners' under their control as a supplementary budget. We should not forget, however, that the second leg of the system, which facilitates these relationships, is situated abroad. It stands firmly on the basis of Western legal institutions.

If it repudiates this prop, the political system really will begin reverting to feudalism, not just metaphorically but in an entirely literal sense. What can be gained by nailing up the gate in the fence, by closing the safety valve and repatriating at least part of the fugitive capital? We can be sure that demands for guarantees of survival and safeguarding of capital within Russia itself will increase. Such guarantees are, however, already in very short supply in a country where they can be given only by one man, who works in the Kremlin. There is, in fact, nothing absolute about even those guarantees, which are neither clear nor unambiguous. An owner may believe his property and liberty are assured only to find that has long ceased to be the case. That his fortunes have changed he will discover only when officials come to visit his company with a search warrant.

The cause might be some minor slip, an infringement of the unwritten rules, or simply that some enemy from the past has risen in favour. One thing, however, is clear: the present guarantees are insufficient to maintain the fragile peace between the holders of major assets. The boyars will inevitably have to rely to an even greater extent than in the past on unofficial ways of resolving their conflicts: on unofficial policing, unofficial courts and unofficial enforcement of their rights. The importance and prices of their unofficial guarantors, the members of the various law enforcement and state security agencies, and possibly of certain of their private-sector competitors, will reach even higher levels. The pressures within the system will inevitably rise.

At this point it will become patently obvious that the building of the home is unfinished. The ruling class will have to choose, either to negotiate as a matter of urgency with the property owners and other active minorities, or to rely solely on the use of force. Whether they resort to one of the older Russian remedies or seek a new way, they will have no choice but to finish building our home. At that moment, the whole history of Russia, with all the attempts by princes, tsars, general secretaries and presidents to find an ideal and permanent solution to the issue of the relationship between the state and private property, will flash before our eyes.

CONCLUSION

Finding the ideal formula for relations between the state and property is a theme that runs through the seemingly very different periods of Russian history. It is a formula that has been sought by tsars, general secretaries of the Communist Party, and post-Soviet leaders.

The relationship between the state and property is a playing field for politics, but relations of a higher order should not be forgotten: those between the state and the individual. Ownership can be understood as ownership of oneself, which makes for a possible approach to the question of how an independent person should be able to live within society and the state. Protecting the rights of the property owner cannot be divorced from protecting civil rights and the right to be independent.

In many countries, the state, property owners and, more broadly, owners of their own lives, free individuals, live in accordance with long traditional rules for coexistence and interaction. When changes are introduced, they are not tectonic shifts. Countries undergoing social transformation often adopt ready-made models for relations between the state and property, choosing rules already in use in cultures close to their own. For example, in the post-Soviet period, Estonia looked to Finland, Poland looked to Germany, and Azerbaijan to Turkey.

Russia is one of those nations that has no one to look to. Relations between the state and property here are changeable and, within the foreseeable planning horizon, unpredictable. This very impermanence is a constant. For how many centuries has the search for the optimal solution been going on? Perhaps that is why the peripeteias in relations between the individual and the state are so acutely sensitive here. When you live in a region of constant seismic activity, it is difficult to plan meetings and travel for the year ahead. In Russia there seem to be no minor problems, only major ones. How are free people to live in this state? What path should they choose in order to retain their self-respect and to provide at least a modicum of domestic comfort for their families? How are they to insure themselves against the next nullification of their personal efforts and savings?

The irony of it all is that life in anticipation of the next earthquake, which everyone in Russia is only too familiar with and which regularly does lead to political earthquakes and the nullification of savings, results from the very cult of stability. Centuries of efforts directed at creating an impregnable and sacrosanct state bring about a new nullification of everything in Russia almost once in every generation. Do we perhaps all want subconsciously to keep starting life from scratch?

The formation of the autocratic Moscow state in the fifteenth to sixteenth centuries was accompanied by a determination to totally subordinate property owners to the grand prince. Ivan the Terrible, the creator of the Muscovite autocracy, was perhaps the most consistent of Russia's rulers, strengthening the state while methodically destroying all centres of autonomy. He crushed the ecclesiastical and secular opposition, annihilated the alternative political systems of Novgorod and Pskov, parried threats from within the dynasty, but, most importantly, made service to the state a condition of owning property. In the second half of the eighteenth century, the regime tried to resolve the issue in exactly the opposite manner, by transferring the land and resources to nobles as their private property. The empire imposed on the nobility the task of 'stewardship' of the peasants, delegating to the upper class the responsibility for managing them, which it could not cope with itself, and thereby consolidating serfdom. This was a gift conferred by a monarch, not a right won by hard bargaining or conflict, and the nobility's new property was not seen as something they had fought for and earned. For the next, final, hundred years of the empire, it was considered appropriate in polite society to deplore private property, both because it was regarded as synonymous with slavery, and because the institution was seen as, in principle, profoundly unjust.

In the twentieth century, the regime again changed its institutional model. The Bolsheviks found a third solution to the problem of private property, quite unlike the solutions of Ivan the Terrible or Catherine the Great: they abolished virtually everything private, leaving only a few personal things and trying to socialize all major property. There was a return under Stalin to Ivan the Terrible's favourite practice of bestowing property in return for service. Orders for apartments in new blocks with turrets and pillars were awarded by the state to those who loyally and 'proximately' served it, as leaders, builders, or representatives abroad of their land at international competitions and film festivals.

It was not long before this property conditional on service began to acquire the characteristics of real property: it could be exchanged, it could be inherited, and, all in all, it could pretty much be regarded as private property. The decision in the early 1990s to transfer ownership of apartments to the citizens occupying them merely formalized the existing state of affairs.

The right to own private property was formally extended (in the case of accommodation people were already occupying) and offered (in the form of investment vouchers) to virtually the entire population. The right of ownership, no matter how vulnerable it was because of the imperfections of the new institutions of the Russian state, was entirely real. It did not, however, prove to be the magic wand that would transform people into citizens and the electorate into the masters of their country.

We can put it like this: Russia became a society of property owners but not an inclusive society of property owners along Western lines. If we consider the minimum set of conditions for forming such a society to be private property, a market economy and the rule of law, Russia clearly did not have the complete set: the third condition was missing, and there were major problems with the second.

The problem was that there were few incentives for these conditions to develop. The post-Soviet 'merchants', with the exception of a few stubborn representatives of that stratum, simply did not put up a fight for the right of property ownership in Russia because, as we have seen, they did not really need it. In the post-Soviet years there reemerged, from the mists of centuries past, elements of the old 'liberty' from before the Moscow state. This had allowed the boyars to retain their rights to fiefdoms even if they ceased to serve the prince. The difference from the ages before Ivan the Terrible is that the post-Soviet 'fiefdoms' were moved outside the borders of the Russian state to where there were effective mechanisms for protecting property rights. Why fight for a right when you can just buy a ticket for a three-hour flight to your property and a legal system that guarantees your rights to it?

But this blessed era of 'hybrid' law, a situation where there are no rules in Russia but you can use the rules of other countries, is becoming a thing of the past. Formal institutions, including the legislature, courts and authorities to enforce observance of the law, are at the very core of Western regimes, which many representatives of the Russian state seek to oppose.

This is not a new issue of present policy but a long-standing and fundamental matter, and it is unlikely Russia will succeed in avoiding tackling it forever. Every country needs continuity, and property ownership is a tried and trusted mechanism for providing it.

Many countries find it difficult to achieve continuity, but Russia is really radical. No form of government has survived in Russia long enough to put down strong roots. For us the rule has been not to preserve links with the past but to trash traditions, people's fortunes and savings (see chapter 1).

Of course, some links survive simply because people tend to pass their skills, knowledge and values on to younger generations, but as a rule these links are personal, individual, kept within the family, rather than social. Russia has families of hereditary musicians, artists, architects, scholars, animal trainers, engineers and doctors. On the level of assets, there is also some continuity of ownership. Among the owners of city apartments, there are not a few children and grandchildren of those who first owned them. Even if these are very modest assets, they are at least providing some experience of the transfer of wealth from one generation to the next.

There are different kinds of continuity in Russia, but there is almost no sign of the one kind most important for the stability of political regimes: continuity of institutions, including the constitution and other basic laws, associations, corporations and political parties. It is the absence of this healthy continuity that makes it possible for 'adverse continuity' to replicate itself.

Russia's regimes have succeeded one another, but the reforms of the pre-revolutionary government, the Soviet experiment and the 'shock therapy' to introduce free-market mechanisms a quarter of a century ago have had no impact on certain constants of Russian life: the peculiarities of the relationship between elite and ruler, or between the private individual and the state. Another constant has been the readiness of successive regimes at any moment to reshuffle the cards and restructure their relationship with property owners and society at large in accordance with some new principle. The inability to provide continuity of ownership, and the social and administrative continuity related to it, has led to the replication again and again in Russia of personalist regimes. This in turn has led to a predominance of emotion in politics, to pseudo-religious messianism, and to a loss of our bond with the land (and the ground beneath our feet).

So it is that today, as work on this book comes to an end, the chances look slim that Russian society will devise a workable scheme of continuity to make possible the peaceful transfer of ownership and power from the first generation of property owners of the post-Soviet republic to the second.

The vast majority of owners and nominal holders of major and medium-sized fortunes in Russia are first-generation owners. In post-Soviet history, there has yet to be a massive transfer of natural resources, manufacturing companies and great conglomerates of assets to a second generation of owners. The status of ownership of big property is at the very heart of Russia's future political agenda.

The transition from a first to a second generation is the first step towards establishing any tradition. The second generation of oligarchs and major property owners will have an opportunity to become Russia's new aristocracy, but for that to happen they will need to ensure sound institutional protection of their rights and privileges, in Russia and not only abroad. In all societies that have undergone a transformation of this kind, the protection of rights was initially a privilege available only to a select few. Pressure from below, the demands of an increasing number of groups of citizens, made it possible over time for this circle of privilege to be expanded. It is a different question whether Russian society will be prepared to accept the existence of such an aristocracy, whether it is prepared to see it return here and take root.

How ironical that, just as Russia has become a nation of property owners, acute problems are appearing in the rest of the world in economies and political systems based over the last 500 years on private ownership. It is only in the last few decades that such societies have begun to reveal doubts about the durability and fairness of their model of development.

The wealthy Western societies that, thanks to their robust protection of property rights, made economic breakthroughs while remaining politically stable are suffering a crisis of deepening inequality. Various alternatives to private property are gaining popularity, various forms of leasing, or joint or alternating use of resources. People are sharing apartments, houses, cars, household appliances and other equipment. It is important to remember, however, that, without the initial institutional framework of protection of individual rights and contractual law, the spread of a new, 'moral' economy would be impossible. The forming of a moral economy is an intriguing area for further research. Another important area is intellectual property, where there are developments analogous to those that affected land ownership 500 years ago.

In the last five centuries, Russia has engaged in a lot of experimentation without arriving at any long-term solution to the issue of property ownership. Today's Russian society has advanced further than any earlier generation towards developing private life. Never before have so many people possessed their own, individual space. Never before has such a huge proportion of the population been free of working for a taskmaster and of marching in line.

We should not forget that, but we need also to understand that, even after we have succeeded in stopping others from interfering in our lives, we will still be members of society.

We may be able to make our interior decor look Japanese, buy a German car and speak English. We may be able to dress so that no one, just from looking us, will be able to tell which culture we were born into. But ultimately we will still need to recognize that we live within the borders of a particular country, because countries differ from each other not in what you can buy there, but in what they have that cannot be bought.

Sometimes we do have to come out of our beloved home, and in the streets we meet our fellow citizens, with whom we are jointly responsible for the environment we live in. All of us together get caught in the traffic jams, resign ourselves to the polluted air, and feel humiliated that for the privilege of enjoying all this we are being fleeced out of ever more money and subjected to efforts to control us more closely.

For no other reason than what is happening in the street, people emigrate. The environment is not dependent on a single person. Abandoning their own country, people buy the environment of a different country. In reality they are paying for things that are the most important product of social development: laws that work, trust between people, hygiene, clean air and security.

A successful individual may not feel the need to emigrate. He or she may move into a gated community, work behind high walls and drive around in a bullet-proof vehicle. Not everyone can afford that. It is expensive because something that ought to be a public good is having to be paid for privately: private air, private safety, private roads. There are people, though, who are prepared to pay because they are being subsidized by the state, through work for the state, through access to resources, through being above the law. That is how the select few in Russia have always lived, the courtiers of the regime who, in the post-Soviet years, it became customary to call, like pedigree cattle, 'elite'.

To earn enough money honestly to afford private air is not a practical proposition, but that is precisely what everybody living in Russia is seeking to do. We are trying to find a place where we can breathe, trying to build a personal healthcare system, to provide private security and private education. Of course, most of us do not have official positions in the state, or epaulettes, or a stake in the oil industry, but we are all trying to do something that is logically impossible: to solve public problems through private efforts. It is like running on the spot, and that is why we get so tired, and spend so much money.

Public development means reducing the price we pay for hygiene, laws and security. When a society rejects development, it must be prepared to build higher and higher fences and pay more and more for a dangerous and unfriendly environment.

The modernization of Russia in the past quarter-century has been undertaken on a private not a public level. Many members of the country's population have become modern human beings, but, taken together, these sophisticated, much-travelled people who are so at home with all the latest technology constitute a wholly archaic social system ruled by a wholly archaic state mechanism.

The separating off of property rights from the right to act independently leads to a system in Russia that allows us to buy a car but does not allow us to 'buy' a functioning road network and freedom from traffic jams. It allows us to put a fence round our home but does not let us ensure we are safe and able to be independent outside it.

EPILOGUE

In Search of Real Ownership

When this book was first published in Russian in 2015, I finished with the thought that Russia would need to build a public sphere and a public environment worthy of the sophistication of its best individuals. The collection of private persons that is today's Russia would need to learn to cooperate better. But learning does not happen overnight and societal changes are slow. The path Russia has taken so far has been to solve public problems by delegating them to the one institution it has been able to consolidate: the state.

I have been very struck by how frequently debate in Russia has focused on the concept of private property since 2015. But it is not the kind of discussion I hoped for. Ownership is often more trouble than it is worth, many people in Russia say these days. Because of the failing economy, a private company or private bank only too often turns into a liability. Privately owned media have continued to lose ground to government-owned or state-run outlets. Even home ownership has proved to be a hindrance as soon as Russia started to tackle the ageing Soviet-built apartment blocks.

The Russian state is expanding, but a return to full state ownership of all major assets is highly unlikely as it would impose an intolerable burden on the government. According to the IMF, some 70% of the country's GDP is already produced by state-owned or state-controlled entities and the government is not happy about it.[1] A sizeable privatization programme is quite likely in the future, but its scope will be limited: legacies of the past and problems of the present collide in Russia to keep the institution of private property under strain in politics, business and even private lives.

Moral hazards of the present

What is striking in Russia is the impermanence of deals and relationships that one would expect to endure. Russia's richest businessmen pledge their readiness to give up their assets, if needed, to the state,[2] but the question mark hovering over the status of their companies is even greater than it seems. The scale of upheaval that regularly follows a change in the Kremlin's occupants means that their pledge is valid only for this particular ruling group. It is not to the crown itself that the oligarchs swear allegiance but to the current wearer of the crown.

As soon as political power changes hands, all the current arrangements will be null and void. The next president and prime minister may renegotiate the terms of 'use' of Russia's largest companies, but they may not. It depends on who they will be and how they come to power. Russia's current political regime has so far failed to evolve clear rules of succession, which is why the level of political uncertainty is so extremely high. Coupled with volatile oil prices and US and European sanctions against Russia, this is a recipe for deep economic malaise. People commanding large assets are simply in the dark about their prospects for the medium- to long-term future. This creates a huge incentive to ensure that all profits accrue to you while losses are borne by the state. There is nothing new about the privatizing of profits and nationalizing of losses, but it does mean that hopes that Russia will move on to fairer relations between large-scale property owners and society have been dashed.

Almost every private bank in Russia is 'too big to fail'. In 2017 alone, Russia's Central Bank and a state-funded foundation specially created to bail out private banks poured more than 1 trillion rubles (US$16.7 billion; £12.7 billion) into three major failing banks: Otkrytie, B&N Bank and Promsvyazbank.[3] There are numerous others. As the prospect of a bailout is almost guaranteed, there is no telling which banks and companies are genuinely failing and which are simply taking advantage of the Kremlin's unwillingness to face the slightest social disturbance, including layoffs and banking crises. Short-term profiteering and moral hazard reign supreme in today's Russia.

Private banks, manufacturing companies, retail outlets, hotels and restaurant chains in Russia are going out of business at a frightening pace. Bankruptcies can be a sign of growing pains, of creative destruction, as it were, but that is not what this looks like. 'During previous crises, new firms were being created to replace those closing down; not so this time,' economist Georgiy Ostapkovich recently told *Vedomosti* daily. 'It is happening across all sectors. Thirty-five per cent more firms are going under than are being replaced, and it is not a lack of funding that most entrepreneurs are citing. Half of them blame the general feeling of uncertainty. They do not know what is going on in the Russian economy.'[4]

Activist investigations of the holdings of Russia's politicians tell us that the wealth they possess is both vast and volatile. The prime minister, Dmitry Medvedev, is a case in point. Alexey Navalny, anti-corruption crusader, recently uncovered palaces, dachas, vineyards and a yacht that had been put at the disposal of Russia's prime minister. Medvedev has the use of these properties but it is impossible to establish any legally provable connection between him and the assets. A lawyer by trade, Medvedev has foxed the campaigning vigilantes by constructing perfect deniability. The ownership is not just difficult but impossible to establish because no owner exists. The paper trail led to a chain of charities that by definition were not profit-making or interest-paying entities.[5]

The charities' managers, currently friendly to the incumbent, are easily replaceable. Most allegations about government officials possessing illegal wealth are thwarted by the fact that any connection between high-ranking players and their real estate and other holdings in Russia is deniable. Those enjoying the use of questionable perks and properties are almost never the people who own them. Why not declare these places official residences or, alternatively, privatize them openly? That is the question, and all the more so when everybody in Russia expects the higher-ups to bask in opulence.

The lack of clear rules of succession is no doubt partly to blame. An opaque, tentative relationship is better suited, given the climate of overall uncertainty. New rulers may come in with an indignant declaration of war against corruption, close down the fake charities and transfer these properties to childcare institutions. Or they may not close them down and instead allow the old players to use them for a fee. Then again, they may take over the amenity of the dachas and vineyards themselves. Temporary possessions conditional on their holders' ability to serve were a feature of Russia in the olden days and when the Soviet Union was at its zenith. The difference from Russia today is that then the rules were clear. A *pomestiye* landholding granted under the seventeenth-century Tsar Alexis or an official dacha under Stalin, while not heritable property, was an asset the ruler's servicemen could use for as long they were able to serve.

These days the rules are considerably less clear. What *is* clear is the incentives this lack of clarity creates. If you are a business person, the incentive is to 'hit and run': siphon off everything you can from your failing business and scoot abroad. If you are an official, the incentive is to keep your property hidden inside the country while securing your rights in other jurisdictions. In Russia, power and property are not separate. To lose power usually means to lose most of the wealth you have accumulated within the country. Those, like myself, who were thinking this was a transitional stage, a step on a path to a more clearly defined regime, are feeling perplexed. The Kremlin still enjoys the provisional nature of its deals with the country's richest and potentially most powerful players. Long-term commitment or a responsible attitude towards owning assets are not the values fostered by the current climate and, unfortunately, it is not only the elites whose relationship with private property is faltering.

The invisible hand of the past

The Soviet past affects Russia's present in numerous ways, but there is one kind of legacy that is literally towering over us. Most Russians still live in prefabricated high-rise blocks arranged in microdistrict schemes, in which buildings do not line streets but are scattered over an open space in a geometrical or asymmetrical manner. Developments of this type cover 70 to 80% of Russia's urban areas. They define the country's cityscapes, determining residents' commutes and generally impacting on their lifestyles.

It is not just dull monotony that is the problem. In fact, some of the better neighbourhoods built in the 1960s or 1970s have become pleasantly overgrown, habitable places loved by their residents. Belyaevo, a group of microdistricts in the southwest of Moscow where I grew up and which is mentioned at the beginning of this book, is just one such neighbourhood. The problem is that more than half the existing housing consists of small one- or two-room apartments devised by Soviet architects and engineers to comply with the rigorously economical norms of the day. More than half the housing existing in Russia and most of the formerly Soviet states was built before 1970. The Soviet government's overarching goal back then was to provide as many people as possible with living space that would represent a marked improvement on the communal apartments and barracks of the Stalin era.

That problem has been solved: the days of communal living are gone. But we are stuck with the solution to a problem that is no longer relevant. Grim-looking factories (DSKs, literally house-building factories) are still churning out reinforced-concrete panels that are used to assemble endless rows of high-rises around the country's major cities. The machine continues to power ahead as if Russia were still a centrally planned economy aiming to provide its citizens with minimal accommodation. The reason the old approach to housing persists is that it has proved easier to monetize the Soviet-created scheme than to come up with anything better suited to the changed economic and social environment. This principle, by the way, is true not only of housing but of many Soviet-heritage institutions, from the law enforcement agencies to Gazprom: they are monetized rather than restructured and rebuilt.

The invisible hand of the past works in ways that are hard to reverse in the absence of strong political direction. Russian cities have inherited hundreds of house-building factories employing millions of people. Authorities need to use this capacity to the full or downsize and face dire social consequences. Every incentive exists for both local and national politicians to keep the market monopolized and the factories running. It helps them both to avoid mass unemployment and to stay – through family or cronies – in highly lucrative business. Most housing construction is controlled by municipal or regional grandees.

This continued industrial production is not just an aesthetic issue. It creates mass housing that is out of date as soon as it is built and will require periodical renovation that municipal authorities in most of Russia's cities, no longer part of a socialist state, are unwilling or unable to provide. They are always interested in the profits to be made from selling homes but have meagre budgets when it comes to maintenance. Despite the fact that the Russian state controls a large part, probably more than half, of the economy, it is far less 'socialist' than those of France or Sweden. In fact, the ageing housing stock built under central planning represents a genuinely difficult problem for the kind of economy, neither socialist nor fully free market, that is today's Russia. A major revamp will be possible only if the authorities see both an imminent social calamity and a money-making opportunity.

Up to 1.6 million Muscovites live in worn-out dwellings that are beyond repair. That was the message delivered by the mayor of Moscow, Sergey Sobyanin, to President Putin during a televised meeting in early 2017.[6] It was an exaggeration, but the kind of rhetoric Moscow's mayor used to draw attention to his 'renovation' initiative. It is not, in fact, a renovation but a major building project that would clear sites of older structures and make use of Moscow's enormous, partly municipally owned construction industry. This industry is involved also in 'renovating' Moscow's central neighbour-hoods, which often means razing detached shops and kiosks, classified as squatter developments, without compensation. The kiosks were considered perfectly legitimate under the previous mayor and most had legal documents confirming their property rights.

Under Sobyanin's plan, up to 4,500 of the five-storey prefabricated apartment blocks built under Khrushchev will be razed and replaced by new housing, at least twice as much in terms of square metres as the project needs to pay for itself: the government of Moscow will sell the excess apartments. The project is already under way. It took the Soviet building industry (which could work fast) about ten years to build that much accommodation, and would probably take longer these days. It will still need an enormous concentration of resources to accomplish anything like it.

The centrally planned nature of the original project affects how it develops in the post-Soviet economy. The sheer scale of the undertaking means that the property rights of those owning the apartments become a hindrance to individual rights rather than a bastion for protecting them. Facing eviction and resettlement, some of the residents of these blocks protested, but the majority agreed to surrender their old apartments in return for similarly small newly built ones. The problem that most of the apartments were owned by their residents, while the land under the buildings was municipal property, was legislated away by the government by extending its powers for dealing with property in ageing buildings. Some of the few protesters appealed to their status as owners, but the new law and the majority of other owners easily prevailed. Hundreds of thousands of Moscow residents have chosen their social rights, the right to be given a new flat, over their individual property rights. They saw relinquishing a right as furthering their interests more than asserting it.

We posited in the book that the quality of the right to own things in Russia differed depending on whether the asset in question was a large company or a small property like an apartment or a corner shop. That distinction still holds but it is being eroded. One can no longer say with certainty that owning a flat or a small drinking establishment is significantly more secure than owning an oil company. Ownership of an oil company is contingent on an informal understanding with the Kremlin; ownership of an apartment or shop is contingent on the municipal government's plans for urban improvement. What they all have in common is dependence not just on the government but on the whim of those currently in office.

Still a halfway house

I do not see all of this as necessarily pointing to an imminent crisis. The picture is not entirely bleak, and may not be bleak at all. What the state of government and societal institutions reveals is that the transition Russia is undergoing is far more complex than many thought twenty-five or even ten years ago. Uncertainty is a sign of the times, but the Kremlin is not solely to blame for that. Russian society itself is uncertain. The recurrent attacks of intense nostalgia for Soviet times should not be mistaken for a desire to turn back the clock. There is little disagreement that the Soviet economic and political model was broken beyond repair; the Russian elites who are often seen as militantly revisionist are not seeking to reinstate a Soviet-style totalitarian regime.

That would mean retaking ownership of the entire country, which is the last thing they want. That would be detrimental to their own rational interests, which certainly include personal prosperity but also international recognition for Russia as a strong player on the world stage. Russia's top leaders are said to be furious at being forced to bail out all those banks whose shareholders are hiding in London. The Kremlin ends up owning an increasing chunk of the economy not because it believes in socialism (the Kremlin's current occupants are right-wing politicians) but because of its fixation on security, which we described in chapter 6. The Russian elites' behaviour – their attempts at technical and technological modernization, their use of Western institutions and jurisdictions, their continued engagement with the West despite the conflict over Ukraine – is an indication of a will to be an independent player in the world, not an enemy to everyone. To say this is not to defend their means, of which I have never approved, but merely to interpret their intentions.

As for society at large, its position is even more complex. It is not that Russians for some reason hate private property and the rule of law. Years of forced collectivism and precarious living under a totalitarian state made us intensely private and deeply concerned with security. To have a house of their own and to live a full life despite the insecurities of the outside world are the dreams of the majority of Russians. The current state of the institution of private property within the framework of Russia's other institutions is, however, fragile and problematic.

In general, small and medium property does bring security, and the court system is sufficiently developed to provide reliable protection in a majority of cases. There are, though, many situations where property does not bring security, and the powerful and the rich can use the courts for their own purposes. Property thus can be seen as a liability. It may attract the attention of a greedy adversary or, more to the point, of a law enforcement officer offering 'protection' in return for a share in your business; it can be used by a dishonest partner to sue you for a non-existent crime and get you out of the way; it can be confiscated by the state. In other words, shying away from property ownership is often a means of eluding the state and its deceitful servants.

I do, nevertheless, believe there are many redeeming aspects to Russia's current state of insecurity and uncertainty. It does, at the very least, provide ample material for citizens of Russia wishing to work on improving it. Many of the issues Russia is struggling with are not unique to this country, which means the experiences we are living through may later be of use to others. The current phase in Russian history started as a transition and that is what it still is. Despite repeated lapses, Russia has left its totalitarian past behind and is not going to return to it. There is little argument about the point of departure: it is the uncertainty of purpose that is so unnerving.

By trial and error, Russian society and the Russian state – often at cross-purposes – are moving towards a distinct property regime and a political model built on that foundation that will be neither 'Western', nor 'Eastern' but their very own. Being responsible for one's nearest and dearest, being a proud part of a prosperous community, owning one's life and ultimately one's country are the goals. The ongoing uncertainty only makes these goals all the clearer.

NOTES

Introduction: The Tragedy of Property

1 Richard Pipes, *Russia under the Old Regime* (New York: Charles Scribner's Sons, 1974); Richard Pipes, *Property and Freedom* (New York: Harvill, 1999).
2 S.L. Frank, 'Sobstvennost i sotsializm', in *Russkaia filosofiia sobstvennosti*, eds K. Isupov and I. Savkin (St Petersburg: 'Ganza', 1993), pp. 311–12.
3 Vladimir Bibikhin, 'Svoe, sobstvennoe', *Voprosy filosofii*, no. 2, 1992 (http://www.bibikhin.ru/svoe_sobstvennoe).

Chapter 1 The Entrance

1 According to the first *General Census of the Population of the Russian Empire*, conducted in 1897, less than 15% of the population living within the present-day borders of Russia were urban. See 'Byla Rossiia sel'skoi – stala gorodskoi', *Demoskop Weekly*, nos 33–4, 10–23 September 2001 (http://demoscope.ru/weekly/033/tema01.php). On the contemporary situation, see 'Vot kakie my, rossiiane: Ob itogakh Vserossiiskoi perepisi naseleniia 2010 goda', *Rossiiskaia gazeta*, 26 December 2011.
2 Rosstat, *Chislennost' naseleniia Rossiiskoi Federatsii po polu i vozrastu na 1 ianvaria 2014 goda* (http://www.gks.ru/bgd/regl/b14_111/Main.htm).
3 Mikhail Heller and Aleksandr Nekrich, *Utopia in Power: The History of the Soviet Union from 1917 to the Present*, tr. Phyllis B. Carlos (New York: Summit, 1986), p. 233.
4 Nicholas Riasanovsky, *Russian Identities: A Historical Survey* (Oxford: Oxford University Press, 2005), p. 216.
5 Ibid., p. 228.
6 From a personal conversation with Vasilii Rudich, Yale University.
7 Gur Ofer, 'The Soviet Growth Record Revisited', paper presented at the ACES–AEA meetings, Boston, 5–8 January 2006. Quoted in Konstantin Sonin, 'Svoi opyt', *Vedomosti*, 9 September 2008.
8 Ibid.

9 Martin Malia, *The Soviet Tragedy: A History of Socialism in Russia, 1917–1991* (New York: Free Press, 1994), p. 15.
10 This does not contradict Martin Malia's view. He saw Russia not as a kind of anti-West but as one of a number of Europes. There is not, and never has been, a single, culturally homogeneous Europe as distinct from Russia. Europe should be studied as a whole series of *Sonderwege*, 'special paths', including the Russian path. See Martin Malia, '*Non possumus*. Réponse à Alain Besançon', *Commentaire*, vol. 3, no. 87, 1999, pp. 615–18 (http://www.cairn.info/revue-commentaire-1999-3-page-615.htm).
11 Maksim Trudoliubov, 'Perevernutyi dvorets ili shkola gibkosti', *Openspace.ru*, 1 June 2011 (http://os.colta.ru/society/russia/details/22789).
12 Vladimir Iuzhakov, 'Kapitalizatsiia pokolenii', *Vedomosti*, 22 August 2011.
13 Ibid.
14 Pavel Sedakov, 'Pamiatnik epokhe: Dvorets podriadchika "Gazproma"', *Forbes*, no. 82, 2010. For further detail on 'Miller's Palace', see chapter 3 below, pp. 39–40.
15 Roman Shleinov, 'Sor iz dvortsa', *Vedomosti*, 29 December 2010.
16 Maksim Trudoliubov, 'Programma Putina v deistvii', *Vedomosti*, 18 February 2011.

Chapter 2 The Fence: Russian Title

1 Mikhail Zenkevich's translation was first published in issue no. 4 of *Internatsional'naia literatura*, 1963, and periodically thereafter, including in Robert Frost, *Iz deviati knig* (Moscow: Izdatel'stvo inostrannoi literatury, 1963). The poem in English can be found at https://www.poetryfoundation.org/poems/44266/mending-wall.
2 Lawrence Raab, 'On "Mending Wall"', in *Touchstone: American Poets on a Favorite Poem*, eds Robert Pack and Jay Parini (Hanover, NH: University Press of New England, 1996) (http://www.english.illinois.edu/maps/poets/a_f/frost/wall.htm).
3 Ibid.
4 The conversation is reported by Franklin D. Reeve, a Slavist who accompanied Frost. F.D. Reeve, *Robert Frost in Russia* (Brookline, MA: Zephyr Press, 2001 [1964]), p. 136.
5 Ibid., p. 143; Stewart L. Udall, 'Robert Frost's Last Adventure', *The New York Times*, 11 June 1972 (http://www.nytimes.com/books/99/04/25/specials/frost-last.html?mcubz=0).
6 Solomon Volkov, *Conversations with Joseph Brodsky* (New York: Free Press, 1998), p. 100.
7 Anatolii Naiman, *Rasskazy o Anne Akhmatovoi* (Moscow: Vagrius, 1999), p. 162.
8 Reeve, *Robert Frost in Russia*.
9 Blair A. Ruble, *St Petersburg's Courtyards and Washington's Alleys* (Washington, DC: Woodrow Wilson International Center for Scholars, 2003).
10 Alexander Etkind, *Internal Colonization: Russia's Imperial Experience* (Cambridge: Polity, 2011), p. 101.

11 Vladimir Papernyi, *Kul'tura Dva* (Moscow: Novoe literaturnoe obozrenie, 2006), p. 75.
12 Maksim Tovkailo, 'Dachnyi nalog', *Vedomosti*, 17 January 2011.
13 Winter King, 'Illegal Settlements and the Impact of Titling Programs', *Harvard International Law Journal*, vol. 44, no. 2, 2003, pp. 433–71.
14 Maksim Trudoliubov, 'Ekonomika – eto ne kul'turnoe iavlenie', *Vedomosti*, 17 September 2007.
15 Ibid.
16 Erica Field and Maximo Torero, 'Do Property Titles Increase Credit Access Among the Urban Poor? Evidence from a Nationwide Titling Program' (March 2006) (https://scholar.harvard.edu/files/field/files/fieldtorerocs.pdf).
17 See the table of the main characteristics of three types of state, personalistic, modern and new, in Maksim Trudoliubov, 'Liniia Medvedeva', *Vedomosti*, 1 October 2010.
18 'Chestnyi nalog: Ot redaktsii', *Vedomosti*, 31 August 2011.
19 Maksim Trudoliubov, 'Zadacha novogo pokoleniia', *Vedomosti*, 2 September 2011.
20 Press release of the RF Ministry of Internal Affairs, 18 November 2010 (http://www.mvd.ru/anounce/8524). On the state of the market for security services in 2003, see a press release of 27 May 2003 (https://мвд.рф/news/637).
21 Materials of the *World Values Survey* (http://www.worldvaluessurvey.org/wvs.jsp).
22 Robert D. Putnam, *Making Democracy Work* (Princeton: Princeton University Press, 1993), p. 177.
23 Maksim Trudoliubov, 'Karta tsennostei', *Vedomosti*, 2 February 2007.
24 Philippe Aghion, Yann Algan, Pierre Cahuc and Andrei Shleifer, 'Regulation and Distrust', *Quarterly Journal of Economics*, August 2010, pp. 1015–48. See also Oleg Tsyvinskii and Sergei Guriev, 'Ratio economica: Lovushka nedoveriia', *Vedomosti*, 9 June 2009.

Chapter 3 Behind the Fence: The Privatization of Utopia

1 Maksim Galkin, 'V svoem dvortse ia budu zhit' vdvoem s Alloi', *Trud7* (Moldova), 25 August 2010 (https://news.rambler.ru/starlife/7369192-maksim-galkin-budet-zhit-v-svoem-dvortse-vdvoem-s-alloy/).
2 Open letter from Sergei Kolesnikov (http://www.anticompromat.org/gorelov/kolesn_pismo.html).
3 Roman Anin, 'Dvortsovaia ploshchad' 740 tysyach kvadratnykh metrov', *Novaia gazeta*, 14 February 2011.
4 Roman Shleinov and Dmitrii Dmitrienko, 'Zakazchikami "dvortsa Putina" vystupali upravdelami i FSO', *Vedomosti*, 14 February 2011.
5 Mariia Dranishnikova, 'Putin bez dvortsa', *Vedomosti*, 2 March 2011.
6 Aleksei Boiarskii et al., 'Taina za sem'iu zaborami', *Kommersant"–Den'gi*, 21 January 2011.
7 Sedakov, 'Pamiatnik epokhe: Dvorets podriadchika "Gazproma"'.
8 See 'Russian Opposition Politician Navalny Links PM Medvedev to Billion Euro Property Empire', *DW*, 2 March 2017 (http://www.dw.com/en/russian-opposition-politician-navalny-links-pm-medvedev-to-billion-euro-

property-empire/a-37787539); or Howard Amos, 'Putin "Holiday Mansion" Revealed by Russian Opposition Leader', *Guardian*, 31 August 2017 (https://www.theguardian.com/world/2017/aug/31/putin-holiday-mansion-revealed-russian-opposition-leader-alexei-navalny).

9 Oleg Deripaska, the owner of the Rusal aluminium corporation, told the *Financial Times* on 13 July 2007 that he did not see himself as separate from the state and would unhesitatingly surrender his assets to it. Vladimir Potanin, the majority owner of the Nornickel corporation, has regularly confirmed that he will not bequeath all his property to his children. Oligarch Gennadii Timchenko said in a 2014 interview with Itar-Tass that he was entirely prepared to make his assets over to the state (http://tass.ru/opinions/top-officials/1353227?page=7).

10 Vladimir Papernyi, 'Muzhchiny, zhenshchiny i zhiloe prostranstvo', in *Zhilishche v Rossii, vek XX: Arkhitektura i sotsial'naia istoriia* (Moscow: Tri kvadrata, 2002).

11 Mark Meerovich, *Nakazanie zhilishchem: Zhilishchnaia politika v SSSR kak sredstvo upravleniia liud'mi* (Moscow: ROSSPEN, 2008), p. 16.

12 Sheila Fitzpatrick, *Everyday Stalinism* (Oxford: Oxford University Press, 1999), p. 47.

13 Benedikt Sarnov, *Nash sovetskii novoiaz: Malen'kaia entsiklopediia real'nogo sotsializma* (Moscow: EKSMO, 2005).

14 Papernyi, *Kul'tura Dva*, pp. 148–9.

15 Thomas More, *A Truly Golden Booklet, No Less Beneficial Than Entertaining, of the Best State of a Republic and of the New Island of Utopia*. '[T]hey make their chamber-pots and close-stools of gold and silver. . . . Of the same metals they likewise make chains and fetters for their slaves. . . . They find pearls on their coasts, and diamonds and carbuncles on their rocks; they do not look after them, but, if they find them by chance, they polish them, and with them they adorn their children, who are delighted with them, and glory in them during their childhood.' The Cassell edition of 1901, ed. Henry Morley and transcribed by David Price, is available from Project Gutenberg (http://www.gutenberg.org/files/2130/2130-h/2130-h.htm).

16 Vladimir Lenin [Ul'ianov], 'O znachenii zolota teper' i posle polnoi pobedy sotsializma', in *Polnoe sobranie sochinenii*, vol. 44 (Moscow: Izdatel'stvo politicheskoi literatury, 1964), p. 225.

17 Jonathan Cheng, 'A Palace of Gold Is Sold Off for Its Melt Value, but Not the Throne', *Wall Street Journal*, 7 July 2008.

18 Lewis Mumford, *The Story of Utopias* (New York: Viking Press, 1962), pp. 25–6.

19 Bill Bryson, *At Home: A Short History of Private Life* (New York: Doubleday, 2010), p. 323.

20 Shakespeare, *Twelfth Night*, Act 3, Scene 2.

21 Witold Rybczynski, *Home: A Short History of an Idea* (Harmondsworth: Penguin Books, 1986), p. 32.

22 Ibid., p. 59.

23 J.H. Huizinga, *Dutch Civilization in the Seventeenth Century and Other Essays*, tr. Arnold Pomerans (New York: Frederick Ungar, 1968).

24 Steen Eiler Rasmussen, *Towns and Buildings Described in Drawings and Words*, tr. Eve Wendt (Liverpool: University Press of Liverpool, 1951), p. 80. Quoted by Rybczynski, *Home*, p. 61.

Chapter 4 Private Property: My House Is My Castle

1 Plutarch, *Lives*, vol. 1, tr. Bernadotte Perrin, Loeb Classical Library (London: Heinemann, 1914), p. 229 (http://penelope.uchicago.edu/Thayer/e/roman/texts/plutarch/lives/lycurgus*.html).

2 Ibid., p. 447 (http://penelope.uchicago.edu/Thayer/e/roman/texts/plutarch/lives/solon*.html).

3 Ibid., p. 466.

4 See Xenophon, 'The Constitution of the Lacedaemonians', *Scripta minora*, tr. E.C. Marchant, Loeb Classical Library (London: Heinemann, 1946), pp. 135–89 (https://ryanfb.github.io/loebolus-data/L183.pdf).

5 Thucydides, *History of the Peloponnesian War*, tr. Richard Crawley (London: Dent, 1910; repr.: New York: Dover, 2004), chapter 14, p. 203.

6 Iurii Andreev, *Arkhaicheskaia Sparta: Iskusstvo i politika* (St Petersburg: Nestor-Istoriia, 2008), p. 280.

7 'The Speech of M.T. Cicero for His House. Addressed to the Priests', in *The Orations of Marcus Tullius Cicero*, vol. 3, tr. C.D. Yonge (London: G. Bell & Sons, 1913), para. XLI (http://oll.libertyfund.org/titles/cicero-orations-vol-3).

8 St Augustine, 'City of God and Christian Doctrine', in *A Select Library of the Nicene and Post-Nicene Fathers of the Christian Church*, II, tr. J.F. Shaw and Marcus Dods, ed. Philip Schaff (Buffalo, NY: The Christian Literature Company, 1887), chapter 8 (http://oll.libertyfund.org/titles/schaff-a-select-library-of-the-nicene-and-post-nicene-fathers-of-the-christian-church-vol-2).

9 Publius Ovidius Naso, *Ovid's Fasti*, tr. James Frazer (London: Heinemann, 1931; repr.: eds T.E. Page et al., Cambridge, MA: Harvard University Press, 1959), book V, 143–6 (https://archive.org/stream/ovidsfasti00oviduoft/ovidsfasti00oviduoft_djvu.txt).

10 Susan Treggiari, *Roman Social History* (London: Routledge, 2002), p. 88.

11 Marcus Tullius Cicero, 'The Fifth Book of the Second Pleading in the Prosecution Against Verres. The Speech on the Punishments', in *The Orations of Marcus Tullius Cicero*, vol. 1, tr. C.D. Yonge (London: G. Bell & Sons, 1916), para. XXXVI (http://oll.libertyfund.org/titles/cicero-orations-vol-1).

12 'The Speech of M.T. Cicero for His House', para. LVI.

13 Treggiari, *Roman Social History*, p. 92; 'Semayne's Case', in *The Selected Writings and Speeches of Sir Edward Coke*, vol. 1, ed. Steve Sheppard (Indianapolis: Liberty Fund, 2003) (http://oll.libertyfund.org/titles/911).

14 *Speech on the Excise Bill*, House of Commons (March 1763), quoted in Lord Brougham, *Historical Sketches of Statesmen Who Flourished in the Time of George III* (1855), I, p. 42.

15 Treggiari, *Roman Social History*, p. 93.

16 Hannah Arendt, *The Human Condition*, 2nd edition (Chicago: University of Chicago Press, 1998), pp. 61–2.

17 Plato, 'Laws', in *The Dialogues of Plato*, vol. v, 3rd edition, tr. Benjamin Jowett (Oxford: Oxford University Press, 1892), Steph. 739 (http://oll.libertyfund.org/titles/plato-dialogues-vol-5-laws-index-to-the-writings-of-plato).

18 Richard Schlatter, *Private Property: The History of an Idea* (New Brunswick, NJ: Rutgers University Press, 1951), p. 14.

19 Aristotle, *Politics*, tr. Benjamin Jowett (Oxford: Clarendon Press, 1885),

book 2, section III (https://ebooks.adelaide.edu.au/a/aristotle/a8po/book2. html).

20 Ibid., book 2, section V.
21 Virgil, *The Georgics*, book 4, Georgic I, tr. H. Rushton Fairclough, ed. Anthony Uyl (Woodstock, Ont.: Devoted Publishing, 2016), p. 6.
22 Lucius Annaeus Seneca, *Moral Letters to Lucilius*, vol. 2, tr. Richard M. Gummere (1920), epistle XC, para. 38 (https://en.wikisource.org/wiki/Moral_letters_to_Lucilius/Letter_90).
23 Ibid.
24 Thomas Hobbes, *Leviathan*, 2nd revised edition, ed. Richard Tuck (Cambridge: Cambridge University Press, 1996), ch. 13, pp. 88–9.
25 Andro Linklater, *Owning the Earth: The Transforming History of Land Ownership* (London: Bloomsbury, 2013), p. 36.
26 Thomas Becon, *Works*, 1564, vol. ii, fols xvi, xvii. Quoted in Richard H. Tawney, *The Agrarian Problem in the Sixteenth Century* (London, 1912), Introduction, n. 23 (repr.: New York: Burt Franklin n.d.) (http://www.guten berg.org/files/40336/40336-h/40336-h.htm#Footnote_23_23).
27 John Locke, *Two Treatises of Government*, ed. Peter Laslett (Cambridge: Cambridge University Press, 1988), pp. 350–1.
28 Douglass North, *Institutions, Institutional Change and Economic Performance* (Cambridge: Cambridge University Press, 1990), p. 3.
29 Acts of the Apostles, 2: 44–5.
30 Matthew, 19: 16–24.
31 See, for example, the parable of the householder and the husbandmen (Matthew, 21: 33–41) or of the wakeful servants and their lord (Luke, 12: 37).
32 Maksim Trudoliubov, 'Prokhod cherez igol'noe ushko', *Forbes*, no. 8, 2004.
33 'Tell me, pray, how many inhabitants are there now dwelling in our city. How many of them do you suppose to be Christians? One hundred thousand, do you suppose, and the rest Jews and Gentiles? How many thousand gold coins might be collected? And how great is the number of the poor? I think no more than fifty thousand. And to feed them every day, would much be needed? If all were maintained in common and at a common table the cost would not, of course, be high.' *Tvoreniia sv. ottsa nashego Ioanna Zlatousta, arkhiep. Konstantinopol'skogo*, 12 vols, book 1, vol. 9 (St Petersburg, 1903), p. 113.
34 Schlatter, *Private Property*, pp. 49–50.
35 Ibid., p. 87.
36 Alexander Gerschenkron, 'City Economies: Then and Now', in *The Historian and the City*, eds Oscar Handlin and John J. Burchard (Cambridge, MA: MIT Press, 1963), pp. 57–8.
37 *Utopia* is written in Latin, but More's wordplay was with Greek.
38 '[W]hen an insatiable wretch, who is a plague to his country, resolves to enclose many thousand acres of ground, the owners, as well as tenants, are turned out of their possessions by trick or by main force, or, being wearied out by ill usage, they are forced to sell them.' More, *Utopia* (see chapter 3, n. 15 above).
39 Jean-Jacques Rousseau, 'What Is the Origin of Inequality Among Men, and Is It Authorised by Natural Law?', in *The Social Contract and Discourses*, tr.

G.D.H. Cole (London: Dent, 1923) (http://oll.libertyfund.org/titles/rousseau-the-social-contract-and-discourses).
40 Ibid.
41 Maksim Trudoliubov, 'Dogovor s Leviafanom', *Vedomosti*, 5 August 2011.

Chapter 5 Territory: Ambitions of Colonialism and Methods of Subjugation

1 Etkind, *Internal Colonization*, p. 5.
2 Sergei Solov'ev, *Istoriia Rossii s drevneishikh vremen*, vol. 4 (Moscow: Mysl', 1988), p. 631.
3 Etkind, *Internal Colonization*, p. 5.
4 Raymond H. Fisher, *The Russian Fur Trade, 1550–1700* (Berkeley: University of California Press, 1943), p. 122. Quoted by Etkind, *Internal Colonization*, p. 80.
5 Oleg Vilkov, 'Pushnoi promysel v Sibiri', *Nauka v Sibiri*, 19 November 1999.
6 Nikolai Iadrintsev, *Sibir' kak koloniia v geograficheskom, etnologicheskom i istoricheskom otnosheniiakh*, 2nd edition (St Petersburg: Izdanie I.M. Sibiriakova, 1892; Philip D. Curtin, *Cross-Cultural Trade in World History* (Cambridge: Cambridge University Press, 1984). Quoted by Etkind, *Internal Colonization*, pp. 77, 78.
7 Vladislav Inozemtsev, Il'ia Ponomarev and Vladimir Ryzhkov, 'Kontinent Sibir' na puti ot kolonial'noi k global'noi paradigme razvitiia', *Rossiia v global'noi politike*, vol. 6, no. 10, 2012 (http://www.globalaffairs.ru/number/Kontinent-Sibir-15789).
8 Ibid.
9 Linklater, *Owning the Earth*, p. 77.
10 Daron Acemoğlu, Simon Johnson and James A. Robinson, 'The Colonial Origins of Comparative Development: An Empirical Investigation', *American Economic Review*, vol. 91, no. 5, 2001, pp. 1369–1401.
11 Daron Acemoğlu, Simon Johnson and James A. Robinson, 'Reversal of Fortune: Geography and Institutions in the Making of the Modern World Income Distribution', *Quarterly Journal of Economics*, vol. 117, no. 4, 2002, pp. 1231–94.
12 Daron Acemoğlu and James Robinson, *Why Nations Fail: The Origins of Power, Prosperity, and Poverty* (New York: Crown, 2012), p. 70.
13 Ibid., p. 75.
14 Vasilii Kliuchevskii, *Kurs russkoi istorii*, in *Sochineniia*, 9 vols, vol. 1 (Moscow: Mysl', 1987), p. 50.
15 Sergei Solov'ev, *Istoriia Rossii*, p. 631.
16 Kliuchevskii, *Kurs russkoi istorii*, in *Sochineniia*, vol. 3, p. 8.
17 Vladimir Mau, 'Vernost' ordynskoi traditsii', *Vedomosti*, 5 March 2007.
18 Maksim Trudoliubov and Pavel Aptekar', 'Ot "matritsy" do "kryshi"', *Vedomosti*, 27 March 2009. For a detailed analysis of the formation of the elite, see Lev Gudkov, Boris Dubin and Iurii Levada, *Putinskaia 'elita'* (Moscow: Inostranka, 2008).
19 David Remnick, *Lenin's Tomb* (New York: Random House, 1993), p. 185.
20 Ol'ga Kryshtanovskaia, 'Transformatsiia staroi nomenklatury v novuiu

rossiiskuiu elitu', *Obshchestvennye nauki i sovremennost'*, no. 1, 1995, pp. 51–65.
21 Vladislav Inozemtsev, 'Investitsionnaia politika: Slovo i delo', *Vedomosti*, 4 April 2011.
22 Etkind, *Internal Colonization*, p. 88.

Chapter 6 The Lock on the Door: The Priority of Security

1 Pipes, *Property and Freedom*, pp. 32–4.
2 Kliuchevskii, *Kurs russkoi istorii*, in *Sochineniia*, vol. 1, p. 359.
3 Donald G. Ostrowski, *Muscovy and the Mongols: Cross-Cultural Influences on the Steppe Frontier* (Cambridge: Cambridge University Press, 1998), p. 62.
4 Vasilii El'iashevich, *Istoriia prava pozemel'noi sobstvennosti v Rossii*, vol. 2 (Paris, 1951), p. 27.
5 Ibid., p. 32.
6 Ibid., p. 36.
7 Sergei Platonov, *Lektsii po russkoi istorii* (Moscow: Vyschaya shkola, 1993), p. 231.
8 Daniil Al'shits, *Nachalo samoderzhaviia v Rossii* (Moscow: Nauka, 1988), pp. 120–2.
9 Elena Liakhova, 'Russkie monastyri kak faktor vliianiia na derzhavnuiu gosudarstvennost'', *Molodoi uchenyi*, vol. 2, no. 6, 2011, pp. 73–5.
10 Andrei Teslia, *Istoria zakonodatelstva o prave pozemelnoi sobstvennosti v Rossii c IX po nachalo XX veka* (Khabarovsk: Dalnevostochny gosudarstvenny universitet putei soobshchenia, 2004), p. 44 (http://5fan.ru/wievjob.php?id=16025).
11 Acemoğlu and Robinson, *Why Nations Fail*, pp. 98–9.
12 Ibid., pp. 99–100.
13 Etkind, *Internal Colonization*, p. 125.
14 Stefan Hedlund, *Russian Path Dependence* (London: Routledge, 2005), p. 97.
15 Edward Keenan, 'Muscovite Political Folkways', *Russian Review*, vol. 45, no. 2, 1987, p. 130.
16 Marshall T. Poe, *A People Born to Slavery* (Ithaca, NY: Cornell University Press, 2000), pp. 220–1.
17 Ibid., p. 219.
18 Rein Taagepera, 'An Overview of the Growth of the Russian Empire', in *Russian Colonial Expansion to 1917*, ed. Michael Rywkin (London: Mansell, 1988), p. 6. I would like to thank Alexander Etkind for drawing my attention to this essay.
19 Hedlund, *Russian Path Dependence*, pp. 47, 132.
20 Ibid., p. 310.
21 Tamara Kondrat'eva, *Kormit' i pravit': O vlasti v Rossii XVI–XX vv.* (Moscow: ROSSPEN, 2006), p. 10.
22 Simon Kordonskii, 'Klassifikatsiia i ranzhirovanie ugroz', *Otechestvennye zapiski*, no. 2, 2013 (http://www.strana-oz.ru/2013/2/klassifikaciya-i-ranzhirovanie-ugroz).
23 Ibid.

24 Boris Dubin, 'Nartsissizm kak begstvo ot svobody', *Vedomosti*, 27 August 2014.

Chapter 7 Labourers: Moral Economics and the Art of Survival

1 From 'Rossiia' (1854), a poem by Aleksei Khomiakov.
2 El'iashevich, *Istoriia prava pozemel'noi sobstvennosti*, vol. 1, pp. 46–64, 112–13.
3 Nikolai Druzhinin, *Gosudarstvennye krest'iane i reforma P.D. Kiseleva*, vol. 1 (Moscow–Leningrad: Izdatel'stvo AN SSSR, 1946), pp. 28–9. Quoted in Teslia, *Istoriia zakonodatel'stva o prave pozemel'noi sobstvennosti*, p. 24.
4 El'iashevich, *Istoriia prava pozemel'noi sobstvennosti*, vol. 2, p. 95.
5 Tracy Dennison, *The Institutional Framework of Russian Serfdom* (Cambridge: Cambridge University Press, 2011). Quoted in Igor' Fediukin, 'Muzhik i institut', *Kommersant"–Vlast'*, 27 July 2009.
6 Teslia, *Istoriia zakonodatel'stva o prave pozemel'noi sobstvennosti*, p. 75.
7 Ibid., p. 72.
8 David Moon, *The Russian Peasantry, 1600–1930: The World the Peasants Made* (London: Longman, 1999), p. 99. See also Teslia, *Istoriia zakonodatel'stva o prave pozemel'noi sobstvennosti*, table on pp. 75–6.
9 Nicholas I, 'Rech' Nikolaia I v zasedanii Gosudarstvennogo Soveta 30 marta 1842 goda. (Po zapisi barona M.A. Korfa)', in *Nikolai I i ego epokha*, ed. Mikhail Gershenson (Moscow: Zakharov, 2001), p. 82.
10 Nikita Sokolov, Lecture at the Moscow School of Political Research, April 2012.
11 Fediukin, 'Muzhik i institut'.
12 Herzen quoted and analysed by August von Haxthausen in Aleksandr Gertsen, 'Rossiia', in *Sobranie sochinenii*, 30 vols, vol. 6 (Moscow: Izdatel'stvo Akademii nauk SSSR, 1955), pp. 187–223. Herzen compared von Haxthausen's trip to Russia, which resulted in his writing a 'positive' book, with that of the Marquis de Custine, who had written negatively.
It is more interesting, however, to compare the Prussian lawyer von Haxthausen's tour of the Russian Empire with the tour of America by the French lawyer and politician Alexis de Tocqueville. Both foreign visitors were full of benign curiosity, both wanted to see for themselves and understand how a distant country lived, and both, on the basis of their travels, wrote highly influential books. Von Haxthausen's account of the commune made a deep impression on the regime and intellectuals in Russia, and de Tocqueville's *Democracy in America* proved extraordinarily popular. The approaches of the German and the Frenchman were, however, drastically different. Unlike von Haxthausen, de Tocqueville based his book on observation of reality and sought to interpret it.
13 Pavel Biriukov, *Biografiia L.N. Tolstogo*, 4 vols, vol. 2 (Berlin: Izdatel'stvo I.P. Ladyzhnikova, 1921), p. 81.
14 Etkind, *Internal Colonization*, p. 141.
15 Paul H. Rubin, *Darwinian Politics: The Evolutionary Origin of Freedom* (New Brunswick, NJ: Rutgers University Press, 2002).
16 James C. Scott, *The Moral Economy of the Peasant: Rebellion and Subsistence in Southeast Asia* (New Haven: Yale University Press, 1976).

17 Stephen F. Williams, *Liberal Reform in an Illiberal Regime: The Creation of Private Property in Russia, 1906–1915* (Stanford: Hoover Institution Press, 2006), p. 39.

18 Scott, *The Moral Economy of the Peasant*, p. 2.

19 Jerome Blum, 'The Internal Structure and Polity of the European Village Community from the Fifteenth to the Nineteenth Century', *Journal of Modern History*, vol. 43, no. 4, 1971, pp. 541–76.

20 Moon, *The Russian Peasantry, 1600–1930*, p. 80.

21 Williams, *Liberal Reform in an Illiberal Regime*, p. 41.

22 Stephen L. Hoch, *Serfdom and Social Control in Russia: Petrovskoe, a Village in Tambov* (Chicago: University of Chicago Press, 1986), pp. 177–86. On state and appanage peasants, see Moon, *The Russian Peasantry, 1600–1930*, pp. 217–18. For a comparison with industrial production, see Williams, *Liberal Reform in an Illiberal Regime*, p. 46.

23 Hoch, *Serfdom and Social Control in Russia*, p. 134.

24 Ibid., p. 128.

25 Ibid., pp. 154–7.

26 Ibid. For statistics on punishments and their purposes, see pp. 162–4.

27 Ol'ga Sukhova, *Desiat' mifov krest'ianskogo soznaniia: Ocherki istorii sotsial'noi psikhologii i mentaliteta russkogo krest'ianstva (konets XIX–nachalo XX v.) po materialam srednego Povolzh'ia* (Moscow: ROSSPEN, 2008), p. 160.

28 Nina Rogalina, 'Agrarnyi krizis v rossiiskoi derevne nachala XX veka', *Voprosy istorii*, no. 7, 2004, pp. 13–14. Quoted by Sukhova, *Desiat' mifov krest'ianskogo soznaniia*, p. 160.

29 Aleksandr Nikolaevich Engelgardt, *Letters from the Country, 1872–1887*, tr. Cathy Frierson, (Oxford: Oxford University Press, 1993), p. 232.

30 Aleksandr A. Chuprov, 'Unichtozhenie sel'skoi obshchiny v Rossii', *Voprosy ekonomiki*, no. 10, 2010, pp. 135–46 (p. 141). (The English version appeared as A.A. Chuprov, 'The Break-Up of the Village Community in Russia', *The Economic Journal*, vol. 22, 1912, pp. 173–97.)

31 Ibid.

32 Richard Wortman, 'Property Rights, Populism, and Russian Political Culture', in *Civil Rights in Imperial Russia*, eds Olga Crisp and Linda Edmondson (Oxford: Oxford University Press, 1989), p. 31.

33 Williams, *Liberal Reform in an Illiberal Regime*, pp. 148–9.

34 'Nelepye tolki i nadezhdy pomeshchich'ikh krest'ian: Zapiska Koribut-Dashkevicha', *Russkii arkhiv*, no. 8, 1874, p. 452. Quoted by Sukhova, *Desiat' mifov krest'ianskogo soznaniia*, p. 160.

35 Illarion Chernyshev, *Obshchina posle 9 noiabria 1906 g.* (Petrograd, 1917), part 2, p. 38. Quoted by Sukhova, *Desiat' mifov krest'ianskogo soznaniia*, p. 160.

36 Ibid., pp. 271–2.

37 Ibid., p. 304.

38 Oleg Vronskii, *Krest'ianskaia obshchina na rubezhe XIX–XX vv.: Struktura upravleniia, pozemel'nye otnosheniia, pravoporiadok* (Moscow: Moskovskii pedagogicheskii gosudarstvennyi universitet, 1999), p. 138. Also Sukhova, *Desiat' mifov krest'ianskogo soznaniia*, p. 227.

39 George M. Fredrickson and Christopher Lasch, *Resistance to Slavery* (Kent,

OH: Kent State University Press, 1967), pp. 230–2. Quoted by Hoch, *Serfdom and Social Control*, p. 184.

40 Gresham M. Sykes, *Society of Captives: A Study of a Maximum Security Prison* (Princeton: Princeton University Press, 1958), p. 28. Quoted by Hoch, *Serfdom and Social Control*, p. 184.

41 Alexander Solzhenitsyn, *One Day in the Life of Ivan Denisovich*, tr. H.T. Willetts (London: Vintage, 2005), p. 10.

42 Ibid., pp. 48–9.

43 Fredrickson and Lasch, *Resistance to Slavery*, p. 241.

44 E.O. Osokina, 'O sotsial'nom immunitete, ili Kriticheskii vzglyad na kont-septsiiu passivnogo (povsednevnogo) soprotivleniia. Rasshirennyi variant doklada, predstavlennogo na mezhdunarodnoi konferentsii "Istoriia stalin-izma. Itogi i problemy izucheniia"', Moscow, 5–7 December 2008.

45 Solzhenitsyn, *One Day in the Life*, pp. 34–5.

46 Osokina, 'O sotsial'nom immunitete'.

47 Francis Fukuyama, *The Origins of Political Order: From Prehuman Times to the French Revolution* (New York: Farrar, Straus and Giroux, 2011), p. 7.

Chapter 8 Masters: The Tragedy of Domination

1 Ivan Pnin, *Sochineniia* (Moscow: Izdatel'stvo Vsesoiuznogo Obshchestva politkatorzhan i ssyl'noposelentsev, 1934), p. 130.

2 Although Catherine's Letters Patent were not the first, they were among the first legislative acts relevant to our topic, and were to prove the most important and to have the most far-reaching effects. In 1762, Peter III had, with his Manifesto of Liberty for the Nobility, relieved the nobility of their service obligations, which effectively made ownership of land unconditional. They could renounce their service ties without having to give back their patrimonial lands and estates. There was, however, no explicit confirmation of property and individual rights in the manifesto.

3 For the text of the Letters Patent, see http://www.hist.msu.ru/ER/Etext/dv_gram.htm.

4 Aleksandr Gertsen, *Kreshchenaia sobstvennost'* (London: Vol'naia russkaia knigopechatal'nia, 1853), pp. 3-4.

5 Fukuyama, *The Origins of Political Order*, p. 142.

6 Walter M. Pintner, *Russian Economic Policy under Nicholas I* (Ithaca, NY: Cornell University Press, 1967), p. 37.

7 The proposal was to issue loans for terms of eight, twelve or twenty-four years. Loans for twelve and twenty-four years were to be at a rate of 6% per annum, with an additional 2% on repayment of the loan. The size of the loans was to be from 5,000 to 500,000 rubles, depending on the number of registered 'souls' available as security. One 'soul' could stand as security for a loan of 150–200 rubles, depending on the status of the province. Aleksandr Bugrov, 'Iz istorii Banka Rossii: Zaemnyi bank' (http://www.vep.ru/bbl/history/cbr10.html).

8 Ibid.

9 Ibid.

10 Tomas Ouen [Thomas Owen], 'Pravo sobstvennosti v istorii Rossii', *Vedomosti*, 14 December 2012.

11 Pintner, *Russian Economic Policy*, pp. 37–42.

12 Ibid., p. 30.

13 Even if we discount the fact that Catherine's Letters Patent of 1785 only confirmed what had already been in practice for a couple of decades, we obtain a total of 155 years of unconditional ownership of land, between 1762 and 1917. This is less than the Moscow period (from the reign of Ivan IV until Peter the Great) and less than the Mongol period. In other words, it is a very brief period of time in historical terms.

14 Lee A. Farrow, *Between Clan and Crown: The Struggle to Define Noble Property Rights in Imperial Russia* (Newark: University of Delaware Press, 2004), p. 208.

15 Ibid., p. 193.

16 Teslia, *Istoriia zakonodatel'stva o prave pozemel'noi sobstvennosti*, pp. 7–9.

17 Derek Offord, 'Alexander Herzen and James de Rothschild', *The Rothschild Archive: Review of the Year*, April 2005–March 2006, pp. 39–47.

18 Andrei Shipilov, 'O bednosti i bogatstve', *Obshchestvennye nauki i sovremennost'*, no. 5, 2008, pp. 163–75.

19 Offord, 'Alexander Herzen and James de Rothschild', p. 42.

20 Ibid., pp. 42–3.

21 Aleksandr Gertsen, *Byloe i dumy*, in *Sobranie sochinenii*, 30 vols, vol. 10 (Moscow: Izdatel'stvo Akademii nauk, 1956), p. 132.

22 Offord, 'Alexander Herzen and James de Rothschild', p. 44.

23 Pavel Basinskii, *Lev Tolstoi: Begstvo iz raia* (Moscow: AST, 2011), p. 65.

24 Biriukov, *Biografiia L.N. Tolstogo*, vol. 2, pp. 558–9.

25 Leo Tolstoy, *Strider: The Story of a Horse*, tr. Louise and Aylmer Maude, chapter 6 (https://en.wikisource.org/wiki/Strider:_the_Story_of_a_Horse).

26 Etkind, *Internal Colonization*, p. 17.

27 Ekaterina Pravilova, *A Public Empire: Property and the Quest for the Common Good in Imperial Russia* (Princeton: Princeton University Press, 2014), p. 25.

28 Ibid. See also *Zhurnal Vysochaishe utverzhdennoi komissii dlia peresmotra deistvuiushchikh zakonov o bechevnikakh i o poriadke ob"iavleniia rek sudokhodnymi i vplavnymi* (St Petersburg: Tipografiia Ministerstva putei soobshcheniia, 1878).

29 Pravilova, *A Public Empire*, pp. 43–5.

30 Felix Yusupov, *Lost Splendour and the Death of Rasputin* (London: Adelphi, 2015), pp. 129–30.

31 Ibid., p. 130; E. Iudin, 'Rossiiskaia modernizatsiia i aristokratiia: sostoianie sem'i Iusupovykh v nachale XX v.', *Novyi istoricheskii vestnik*, no. 1, 2006.

32 Francis Fukuyama is inclined to see this as a choice. 'Left to their own devices, elites tend to increase the size of their latifundia, and in the face of this, rulers have two choices. They can side with the peasantry and use state power to promote land reform and egalitarian land rights, thereby clipping the wings of the aristocracy. This is what happened in Scandinavia, where the Swedish and Danish monarchs made common cause with the peasantry at the end of the eighteenth century against a relatively weak aristocracy. Or the rulers can side with the aristocracy and use state power to reinforce the hold of local oligarchs over their peasants. This happened in Russia, Prussia, and other lands east of the Elbe River from the seventeenth century on, as a generally free peasantry was reduced to serfdom

with the collusion of the state.' Fukuyama, *The Origins of Political Order*, pp. 182–3.

33 Pravilova, *A Public Empire*, p. 32.
34 Ibid., p. 30.
35 Wortman, 'Property Rights, Populism, and Russian Political Culture', p. 32.

Chapter 9 Architecture, Happiness and Order

1 Le Corbusier, *Toward an Architecture*, tr. John Goodman (Los Angeles: Getty Research Institute, 2007), pp. 88–9.
2 Ibid., p. 94.
3 Nikolai Erofeev, 'Istoriia khrushchevki', *Otkrytaia levaia*, 24 December 2014 (http://openleft.ru/?p=4962).
4 Selim Khan-Magomedov, *Arkhitektura sovetskogo avangarda* (Moscow: Stroiizdat, 2001), vol. 2: *Sotsial'nye problemy*, p. 322.
5 Ibid.
6 Papernyi, *Kul'tura Dva*, p. 169.
7 Translated by Arch Tait. For a brilliant commentary and analysis of the literary sources of this poem, see Fedor Uspenskii, 'Molotok Nekrasova: "Kvartira" O. Mandel'shtama mezhdu stikhami o stikhakh i grazhdanskoi poezii 1933 goda', in *Dar i krest. Pamiati Natal'i Trauberg: Sbornik statei i vospominanii* (St Petersburg: Izdatel'stvo Ivana Limbakha, 2010), p. 319.
8 Nadezhda Mandelstam, *Hope Against Hope*, tr. Max Hayward (London: Collins and Harvill, 1971), p. 150.
9 Ibid.
10 Alain de Botton, *The Architecture of Happiness* (New York: Vintage, 2006), p. 98.
11 A.I. Shneerson, *Chto takoe zhilishchnyi vopros* (Moscow: Izdatel'stvo VPSh i AON pri TsK KPSS, 1959), p. 63; See also Gregory D. Andrusz, *Housing and Urban Development in the USSR* (London: Macmillan, 1984), p. 19.
12 Nikita Khrushchev, *Vremia. Liudi. Vlast': Vospominaniia*, 4 vols, vol. 2 (Moscow: Moskovskie novosti, 1999), p. 390.
13 Ibid., p. 547.
14 Steven E. Harris, *Communism on Tomorrow Street: Mass Housing and Everyday Life after Stalin* (Washington, DC: Woodrow Wilson Center Press, 2013), p. 90. See also the table on pp. 89–91.
15 Mark B. Smith, *Property of Communists: The Urban Housing Program from Stalin to Khrushchev* (DeKalb: Northern Illinois University Press, 2010), p. 100.
16 Calculated by Steven Harris, *Communism on Tomorrow Street*, p. 5; see also Jane R. Zavisca, *Housing the New Russia* (Ithaca, NY: Cornell University Press, 2012), Kindle edition, loc. 665.
17 Pavel Blokhin, *Maloetazhnyi zhiloi dom* (Moscow: Izdatel'stvo Akademii arkhitektury SSSR, 1944), p. 59.
18 Harris, *Communism on Tomorrow Street*, p. 80.
19 Ibid., pp. 82–3.
20 Andrei Kaftanov, 'Elitnye vyselki', *Kommersant"–Vlast'*, 2 May 2000.
21 Zavisca, *Housing the New Russia*, loc. 891.

22 Smith, *Property of Communists*, pp. 144–5.
23 Mariia Sergeenko, *Zhizn' Drevnego Rima* (St Petersburg: Letnii Sad–*Neva*, 2000), pp. 78–9.
24 There is wonderful book about the Russian dacha written by British researcher Stephen Lovell: *Summerfolk: A History of the Dacha, 1710–2000* (Ithaca, NY: Cornell University Press, 2003).
25 Maksim Trudoliubov 'Vystavka schast'ia', *Vedomosti*, 14 July 2006.
26 La Rue Van Hook, *Greek Life and Thought* (New York: Columbia University Press, 1930), p. 39.
27 Seneca, *Letters from a Stoic*, Epistle XC, p. 115.
28 Mikhail Gasparov, *Zanimatel'naia Gretsiia* (Moscow: B.S.G.-Press, 2009), p. 450.
29 Iuliia Petrova and Anastasia Agamalova, 'Naval'nyi: Kvartira docheri Sobianina stoit v 6 raz bol'she desiatiletnego zarabotka sem'i', *Vedomosti*, 9 August 2013.
30 Stepan Kravchenko, Evgeniia Pismennaia and Irina Reznik, 'Putin's $50 Million Luxury Apartments for Powerful Allies', Bloomberg, 10 July 2013 (https://www.bloomberg.com/news/articles/2013-07-11/putins-50-million-luxury-apartments-for-powerful-allies).
31 Anastasiia Kornia, 'Putin predlozhil zapretit' chinovnikam imet' za rubezhom scheta i tsennye bumagi', *Vedomosti*, 12 February 2013.
32 See chapter 1; also Iuzhakov, 'Kapitalizatsiia pokolenii'.

Chapter 10 The Halfway House

1 David Broner, *Zhilishchnoe stroitel'stvo i demograficheskie protsessy* (Moscow: Statistika, 1980), p. 25.
2 Ilya Ehrenburg, *The Thaw*, tr. Manya Harari (London: Harvill, 1955), p. 20.
3 Harris, *Communism on Tomorrow Street*, pp. 95–6.
4 Ibid., p. 151.
5 Christine Varga-Harris, 'Forging Citizenship on the Home Front', in *The Dilemmas of De-Stalinization: Negotiating Cultural and Social Change in the Khrushchev Era*, ed. Polly Jones (London: Routledge, 2006), pp. 101–16.
6 Zavisca, *Housing the New Russia*, loc. 4210–15.
7 Ibid., loc. 1030–4.
8 According to a 1989 report by the Higher School of Economics, Moscow, provision of residential floor space in Russia was 26% of that in the United States (16.1 and 61.3 m2 per head of the population respectively). In 2009 it was 32% (22.5 and 69.7 m2 per head respectively). 'Rost nedostupnosti zhil'ia v sravnenii s SSSR preuvelichen', *Kommersant"*, 11 April 2011. There are other, more stringent assessments. 'Provision of residential accommodation in Russia is 40% of the level in developed countries, if we count all housing, including hostels,' says Vladimir Hamza, vice-president of the Association of Regional Banks of Russia. 'If we exclude buildings not regarded as habitable in developed countries, the provision in Russia is 20%' (http://ria.ru/society/20111201/503610992.html).
9 The quotation about overcrowding is taken from 'Kvartirnaia blagodat", Iakov Krotov's blog on the Radio Liberty website (http://www.svobodanews.

ru/content/blog/24556918.html); see data on the relative number of apartments in a report by the Research and Branding Group (http://www.rb.com. ua/rus/marketing/tendency/8232).

10 Mikhail Dmitriev, 'Pochemu rost dokhodov ne spasaet reiting Putina', *Forbes.Ru*, 28 February 2013 (http://www.forbes.ru/mneniya-column/ vertikal/234935-pochemu-rost-dohodov-ne-spasaet-reiting-putina).

11 'Ot redaktsii: Skol'ko stoit rai v shalashe', *Vedomosti*, 1 June 2012.

12 Jane Zavisca believes that failures of the market in Russia are the fault of American consultants who unintelligently attempted to transplant US institutions to Russian soil. In the United States, banks grant mortgages and then sell them on to enterprises supported by the state, like Fanny Mae and Freddy Mac, and to other financial institutions. These in turn convert the mortgage payments into 'mortgage-backed securities', which they issue for free circulation on the market. The initial loan thus disappears from the balance sheet of the bank that issued it. The situation has irresponsibility built into it: the bank does not have to fear issuing the loans, borrowers are not afraid to take them if they are cheap and do not require savings or any great effort on their part. This is a royal road to the formation of a market bubble and, as became evident in 2007, a recipe for a global financial crisis.

In Europe, various forms of encouraging saving to buy a house are commonplace, where the investor is dealing with a special system of building societies (*Bausparkassen, épargne logement*) separate from the 'big' financial market. After saving up a substantial deposit of 40 to 60%, depositors gain access to inexpensive loans. In this instance, the market is capitalized in savings, not securities.

13 Nadezhda Kosareva, Tat'iana Polidi, Aleksandr Puzanov and Evgenii Iasin, 'Novaia zhilishchnaia strategiia' (Moscow: VShE, 2015), p. 7 (https://www. hse.ru/org/hse/expert/industrial/news/147033496.html).

14 Tat'iana Polidi, 'Zhilishchnoe stroitel'stvo v Rossii: Mify i real'nost', Nauchnyi seminar Fonda 'Liberal'naia missiia', 31 March 2015 (http://www. liberal.ru/articles/6745).

15 Data from a report by Deloitte. On average, across the EU the proportion of mortgage loans to GDP is 51.7%. The highest level is in the Netherlands and Denmark and the lowest is in the Czech Republic. In Russia the proportion of mortgage loans is five times lower than in the Czech Republic at just 2.6% of GDP. The level of mortgage debt per capita in Russia is also the lowest, which, at €311, is seven times lower than in Poland (which is the lowest in the EU, at €2,280). See 'Rossiiane svobodny ot ipoteki', *Vedomosti*, 27 August 2013. 'Dannye oprosa NAFI o dostupnosti ipoteki: Lish' 2% rossiian gotovy priobresti kvartiru v kredit', *Vedomosti*, 26 April 2012. (https://www. vedomosti.ru/realty/articles/2012/04/26/lish_2_rossiyan_gotovy_vzyat_ipote chnyj_kredit).

16 Calculations of the Institute for Urban Economics (Moscow).

17 Wendell Cox and Hugh Pavletich, *9th Annual Demographia International Housing Affordability Survey: 2013, Ratings for Metropolitan Markets* (http://demographia.com/dhi2013.pdf). We should note that in its calculations the World Bank uses the median rather than the average price of a family house; household income for the preceding three years is also the median rather than the average. The median value of income in countries with a high level of stratification is usually significantly lower than the average.

18 The World Bank index is based on how many annual median incomes of a (whole) family would be needed to purchase a median-priced apartment. The calculations for Russia and Belarus (9.5 years) were arrived at by Giuseppe Torluccio of the University of Bologna and Elena Dorokh of the Belarusian State University. Elena Dorokh and Giuseppe Torluccio, 'Housing Affordability and Methodological Principles: An Application', *International Research Journal of Finance and Economics*, no. 79, 2011, p. 64. See also 'Ot redaktsii: Skol'ko stoit rai v shalashe'; Cox and Pavletich, *9th Annual Demographia*.

19 With the development of market relations, the residential building sector in Russia, in terms of the main market players – professional property developers and non-professional developers (citizens) – returned to what it had been seventy years earlier. See Kosareva et al., 'Novaia zhilishchnaia strategiia', p. 8.

20 Ibid., p. 18.

21 Vladimir Shlapentokh and Anna Arutunyan [*sic*], *Freedom, Repression, and Private Property in Russia* (Cambridge: Cambridge University Press, 2013), p. 40.

22 The reason for this is explained in Rostislav Kapeliushnikov, *Sobstvennost' bez legitimnosti?* (Moscow: Vysshaia shkola ekonomiki, 2008) (http://polit.ru/article/2008/03/27/sobstv/).

23 See, for example, Iana Iakovleva's articles 'Pribyl'' kak prestuplenie', *Vedomosti*, 9 February 2012; 'Russkii diskont', *Vedomosti*, 26 April 2010; and 'Ne prosto rybki', *Vedomosti*, 14 September 2009.

24 For the full story as related by William Browder, see 'Uil'iam Brauder: V Rossii net gosudarstva', ed. Masha Gessen, *Snob*, vol. 6, no. 33, June 2011 (http://www.snob.ru/thread/71); see also Tat'iana Seiranian and Aleksei Nikol'skii, 'Iurist Hermitage Magnitskii umer v tiur'me', *Vedomosti*, 17 November 2009; Sergei Guriev and Oleg Tsyvinskii, 'Modernizatsiia-37', *Vedomosti*, 24 November 2009.

25 Vladimir Radchenko and Al'fred Zhalinskii, 'Ugolovno-investitsionnyi klimat', *Vedomosti*, 24 June 2011.

26 Dmitrii Kaz'min, 'Ofshornye kompanii – otdushina dlia biznesa: Interv'iu predsedatelia Vysshego arbitrazhnogo suda Antona Ivanova', *Vedomosti*, 25 January 2012 (https://www.vedomosti.ru/politics/articles/2012/01/25/ne_nado_borotsya_s_anglijskimi_sudami_anton_ivanov).

27 'O chem umolchal Putin: Ot redaktsii', *Vedomosti*, 12 April 2012.

28 Ol'ga Kuvshinova, 'Investitsii v Rossiiu: den'gi est', uverennosti net', *Vedomosti*, 20 June 2013.

29 Maksim Trudoliubov, 'Kolonial'nye budni Rossii', *Vedomosti*, 29 April 2011.

Chapter 11 Two Options: Finish Building the Home, or Emigrate

1 Samuel P. Huntington, *The Third Wave: Democratization in the Late Twentieth Century* (Norman: University of Oklahoma Press, 1991), p. 137.

2 Ivan Krastev, 'Paradoxes of the New Authoritarianism', *Journal of Democracy*, vol. 22, no. 2, April 2011, p. 12.

221

3 Maxim Boycko, Andrei Shleifer and Robert W. Vishny, 'Privatizing Russia', *Brookings Papers on Economic Activity*, vol. 24, no. 2, 1993, p. 142.
4 Ol'ga Kuvshinova, 'Tsena otlozhennykh reform', *Vedomosti*, Forum supplement, 20 November 2012.
5 Joseph A. Schumpeter, *Capitalism, Socialism and Democracy* (London: George Allen and Unwin, 1976), p. 269.
6 Maksim Trudoliubov, 'Liniia Medvedeva', *Vedomosti*, 1 October 2010.
7 Adam Przeworski, *Democracy and the Market* (Cambridge: Cambridge University Press, 1991), p. 10.
8 Reasons why democratization in Russia failed are suggested in Vladimir Gel'man, 'Out of the Frying Pan, into the Fire? Post-Soviet Changes in Comparative Perspective', *International Political Science Review*, vol. 29, no. 2, March 2008, pp. 157–80.
9 Vladimir Pastukhov, 'Predannaia revoliutsiia', *Novaia gazeta*, 9 January 2013.
10 Aleksandr Auzan, 'Chastnaia sobstvennost' – ne luchshii variant: U kazhdogo rezhima sobstvennosti svoi preimushchestva i problemy', Zapis' vystupleniia na vstreche iz serii 'Dorozhnaia karta grazhdanina' v klube 'Mart' 3 aprelia 2012 goda (https://snob.ru/profile/5340/blog/page/2?v=1447658658).
11 The economic commentator Boris Grozovskii, after reading the memoirs and arguments of the Russian reformers collected in *Revoliutsiia Gaidara: Istoriia reform 1990-kh iz pervkh ruk*, remarks, 'The Gaidar government had no mandate to reform society's institutions – the courts, the army, the bureaucracy – and in any case it had no idea how to go about it.' Boris Grozovskii, 'Nedorevoliutsiia: Kto vinovat v provale reform nachala 1990-kh', *Forbes. ru*, 27 June 2013 (http://www.forbes.ru/mneniya/istoriya/241265-nedore volyutsiya-kto-vinovat-v-provale-reform-nachala-1990-h).
12 The following few paragraphs are excerpts from an article co-authored with Pavel Aptekar': 'Stalinskii proekt: Chrezvychainoe pravo', *Vedomosti*, 4 September 2009 (https://www.vedomosti.ru/opinion/articles/2009/09/04/ stalinskij-proekt-chrezvychajnoe-pravo).
13 *Dekrety Sovetskoi vlasti*, vol. 1 (Moscow: Gospolitizdat, 1957), pp. 124–6.
14 Martin Latsis, *Chrezvychainye komissii po bor'be s kontrrevoliutsiei* (Moscow: Gosudarstvennoe izdatel'stvo, 1921), pp. 8–9.
15 An encrypted telegram from I.V. Stalin to the secretaries of provincial and regional Party committees and to the heads of the NKVD-UNKVD on the use of 'physical methods of inducement' against 'enemies of the people', 'Lubyanka: Stalin i NKVD–NKGB–GUKR "Smersh". 1939–mart 1946', Fond Aleksandra Yakovleva (http://www.alexanderyakovlev.org/fond/ issues-doc/58623).
16 Vadim Volkov, 'Palochnaia sistema: instrument upravleniia', *Vedomosti*, 19 February 2010.
17 Ibid.
18 Ibid.
19 For example, in the five years from 1987 to 1991, 2.5 million individuals were convicted in the RSFSR. In modern Russia, in the five years from 2004 to 2008, according to the Judicial Department of the Supreme Court, 4.4 million people were convicted.

20 Ella Paneiakh and Mariia Shkliaruk, 'Do suda vinovatye', *Vedomosti*, 12 March 2013.
21 Vadim Volkov, *Silovoe predprinimatel'stvo, XXI vek: Ekonomikosotsiologicheskii analiz* (St Petersburg: Izdatel'stvo Evropeiskogo universiteta v Sankt-Peterburge, 2012).
22 Anastasiia Kornia, 'Neuiutnaia Rossiia', *Vedomosti*, 10 June 2011.
23 Maksim Trudoliubov, 'Svoia doroga v ad', *colta.ru*, 6 August 2012 (http://archives.colta.ru/docs/3588).
24 Albert O. Hirschman, *Exit, Voice, and Loyalty: Responses to Decline in Firms, Organizations, and States* (Cambridge, MA: Harvard University Press, 1972).
25 Krastev, 'Paradoxes of the New Authoritarianism', p. 12.
26 Aleksei Mikhailov, 'Nikto siuda ne ponaekhal', *gazeta.ru*, 25 December 2012 (http://www.gazeta.ru/comments/2012/12/25_a_4905321.shtml).
27 Vladislav Inozemtsev, 'Russkii mir I protiv Russkogo mira II', *Vedomosti*, 29 July 2014.

Epilogue: In Search of Real Ownership

1 Richard Hughes, Tom Josephs, Viera Karolova, Vladimir Krivenkov, and Gösta Ljungman, *Russian Federation: Fiscal Transparency Evaluation* (IMF Country Report No. 14/134) (Washington, DC: International Monetary Fund, 2014) (https://www.imf.org/external/pubs/ft/scr/2014/cr14134.pdf).
2 The aluminium magnate Oleg Deripaska, the former owner of one of the world's largest crude oil companies, Gennadii Timchenko, and the nickel mogul Vladimir Potanin have all stated this publicly. See chapter 3, note 9 above.
3 Anna Mikheeva Ekaterina Litova, Anastasia Krivorotovaet, and Anna Kholiavko, 'Tret'ii ne lishni', *RBC Daily*, 17 December 2017 (https://www.rbc.ru/finances/17/12/2017/5a33c63c9a79477c6265a33e).
4 Vladimir Ruvinskii, 'Nikto ne khotel predprinimat'', *Vedomosti*, 1 October 2017 (https://www.vedomosti.ru/opinion/articles/2017/10/02/736034-nikto-ne-hotel).
5 Leonid Bershidsky, 'There's No Separating Wealth and Power in Russia', *BloombergView*, 3 March 2017 (https://www.bloomberg.com/view/articles/2017-03-03/there-s-no-separating-wealth-and-power-in-russia).
6 Maxim Trudolyubov, 'Moscow's New Housing Megaproject Confronts Soviet History', *The Moscow Times*, 2 March 2017 (https://themoscowtimes.com/articles/moscows-new-housing-megaproject-confronts-soviet-history-57312).

INDEX

Acemoğlu, Daron 80
Acts of the Apostles 66
Adams, John Quincy 124
Aeneid (Virgil) 54
Affordable Housing Project 165
agriculture
    1905 Revolution and 110–13
    collectivization of 18
    communal 104–9
    'due toil' 101
    Five Ears of Corn Law 180
    private farmer reforms 109–13
    Soviet collectives 113–17
Akhmatova, Anna 23, 24
Alcibiades 152
Alexander I, Tsar
    Enlightenment thought 120
    gradual release of serfs 103–4
    holds back development 123–4
    liberal policies 122
    Pnin and 118, 119
Alexander II, Tsar
    judicial reforms 179
Alexeyev, Mikhail 24
Alexis, Tsar
    property for service 200
Alshits, Daniil 90
Anabaptists 67, 72
Anna, Empress
    tears up nobles' conditions 120

Aquinas, St Thomas 67
Arbitration, Supreme Court of 170
Architects' Club
    'Rapid Construction in the United
        States' exhibition 146
architecture
    for elites 143–4
    engineers and 138–9, 151
    mass-produced housing 136–9
    order and moderation 152–4
    Russian order 154–6
    Russian understanding of 144–5
    simplicity/complexity 145
    Soviet fencing policy 26–7
    Stalinist 140–4
    see also housing
Architecture of Happiness, The (de
    Botton) 144–5
Arendt, Hannah 58–9
Aristotle
    human self-interest 59, 60
    worthy use of land 67
art
    'free' 15–16
    portraying private life 49
Arutyunyan, Anna 168–9
Athens, ancient 50–3
Augustine of Hippo, St
    on home 54
    on property 66

224

Australia 79
authoritarianism
democratic grey zone 173
high mistrust levels and 34–5
in mistrustful society 34
private property and 31, 168–9
Auzan, Alexander 177
Azerbaijan 191
Aztecs, colonization of 77–9

banks and banking
credit to slum owners 28–9
crises and failing 199–200
emigration of capital 204
Krankin and 123
Baptized Property (Herzen) 128
Becon, Thomas 63
Bestushev, Alexander 118
Bibikhin, Vladimir 6
Blokhin, Pavel 147
B&N bank 199
Bolivia 78
Botton, Alain de
The Architecture of Happiness
144–5
Brezhnev, Leonid
elites under 143, 144
housing policies 157, 161
Britain
becomes modern state 87–8
buys Russian furs 75
colonialism 78–9, 94
context of More's *Utopia* 70
economic institutions 62–5
freeing of labour 91–2
gas from Russia 86
home and 2, 57–8
Locke and social contract 63–4
Magna Carta and 87
monarchy versus parliament 62
social contract 61
Brodsky, Alexander 35
Brodsky, Joseph 24
bureaucracy
development of 3

eighteenth–nineteenth century
126–7
business
Alexander I's policies 124
entrepreneurs and bankruptcies
199–200
foreign investment 170
non-Russian 170
offshore companies 169–71
see also industry

Calvin, John 68
Camus, Raymond 138
Canada, colonization of 79
capitalism, half-built in Russia 171
cars, as badge of success 16
Catherine II, the Great, Empress
ambiguous serf structure 101
Charter to the Nobility 103
creates free class 126
demolishes Kremlin Wall 26
Enlightenment thought and 120
fear of peasant mobility 103
natural resources and 132–3
property for service 31–2, 120–1,
135
secularizes Church lands 91
censorship, Pnin and 119
Central Bank
bailing out banks 199
Centres of Scientific and
Technological Creativity of the
Young 84
Chaadaev, Pyotr 131–2
Chayanov, Alexander 106
Chernyshevsky, Nikolai 45
Chicherin, Boris 106
childhood, Soviet 14–16
China
economics of 13
security guards 33
Christianity and Churches
architecture 154
communal utopia and 65–8
Henry VIII takes land from 88

Christianity and Churches (*cont.*)
  as landowner in Russia 91
  property ownership and 12
  Russian Orthodox and 'ours' 177–8
  sanctifies autocracy 94
  Seneca on 66
  Soviet anti-Christianization 13
  utopia and 72
Chukovsky, Korney 23
Chuprov, Alexander Alexandrovich
  111
Cicero, Marcus Tullius
  'Concerning My House' 56–7
  on living conditions 151
  Roman homes 54–5
cinema, shift to characters in 43
citizenship
  rights based on property 51
  see also rights of citizens
Cleobulus 153
Clodius, Publius 56–7
Coke, Sir Edward 57–8
colonialism
  Cortés and Mexico 77–9
  ownership of land 78–9
  Sparta and 52–3
  see also Russia as colonizer and
    colonized
Commercial Bank 123
Commonwealth of Oceana, The
  (Harrington) 72
communes
  behaviour in 114
  private farmers and 109–13
  Soviet collective farms 113–17
  work ethic 114–17
communism/socialism
  1905 revolution reforms 110–13
  Christian utopia and 65–8
  collective life and 41–4
  discredited collectivism 44
  hereditary/redistributive 106–9
  as ideal society 10, 40, 45
  Khrushchev's principles 159
  legislating development 171–2

Marx and 72
More's *Utopia* 69–70
need for economic restructuring
  202
pre-Soviet communes 104–9
Sovietism instead of socialism 14
theorists of 68–72
upheaval in Russia 192–3
Communist Party *see* communism/
  socialism
'Concerning My House' (Cicero)
  56–7
Condorcet, Marquis de 118
corruption
  institutional bribery 28–9
  Magnitsky and 169
  pre-Revolution 125
  rules of succession and 200–1
Cortés, Hernán 73
Credit Bank 123
Crimea, annexation of 81–2, 204
'Crisis, The' (Zoshchenko) 43
Cuban Missile Crisis 25
culture
  post-Soviet cultural capital 19
  secretiveness and openness 26
  Stalin and honorary titles 43
  Stalin's use of humiliation 142–3
  see also art; literature

de Soto, Hernando 28–9, 31
Dead Souls (Gogol) 130
democracy
  authoritarian grey zone 173
  letting go of power 175, 177
  political system in Russia 175–6
  power of property 31
  Veche 95
  without rule of law 176–8
Demosthenes 152
Dennison, Tracy 102–3
Discourse on the Origin of Inequality
  (Rousseau) 71
Dmitriev, Mikhail 163
dbors, guarding 33

economics
British institutions of 62–5
consumption 38–40, 164
decapitalization 18
'depoliticizing' 174
emigration of capital 168, 169–71
entrepreneurs and bankruptcies
199–200
free-market institutions 174
half-built capitalism 171
legislation and 171–2
market and housing 162–8
monopolies 87–8
'moral' communes 104–9, 113
neither market nor socialist 202
non-Russian businesses 170
post-Soviet market 11
privatization programme 198
public development 197
security over development 94–5,
123–5, 174
shortages 16
USSR success 13
widespread debt 124
see also banks; business;
communism/socialism; industry;
private property
education
budget for 98
of elites 128
modernization 13
Soviet maintenance of 40
Edward III
Statue of Labourers 92
Ehrenburg, Ilya
The Thaw 159
elites
affording (non-)public goods
196–7
colonial institutions and 80–1
dependence of peasants and 121
English aristocracy 63
fear of peasants 103
freedom of 127–8
greater space for 161

housing for 154, 155–6, 160
inheritance and 89, 195
loyalty or voice 186–7
nomenklatura unlike aristocracy
83–4
oprichbina and zemshchina land 90
privileged lifestyles 38–40
property for service 93–4, 120–1,
192–3, 200
relation to leaders 194
semi-alien 170–1
stewardship of peasants 108–9,
122, 192
tsarist control and 88–91
widespread debt 124
emigration
access to laws abroad 193–4
the environment and 195
exporting money 184–5, 188–91,
204
loyalty and voice 185–7
Russia's future and 183–4
statistics of 187–8
Engelgardt, Alexander 110
engineers and housing design 138–9,
151, 154–5
Enlightenment thought
Catherine and 120
individual sovereignty 64–5
on injustice 71
Essay on Enlightenment in Respect of
Russia, An (Pnin) 118–19
Estonia 191
Etkind, Alexander
colonizing gas and oil 85–6
Internal Colonization x, 73
eugenics 53
Europe
evolution of private life 46–9
labour slowly freed 91–2
rise of cities 11–12
servants 48
state and natural resources 132
European Union
no admission for Russia 175

Fathers and Sons (Turgenev) 130
fences
  around cemeteries 35
  camps with watchtowers 26–7
  good neighbours and 22–3, 27
  mobility of 32–3
  not a protection 35
Finland 191
Fitzpatrick, Sheila 42–3
France
  Declaration of the Rights of Man 64
  natural resources 132
  rights and liberties 121
Frank, S.L.
  'Property and Socialism' 4
Franklin, Benjamin
  'Time is money' 68
freedom
  disconnected from property 4
  varying aspects of 188
  see also rights of citizens
Frost, Robert
  'The Girl Outright' 25
  'Mending Wall' 22–5
  Soviet Union and 23–5
Fukuyama, Francis
  The Origins of Political Order 117, 122
fur trade 75, 86
furniture, mobility of 46
Fyodor III, Tsar 26

Gaidar, Yegor 4
Gaius the jurist 55, 57
Galkin, Maxim 37–8
gas *see* oil and gas
Gasparov, Mikhail 153
Gazprom 86, 202
  Miller's lifestyle and 39–40
Gelman, Vladimir 175
Germany
  homeownership 2
  natural resources 132
  Nazis admire Sparta 50
  Poland and 191

Gerschenkron, Alexander 68
Ginzburg, Moses 139
'Girl Outright, The' (Frost) 25
Gogol, Nikolai 132
  Dead Souls 130
  The Government Inspector 83
gold rush, Siberian 76
Golden Horde 83
Golovlyov Family, The (Saltykov-Shchedrin) 130
Gorbachev, Mikhail 84
Goremykin, Ivan 111
Government Inspector, The (Gogol) 83
Greece, ancient
  architecture 152–3
  home unit 53–4
  Sparta and Athens 50–3
Guriev, Dmitry 123
Guriev, Sergey 174

Haag, Louise 127, 128
Habermas, Jürgen 148
Hanseatic League 86
Harrington, James
  The Commonwealth of Oceana 72
  land and political power 88
Harris, Steven 160
Haxthausen, Baron August von 104–5, 106
health care
  modernization and 13
  as public good 40–1
Henry VIII 63, 88
Herzen, Alexander 125, 186
  Baptized Property 128
  exports money 127–9, 184–5
  peasant communes and 105–6
  on poverty as slavery 129
Hirschman, Albert 185
History of a Town (Saltykov-Shchedrin) 83, 130
Hobbes, Thomas 63
  human nature 61–2
  Leviathan 62

Hoch, Stephen 107–8
homosexuality, political use of 20, 98
Hooch, Pieter de 49
House on the Embankment 41
housing
  affordability 165–6
  allocating utopia 41–4
  dachas/summer homes 28, 43
  effect of Second World War 145, 158
  elite apartments 155–6
  engineer-designed 138–9, 151, 154–5
  European privacy 46–9
  Everyone's right to 160–2
  Greek home unit 53–4
  home as refuge 54–8, 57–8
  individual building 146
  industry Stalin's priority 149
  as investment 166–7
  Khrushchev and 146–50, 157–62
  need for renewal 201–3
  palaces 38
  as political factor 163
  post-Soviet privatization 167–8
  resettlement 42–3, 203
  Roman stratification 151–2
  rural 163
  sacrificed for industry 10
  self-building 164, 167
  space and crowding 3, 158–9, 161, 165–6
  state monitoring of 10
  unsanctioned 27
  waiting lists 160
  without the market 162–8
  see also architecture; private property
'How Much Land Does a Person Need?' (Tolstoy) 35
Huizinga, Johan 48
human nature, Hobbes on 61–2

Incas, colonization of 78, 79, 85
industry

forced 27
  outdated factories 202
  quality of 15
  second-generation owners 195
  Siberia and 76–7
  Soviet modernization 12–16
  Stalin's priority over housing 149
  upheaval of 9–10
inequalities
  colonization and 79–81
  deepening 195
  legal system and 71
  Roman Stoic egalitarianism 60–1
  in Sparta 52
  Stalin's policies 43
inheritance, no rules for 200–1
injustice
  Rousseau links with property 71
  see also inequalities; legal system
Inozemtsev, Vladislav 187–8
Institute of Urban Economics 165
institutions of state and society
  free-market 174
  Petersburg period 95–6
  un-restructured 202
intelligentsia
  Catherine polices 120
  Pnin and 118–20
  see also literature
Internal Colonization (Etkind) 73, x
International Monetary Fund (IMF) 198
Iofan, Boris 41
Italy 34
Ivan III, the Great, Tsar
  lifetime land grants 89
  no political opposition to 93
Ivan IV, the Terrible, Tsar
  destroys institutions 95
  oprichbina and zemshchina land 90
  peasants' freedom to move 102
  property for service 89–91, 140, 192
  violent oprichniks of 83

John Chrysostom, St 66–7
journalism
    speaking out 125–7
    see also literature
Juvenal, Decimus Iunius 151

Kaftanov, Andrey 150
Kankrin, Yegor 123–4
Kennedy, John F. 23
Keynes, John Maynard 111
Khanin, Grigoriy 14
Khomyakov, Alexey
    landowners as colonials 132
    peasant communes and 105–6
Khrushchev, Nikita
    admires Danish house 145–6
    communist principles of 159
    Cuban Missile Crisis 25
    debate with Nixon 148
    Frost's 'Mending Wall' and 23–5
    housing policies 42, 138, 146–50,
        159–61
    order in a five-storey block 154
King, Winter 28
Kiselyov, Pavel 104–5
Klyuchevsky, Vasiliy x
    Moscow and serfdom 92
    Russian colonization 81–2
Kolesnikov, Sergey 38
Kondratieva, Tamara 95–6
Kordonsky, Simon 96–7
Kostin, Andrey 155
Krastev, Ivan
    authoritarianism and democracy
        173
    on emigration 185
Kryshtanovskaya, Olga 84
Kuchum, Khan 73
Kudrin, Alexey 155
Kurbsky, Prince Andrey 186

La Harpe, Frédéric-César de 118
labour
    Russian surplus 110
    see also communes; peasants

Lagutenko, Vitaliy 138
Lam Sai-Wing 44
Latin America
    colonization of 77–9
    corruption and rights 30
Latsis, Martin 179
Lavrov, Sergey 155
law, rule of *see* legal system
'Laws, The' (Plato) 59–60
Le Corbusier (Charles Jeanneret)
    137–8
legal system 21
    Alexander II's reforms 179
    Bolsheviks/Soviets and 179–80
    confiscation by 169–71
    current practices 181–3
    democracy and 176–8
    English 62
    Enlightenment thought and 120
    homes without legal rights 28–9
    honesty of 29–30
    household boundaries and 65
    judges 181–2
    lack of independence 171
    Napoleonic Code 133
    no rule of law 178–83, 193
    Petersburg period 95
    Roman 55–8
    Rousseau and 71
    uncertainty of ownership 5
    use of other countries 170
    USSR Prosecutor's Office 179–80
    see also police and law enforcement
Lenin, Vladimir Ilych
    Bolshevik domination 83
    formula for resettlement 42
    gold toilet 44
    regression to past 96
Lenin's Tomb (Remnick) 84
Leviathan (Hobbes) 62
literature
    authors speak out 125–31
    dissident writers 17
    economics and 125
    elite and society 83

Frost's 'Mending Wall' 22–5
leisured class and 130–1
Soviet accommodation 159
on Stalinist apartments 141–2
survival ethics 115
on utopias 45
Lithuania 90
Locke, John 68, 120
private property and 71–2
social contract and 63–4
Luther, Martin 67–8
Luzhkov, Yury 155
Lycurgus 50–1

Magnitsky, Sergey 169
Malia, Martin 14
Mandelstam, Nadezhda 141–2
Mandelstam, Osip 141–2
marriage, housing shares and 162
Marx, Karl, Russia and 72
Matthew, Gospel of 66
Mau, Vladimir 82–3
Medvedev, Dmitri
Affordable Housing Project 165
informed about Putin's palace 38
not owner of properties 200
Megginson, William 174
Melnikov, Konstantin
'Sonata of Sleep' 41–2
'Mending Wall' (Frost) 22–5
Methodists 68
Mexico, colonization of 77–9
military
attracting service 127
recruited from poor 108
Soviet maintenance of 40
Miller, Alexey
'Palace' of 19, 39–40
mining, private ownership and 132–3
modernity
European rise of cities 11–12
industrialization and 12–16
More, Thomas
Utopia 44, 69–70
Moscow Pioneers' Palace 41

Mumford, Lewis
The Story of Utopias 45

Naiman, Anatoly 24
natural resources
for benefit of elite 3
colonization of 85–6
European concept of 132
no public ownership 132–4
post-Soviet 5
second-generation owners 195
Navalny, Alexey
housing for elites 155
on Medvedev's properties 200
monitors illegal property 39
Netherlands, carpenter's house in
47–9
Nicholas I, Tsar
continues Alexander's policies 122
emancipation of serfs 104
land grants with serfs 103
Nicholas II, Tsar
Stolypin's land reforms 31
Nixon, Richard 148
NKVD (People's Commissariat of
Internal Affairs) 179
nomenklatura see elites
Novikov, Nikolai 120
Nureyev, Rudolf 186

Offord, Derek 129
oil and gas
colonization of 85–6
privatization and control 97
Soviet modernization 14
volatile prices 199
One Day in the Life of Ivan
Denisovich (Solzhenitsyn) 115,
116
Origins of Political Order, The
(Fukuyama) 117, 122
Osokina, Yelena 116
Ostapkovich, Georgiy 200
Otkrytie bank 199
Ovid 55

palaces
Miller's 19, 39–40
public goods and 40–1
Putin's 19, 38, 154
Yanukovich ix, 41, 44
Palladio, Andrea 154
Papernyi, Vladimir
Culture One and Two 26
Pasternak, Boris 141–2
Pastukhov, Vladimir 176
Paul I, Tsar 118
Paustovsky, Konstantin 23
peasants
colonization of 80–1
danger for regime 100
dependence on nobles 121
'due toil' 110
elite stewardship of 95, 108–9,
122, 192
enserfment of 82
flogging 109
gradual subjugation of 91, 92
husband–wife units 108
military service 108
moral communes 104–9
poll tax and 107–8
post-emancipation reforms
109–13
unable to move 101–3
see also serfdom
Peasants' Revolt (England) 92
Peru, slums and rights 28–9
Peter I, the Great, Tsar
founds St Petersburg 25–6
legal status of peasants 101
mining freedom 132–3
poll tax 107
reforms of 126
shapes Russia 10–11
Peter III, Tsar 101, 126
philanthropy 134
pioneers' palaces 15–16
Moscow Pioneers' Palace
41
as public good 40, 41

Pipes, Richard
Property and Freedom 4
Russia under the Old Regime 4
Pitt, William, the Elder 58
Pittacus 153
Pizarro, Francisco 77–8
Plato
eugenics 53
the ideal society 45
'The Laws' 59–60
property-based citizenship 59
The Republic 70
Sparta and 50–1
Plutarch
on living conditions 151
on Sparta and Athens 51–2
Pnin, Ivan
An Essay on Enlightenment
118–19
life and career 118–20
rule of property owners 134–5
Poe, Marshall 93–4
Poland 191
police and law enforcement 202
Cheka 98
honest of 29–30
as Party combat wing 179, 183
Stalin and torture 180
without rule of law 178–83
see also legal system
politics
no representation 20
power and property gain/loss 200
property qualification 51
see also communism/socialism;
democracy; rights of citizens
poverty
colonization and 79
eating from collectives 180
as slavery 129
prison camps, Solzhenitsyn on 115
private life
in art 49
aspiration to 1–2, 27
currently unsatisfied 43–4

fear and 161
historical perspective on 46–9
mistrust and 27
moderation and 153–4
utopia and 45–6
private property
Akhmatova's perspective of 24
alternatives to 2
authoritarianism and 31, 168–9
Christianity and 65–8
citizenship and 3–4, 51
colonial institutions and 80–1
as conferred 135
cultural evolution of 3–6
current/future issues 204–5
deepening inequality 195
deniability 200
'due toil' 110
elite like foreigners 131–2
emancipation and 109–10,
   109–13
in England 88
English evolution of 62–5
expectation from Soviet state
   16–19
importance today 177
inheritance and 194–5
institutional protection for 29–31
as a liability 205
low Russian figures of 2
More's *Utopia* and 44
obtaining credit and 28–9
palaces 19, 38, 39–40, 154
Petersburg period 95–6
philanthrophy and 134
Pnin on 119
privatization 5, 150
Roman definition of 55–6
Rousseau sees as unjust 71
rule of owners 134–5
Russians abroad 19, 128–9, 184–5,
   188–91
second homes and 28, 43
separate from rights 135
serfs as property 121

sharing 131–5
state upheavals 191–5
taxation and 31
Tolstoy on 131
vulnerable with civic society 20
wealth versus property 58–9
see also elites; housing
Promsvyazbank 199
Property and Freedom (Pipes) 4
'Property and Socialism' (Frank) 4
Protestantism
non-possessors 72
property and wealth 67–8
Przeworski, Adam 175
public goods
development of 196–7
Soviet maintenance of 40
public property, no Russian concept
   of 133–4
Pugashov, Yemelyan 120
punishment
in communes 114–116
prison camps 115
Puritans 68
Putin, Vladimir
architecture for elites 155–6
'getting off our knees' 44
palace of 19, 38, 154
political institutions and 176
Putin's Pals' Club apartments 155
Putnam, Robert, on trust 34

Quakers 68

Radchenko, Vladimir 169
Radishchev, Alexander 120
Rasmussen, Steen Eiler 49
religion
Roman sacred households 54–8
see also Christianity and Churches
Remnick, David
Lenin's Tomb 84
Repnin, Field Marshal Nikolai
Vasilievich 118
Republic, The (Plato) 70

resistance
  or adaptation 116–17
  great authors speak out 125–31
  the Gulag and 115–16
  Pugachov rebellion 120
Riasanovsky, Nicholas 9
rights of citizens
  Catherine and nobility 31–2
  colonization and 79
  disconnected from property 4, 135
  European rise of 64
  to housing 160–2
  no protection of 20
  peasants' 'due toil' 100–1
  post-Soviet 82
  in poverty 59
  security services and 171
  state respect for 30
  taxation and 30–1
  without rule of law 177–8
Robinson, James 80
Roman Catholic Church 63
Rome
  empire calculation 94
  housing stratification 151–2
  laws for households 55–8
  sacredness of homes 54–7
Rothschild, James 128, 129
Rousseau, Jean-Jacques 141
  Discourse on the Origin of Inequality 71
  influence on Soviets 71–2
  social contract 70–2
Ruble, Blair 25–6
rural life
  collectivization and 18
  contemporary housing 163
  farm collectivization 7–9
  neglected provinces 3
  see also agriculture; communes
Russia
  1905 Revolution reforms 110–13
  American market approach 164
  annex of Crimea 81–2
  Bolshevik regression 95–6

  centralization of power 3
  compulsory acquisition 133
  constant upheavals 191–5, 199
  constitution of 175–6
  delegation by property 135
  democracy in 175–6, 176–8
  effect of Second World War 145, 158
  Enlightenment ideals 64–5
  enserfment of peasants 82
  exit/voice/loyalty 185–90
  freedom disconnected from property 4
  historical perspective ix–xi
  infrastructure 167
  loss of territory 82
  national character of 82
  no public land 132–4
  non-inclusive society 193
  people's stoicism 9–10
  Petersburg period 95–6
  population age at Revolution 8–9
  post-Soviet capital and 18–21
  public goods of state 40–1
  rationality of Soviet project 4–5
  rule of property owners 134–5
  security as priority 96–9
  social effect of housing 157–62
  Soviet childhood 14–16
  Soviet modernization 12–16
  square kilometre empire calculation 94
  state as owner 168
  threat of reform 96–7
  today's hands-on control 84–6
  trust/mistrust 27, 34–5, 68
  tsarist control of land 88–91
  tsars consolidate power 92–5
Russia as colonizer and colonized
  decolonization and 21, 86
  exploiting resources 84–6
  fur trade and 75
  historical perspective 83–6
  landowners as colonials 132
  paradox of 3

peasants and 74
people making money 20
structures of 79–81
Yermak takes Siberia 73–7
Russia under the Old Regime (Pipes)
  4
Rybczinski, Witold 47

Saltykov-Shchedrin, Mikhail 115
  The Golovlyov Family 130
  History of a Town 83, 130
Sarnov, Benedict 43
Scandinavian countries, trust in 34
Schlatter, Richard 67
Schumpeter, Joseph 175
science, Soviet 40
Scott, James 106
Sechin, Igor 155
security
  fixation on 204
  guards 33
  over development 94–5, 174
  as priority 96–9
  without reform 171
  without rule of law 178–83
  see also police and law enforcement
Seneca the Younger
  on Christians 66
  on common resources 60–1
serfdom
  ambiguous legal structure of 101–3
  emancipation 31, 95, 104, 121
  gradual release of 103–4
  see also peasants
serfs *see* peasants
servants, European 48
Shakespeare, William
  communal beds in *Twelfth Night*
  47
Shalamov, Varlam 17
Shlyapentokh, Vladimir 168
Siberia
  colonization of 73–7
  ethnic groups within 76
  gold rush 76

industrialization 76–7
  place of exile 76
Sierra Leone 79
Smith, Mark 146, 150
Sobyanin, Sergey
  apartment of 155
  renovating housing 202–3
socialism *see* communes; communism/
  socialism
society
  lack of civic society 20
  levels of trust 34
  restructuring property relations
  194
  social contract and 61, 63–4, 70–2,
  85
Solon 50–1
Soloviov, Sergey 81
  colonization in Russia 73–4
  Russian national character 82
Solzhenitsyn, Alexander 17
  *One Day in the Life of Ivan
  Denisovich* 115, 116
Sorsky, Nil 72
space programme 40
Spain, colonialism of 77–9, 85
Sparta 50–3
Speransky, Mikhail 123
sports 40
Sportsman's Sketches, A (Turgenev)
  130
St Petersburg Journal 118, 119
Stalin, Joseph
  architecture and 140–4
  Great Leap Forward objectives 13
  hierarchical policy 43
  industry over housing 149
  no exit under 186
  order in a skyscraper 154
  personality cult debunked 147
  property for service 192–3, 200
  severity on crimes 180
  use of humiliation 142–3
Steuart, James Denham 118
Stevens, Siaka 79

Stoicism, egalitarianism and 60–1
Stolypin, Pyotr
    agrarian reforms 31, 110, 111–13
Story of Utopias, The (Mumford)
    45
Strider: The Story of a Horse
    (Tolstoy) 131
Stroganov dynasty 73–7
Sukhova, Olga 110
Switzerland 2

Taagepera, Rein 94
taxation
    citizens' rights and 30–1, 65
    communes and 108
    deducted by employers 31
    of dividends 85
    peasant payment of 101
    poll tax study 107–8
    tuning the system 82–3
    without social contract 85
Teslya, Andrey 103
Thucydides 52
time, money and 68
Toledo, Francisco de 78
Tolstoy, Alexey 83
Tolstoy, Leo 125
    'How Much Land Does a Person
        Need?' 35
    peasant communes and 105–6
    spiritual and material wealth
        129–31
    Strider: The Story of a Horse 131
    War and Peace 130
    What Then Must We Do? 130
Tolstoy, Sergey 130
Tolstoya, Sofia Andreyevna 130
town planning
    unreading cities 27
    see also architects; housing
transport
    of grain (*see* peasants)
    Krankin opposes rail 123
    sea versus land 74
    Trans-Siberian railway 76

Trudoviks 111
trust
    high mistrust in Russia 34–5
    privacy and mistrust 27
    religious dissenters and 68
Turgenev, Ivan 125
    Fathers and Sons 130
    A Sportsman's Sketches 130
Turkey 175, 191
Twelfth Night (Shakespeare) 47
Tyler, Wat 92

Ukraine
    1932 famine in 180
    conflict over 204
    Yanukovych's palace ix, 44
United States
    Californian gold rush 76
    colonization of 78
    comparative economics 13
    constitutional human rights 64
    housing space 161
    Locke's influence on 71–2
    Marshall Plan in Berlin 148
    rights and liberties 121
    Russian market approach 164
urbanization 8
    class resettlement 42
    rise of city life 11–12
    Soviet modernization 12–16
    unreadiness for 27
utilitarianism 60
Utopia (More) 44
    communal living 69–70
utopias
    allocation of 41–4
    Christianity and 65–8, 72
    discredited 45–6
    More's 44
    theorists of 68–72

Veblen, Thorstein 40
Vermeer, Johannes 49
Virgil
    Aeneid 54

Volkov, Vadim 181
Vorontsov-Dashkov, Count Illarion
    133
Voznesensky, Andrey 23
Vronsky, Oleg 114

War and Peace (Tolstoy) 130
Weber, Max 68
What Then Must We Do? (Tolstoy)
    130
Wright, Frank Lloyd 154

Xenophon 50

Yadrintsev, Nikolai 76
Yakovlev, Ivan 127, 128
Yakovleva, Jana 169
Yanukovich, Viktor
    palace of 41, 44, ix

Yefremov, Ivan 45
Yeliashevich, Vasilii 100–1
Yeltsin, Boris
    constitution of Russia and 175–6
    nomenklatura elite 84
    private property and 4
Yermak Timofeyavich 73, 75–7
Yesenin, Sergey 7
Yevtushenko, Yevgeny 23
Young Pioneers' camp 47
Yusupov, Prince Felix 134
Yusupov Palace 41
Yuzhakov, Vladimir 18

Zavisca, Jane 161, 162
Zenkevich, Mikhail 23
Zholtovsky, Ivan 155
Zoshchenko, Mikhail
    'The Crisis' 43